A Texas Pioneer
Staging & Freighting on the Texas Frontier

AUGUST SANTLEBEN
EDITED BY I. D. AFFLECK

2024
Copano Bay Press

Originally published in 1910 under the title *A Texas Pioneer: Early Staging and Overland Freighting on the Frontiers of Texas and Mexico.*

ISBN: 978-1-941324-21-9

CONTENTS

Chapter One:

1845—Castroville—Indians—Big-foot Wallace

I was born in the city of Hanover, Germany, on the 28th day of February, 1845, and I was three and a half months old when my parents emigrated from that country and brought me with a sister and brother to America. We made the voyage in a sailing vessel, the *Charles Williams*, which left Bremen with a full crew and one hundred and thirty passengers on board. The city of Galveston, Texas, was sighted about the middle of July, 1845, after making a safe voyage of seven weeks' duration, but many of those who greeted the land of their adoption with joyful expectations were destined to a watery grave when entering the harbor.

I do not know what brought about the catastrophe, but my parents, who gave me this information, said that the ship was stranded when passing through the channel leading into Galveston Bay, about half a mile from shore, where it was broken to pieces, and the wreck could be seen as late as 1885. Only thirty-five of the passengers were saved, and they were rescued by a lifeboat that was sent from the shore. Among them was an infant boy, about two years of age, who was thrown to my parents after they entered the boat, by some one on the vessel, under the impression that the child belonged to our family. Fortunately the boat conveyed its living freight safely to land, but none of the desolate people could comprehend their losses until they congregated on shore, and one of those who realized them least was the author of these memoirs, who at the age of five months was thus transferred from the wreck of a ship and placed on the soil of Texas. Another was the child who had been saved through a mistake, whose parents and his entire family were drowned; but friends took the orphan in charge and conveyed him to Castroville, where he was raised to manhood by a man named Bader, who was perhaps a friend of his family. Christian Schuhart was his name, and he is now a well-to-do farmer and ranchman on the San Geronimo, where I became intimate with him and we often discussed the early misfortunes of our families.

The ship's cargo, including all the belongings of the passengers, was a total loss. The disaster fell heavily on the emigrants who had supplied themselves with wagons, farm implements and other necessaries in Germany, with the expectation of using them in the New World, where their lot had been cast. All were alike destitute of everything except the clothing they wore, but, perhaps, a few had saved small amounts of money that was carried on their persons, and they were thrown on the charity of strangers. Although their pressing wants were supplied by subscriptions, there was no extravagant display of generosity, and a long time passed away before the effects of the calamity ceased to be felt.

My father secured passage, with others of the unfortunate emigrants, for his family on a schooner and sailed for Port Lavaca, where after his arrival he arranged with Plasedo Olivarri, a Mexican, to transport his wife and children, and the few things he possessed, to the Medina River, eight miles above Castroville. There land was assigned for my father's use in the "Castro Corner," but it was unimproved, and as the country was unsettled, we were compelled to live under the canopy of heaven, exposed to all kinds of weather, until a suitable shelter could be erected.

On the opposite side of the river from where we settled was a camp of Lipan Indians, who were then friendly with the whites, and when they visited us, my parents would sometimes allow the two elder children to return with them to their settlement. They were very generous, and they supplied our family with game all the time they lived in our vicinity. Later on the Indians moved elsewhere and immediately, I believe it was in 1847, they went on the war-path. Thereafter they and all the Texas Indians depredated on the white settlements continuously until 1878, during which time many of my acquaintances and some of my dear friends were killed by them. I have endeavored to recall all the names of those who were killed by the hostiles during that period, in connection with the time and place of the murders, which will be presented elsewhere.

The first work my father did, after he became settled, was for Mr. Castro, who employed him and Mr. Huehner, the grandfather of Albert Huth, Bexar County's present Tax Assessor, to dig a ditch on the east side of "Castro's Corner," for which he agreed to pay each of them fifty cents per day. The ditch was eight feet wide and eight feet deep and it took them four months to complete the job. After the ditch was finished Castro leased a piece of land in the Corner to my father for three years, free of charge, except that he was to put it in cultivation.

After that he engaged in farming, but he also made a pit for the purpose of sawing lumber with a whipsaw and at odd times he cut cypress trees along the banks of the Medina River and turned them into lumber and shingles. Such work was very laborious, and as two men were required to run the saw he was only occasionally employed at it because he could not always hire help. By hard toil he managed to support his family with the necessaries of life without any of the luxuries. My parents were affectionate and considerate in the treatment of their children and tried to raise them properly. They were also strictly religious, and they often tried to impress upon the minds of their offspring the importance of thinking and acting in accordance with the Ten Commandments so that they would not come in conflict with the laws of their country.

They were well known throughout west Texas and had many friends on account of their conscientiousness and kind-heartedness. My father was strongly impressed by the obligations and duties of his citizenship, and as he had come to the United States on account of its free institutions, he did not delay, after the expiration of five years, in taking out his naturalization papers which were secured in July, 1850.

He resided on the land he first settled until 1854, and then removed to a tract which he purchased from Samuel Etter, the father of Jacob and Samuel Etter, Jr., both of whom are now substantial farmers and live on Sous Creek, four miles east of Castroville, adjoining the farm bought by my father, which was then situated in Bexar County on the Eagle Pass and El Paso road. In a few years the farm was nicely improved by hard work, and as the land was productive he made good crops, at the same time gathering around him a small number of horses and cattle, so that he was able to live more comfortably.

Free pasturage was abundant, and as there was no expense attached to stock raising every farmer had a few animals, but many owned a thousand or more cattle, besides small herds of horses. The latter were not numerous, because of the risk of having them stolen by Indians. Big-foot Wallace owned the largest number in that region which were principally on Mustang Prairie, four miles below La Coste station, but the Indians succeeded in stealing them all eventually notwithstanding the fact that he kept a constant watch over them and often punished them severely for their thefts.

My childhood years were passed happily and I had a good and easy time, although I helped my father all I could on the farm in light work or in making myself useful in many ways, but I never fancied farming very much. When I was not more than eight years old I would occasionally help him saw lumber when he could get no one else to assist him, because, as I have stated, it required two persons to perform such work with a whipsaw one above and another in the pit below.

My first visit to San Antonio was made with my father in 1854, and it was on this occasion that I was made happy by the wonderful things I saw in the city which filled my childish mind with astonishment. The business portion of the town was then confined to the two plazas, and most of the improvements were in that vicinity. I suppose the population at that time was not more than 3,000 of all classes.

My next trip away from home was when I accompanied my father to Fort Inge on his wagon that was loaded with corn which he sold to the government. It was a part of a certain quantity he had contracted to deliver, at 40c. and 50c. per bushel, as forage for a company of dragoons that was then stationed at said fort, four miles below the present town of Uvalde, and another detachment at Fort Ewell on the Laredo road, both of which have been abandoned many years. All the men in these companies were splendidly mounted on the best horses that Missouri could furnish. Their saddles were the old government pattern, with solid brass stirrups weighing two pounds, and all the mountings were of the same metal. Every soldier was armed with two holster pistols, each with a single barrel, and a Mississippi yager, both of the same caliber, therefore they used the same fixed cartridges loaded with a ball and three buckshot. I was only nine years of age, but I took notice of everything as they were the first soldiers I had ever seen; there I ate my first hard-tack, and there I saw the first playing cards. While my father was unloading the corn, I busied myself gathering the cards that were scattered around the camp. Until then I had never seen painted pictures of any kind, and I thought the cards were the prettiest things my eyes had ever gazed upon.

About that date my father hired Paul Offinger to help him on the farm and he worked for him three years, in which time he saved up enough money to buy fifty acres of land near Quihi, eleven miles west of Castroville. When he moved on his place he had no one to assist him and my father hired me to him to drive his oxen when plowing or hauling for $5.00 per month and my board. I remained with him four months, and though only twelve years of age, my duties were performed to the satisfaction of my employer.

In those days oxen were the only animals that were used on farms on the western frontier for draft purposes, partly because the original outlay and cost of keeping them was less than for horses, and another reason was the risk of losing them on account of Indians who were always stealing horses. The oxen were always necked together, and after a day's work the yoke was removed, a bell was suspended to one of their necks, and they were turned out on the range until wanted, when the tinkling bell indicated their whereabouts.

Generally I found it prosy business wandering through the mesquite bushes in search of my oxen, but one foggy morning I had an exciting experience when I saw a panther in my path feasting on a calf he had killed. He was only a few feet in front of me, but he was so intent on satisfying his hunger that he only looked at me without rising. I, on the contrary, was very much startled, but a spell of fascination crept over me which kept my eyes fixed on him as I slowly backed from his presence a few steps before turning, and then I ran towards home at the top of my speed. I was bare-footed, as was usual with country boys in those days, who only wore shoes on Sundays, and my toes clawed the ground and helped me along. I was making pretty good time when I stepped on a large rattlesnake that was coiled in my path, which filled me with horror, but before he could strike I made a frantic leap in the air and landed beyond his reach. The accident caused my fear of the panther to subside and reduced my gait to a walk. But these adventures did not make me abandon my search, which I continued, though with greater caution, until the musical ox-bell in the distance guided me to the animals I was seeking and I drove them home.

On another occasion Mr. Offinger went out hunting one Sabbath morning, and he allowed me to accompany him. He carried an old-fashioned army musket, which was loaded with the only charge of buckshot that he had, and I was unarmed. On the east side of Quihi prairie we suddenly found ourselves in the midst of a herd of about twenty-five javelinas, or Mexican hogs, that were feeding in a thicket of scrubby live-oak. When they saw us all of them bunched together with their heads towards us while their teeth clashed in a threatening and vicious manner until Mr. Offinger fired into the bunch. As the gun fired they rushed towards him and they moved so quickly that he only had time to climb a small tree beyond their reach. I was standing about twenty steps behind him and knowing the danger I followed his example, but as Mr. Offinger was the aggressor he received all of their attention. He wanted me to descend from my sheltered position and gather rocks with which to drive them away, but I was afraid, consequently we remained in our place of refuge until they disappeared an hour later.

The Mexican or musk hog, which is common in many sections of west Texas, has a sack on its back that contains a secretion which has a strong odor. They are aggressive, often attacking persons without provocation, and when wounded they are dangerous. Their long, sharp tusks cut like a knife and it is difficult to avoid them when on foot because of their quick movements and manner of fighting.

During the time I served Mr. Offinger I had many hours of recreation and my tasks were never heavy. My personal expenditures amounted to only twenty-five cents a month, that went for candy which I bought at Mr. Bailey's store in Quihi, and frequently my friend and playmate, Frank Rieden, now living in San Antonio, helped me to eat it. My wages were well earned, and when I received the nineteen dollars that was due me I returned home with the money and placed it in my father's hand with a great deal of pleasure.

Mr. Bowles was another old friend of my father's who lived at Sabinal, in 1856, and I remember the old double barrel shot-gun he showed my father soon after killing three Indians with it by discharging both barrels at the same instant. The gun was then out of order, and he was taking it to San Antonio to have it repaired. The particulars of the killing, as Mr. Bowles related them to my father, are about as follows: The Indians had made a raid into the settlements, and after the fact became generally known, every one was on the watch for them. Mr. Bowles loaded his gun very heavily with buck-shot and took a position after dark on an elevation near his house, where he stood guard. He had only waited a short time when he saw three Indians approach on foot, following each other in single file along a foot trail. After bringing his weapon to his shoulder he waited until they were in close range and then fired both loads simultaneously. The recoil of the gun threw him on his back and it flew out of his hands behind him. After recovering from the shock the Indians had disappeared, and he made an investigation with the result that one Indian was found dead in his tracks and another where he fell a short distance beyond. The search was continued next morning along a bloody trail, and after following it about three hundred yards, the corpse of the third Indian was found.

This remarkably successful shot has never been recorded, or if it has I am unaware of the fact, but the tragic act is well known to others now living who will vouch for the truth of my story. Perhaps they know more of the circumstances than I can recall, because Mr. Bowles has many relatives living in Uvalde County. He was killed by Indians in the Sabinal Cañon about two years after his adventure, probably by the same tribe, who murdered him to avenge the slaughter of their warriors.

There is no comparison between the number of Indians that were killed by white men that I know of, and the number of white men that were killed by Indians.

Mr. John Bowles killed three Indians in Uvalde County. Xavier Wans killed one Indian and mortally wounded another in Medina County. Jack Hoffmann killed two Indians in Medina County. An Indian was killed by the first settlers at Quihi in Medina County. Nic Habe killed an Indian in Medina County. Ed Tschirheart killed an Indian in San Saba County, near Fort McKavitt. Big-foot Wallace killed two Indians in Medina County. All these Indians were killed by men with whom I was well acquainted.

The following are some stories about Big-foot Wallace:

One time he brought a fifteen-year-old Indian who was probably on his first raid and got lost from his companions and had wandered towards Big-foot's ranch and came in contact with his dogs and to save himself, climbed a tree. Big-foot, hearing the bark of his dogs, went at once to see what kind of an animal they had treed, and to his surprise found a half frightened to death young warrior with his bow and arrows strapped to his back, captured him and put him on his horse in the saddle in front of him, and tied his feet under the horse's stomach and carried him that way to Castroville. Some one in the crowd said, "Say, Big-foot, give me that Indian." Whereupon he said, "No, this is my Indian; if you want an Indian go an' get you one, there are plenty of them left."

Another story that I recollect well happened just before the war, where Big-foot was out horse-hunting and riding a mule when he came upon a fresh trail that was leading in a northerly direction over a divide. He followed the trail to find out if the Indians took the same direction on the other side of the divide, in which case it was his intention to hurry on to Castroville, where he expected to get enough men to cut them off if possible, but as he reached the top of the divide and looking on down the slope he saw to his surprise about twenty-five Indians busy catching the choicest horses out of the herd for their saddle horses. Big-foot saw at once that he was outnumbered and unable to escape, as they had already seen him, whereupon he snatched off his hat and waving it back towards the rear, called at the top of his voice saying, "Come on, boys! Come on, boys! We have got them!" This was too much for Mr. Indian, as they were unable to see Big-foot's imaginary brigade, so they all jumped upon their horses and took to the woods, leaving their stolen animals, which Big-foot afterwards gathered with ease and drove back into the range.

Another story relates that, on one occasion, Big-foot invited several cow-boys, who were hunting cattle, to drink coffee with him and when they accepted his invitation he offered it to them in an Indian skull.

Another anecdote of Big-foot's early days was when he and other men had followed the Indians and overtook them near Bandera, where a battle took place and several Indians were killed. When returning home they all stopped at one of the first settlers' houses and they were invited to dinner. While they were eating they all boasted about their good marksmanship and how many Indians each claimed he had killed. The lady of the house noticed that Big-foot had nothing to say, and she questioned him, saying, "Mr. Wallace, how many Indians did you kill?" And he answered, "None." She then asked, "How is that?" "Just because there were not enough Indians for all of us, and according to the stories that you have heard, there were none left for me."

Chapter Two:

Shenanigans—Mail to Bandera—Civil War

My father always showed a strong affection for me and I was warmly attached to him. I often accompanied him on his journeys away from home, and I am inclined to think that my mischief-making propensities influenced him to remove me from familiar associations when he took me with him. He made frequent trips to Port Lavaca with his ox-wagon, when his team was not needed on the farm, and he received a fair compensation for hauling freight both ways between that point and San Antonio. I was not only his traveling companion on such occasions, but I made myself useful by driving the oxen and was able to do many things that were appreciated.

My father once contracted with a party in San Antonio to haul a load of pine lumber from a mill near Bastrop, on the Colorado River, and I went with him. Bastrop was then a small village with a few scattering houses, and the night we camped in the town a public meeting was held in the open air which I attended. I have no recollection of what it was about, although it was the first political speech I had ever heard, but I do remember that the place was lit up by torches made of pine knots and that they furnished the most beautiful light I had ever seen. I was only about eight years old then, and when I learned that I could get pine knots for the trouble of gathering them, I lost no time the next day in collecting all I wanted, although the task was not as easy as I expected. On the way home I illuminated our camp every night and had some left with which I lit up the premises to please a few of my young friends. They were delighted, because they had never seen anything so brilliant before, but the exhibition closed when I barely missed setting fire to the corn-crib.

The light they had been accustomed to see was made by wrapping a rag around a stick and saturating it with lard; the lower end was then stuck in a coffee-cup half full of sand, and the cup was filled with rendered lard or melted tallow. It made a very dim light, but it was the best we could do before candle molds were introduced, which were used by everybody who made tallow candles, until sperm candles of northern manufacture were placed on the market. The first I ever saw was in Castroville, in 1855, when three of them sold for twenty-five cents; but they were too high-priced for common use and more than the poorer people of that region could afford to pay.

My father was an indulgent parent and he allowed his children many privileges, but he could be severe in his punishments when their misconduct made it necessary, and our mother was equally kind and affectionate. Under such influences the hardships that circumstances imposed upon us were not felt and we retained pleasant memories of our childhood. Our opportunities for an education were limited, and in my case frequent interruptions occurred so that my school days if added together would represent a very short period.

I remember a donkey which was identified with my school experiences that, incidentally, was the cause of many fights and any amount of trouble, but it is not worthwhile to discuss them. He had a disposition that was rather eccentric and he indulged his whims whenever it suited him. He was always in request on week days, and on Sundays some one of the children rode him to church. I will never forget the sensation he created one Sabbath morning when the services were being conducted. The minister was reading from the Bible and the congregation was devoutly listening to the lesson in which the word "Hallelujah" appears. As he raised his voice to an usually loud pitch when repeating the word, the donkey, that was grazing near the window, thought, perhaps, that the exclamation invited a response. A moment later his head appeared in the opening and he uttered a refrain in prolonged strains such as only a donkey can express, until the solemnities were disturbed and the preacher even, although somewhat disconcerted, could not suppress a smile.

My father owned a small bunch of horses that were not easily controlled and the donkey was our stand-by until we got rid of a wild gray mare that could rarely be penned and she always led the herd. One Sunday, when my parents were at church, we managed to get her in the pen, and after roping and throwing her, with the assistance of several visiting boys, I tied a dry cow's hide securely to her tail. When I turned her loose she dashed out of the enclosure and as the rattling raw-hide drove her frantic with fright her headlong flight was continued until she was lost to view. She was never seen afterwards and we came to the conclusion that she was drowned in the Medina River or else she had run herself to death. My father was kept in ignorance of our performance for some time until he missed her, and he did not appear to regret her disappearance because he knew her to be worthless.

Another escapade of mine was more serious in its consequences, and it caused my father and several of his neighbors considerable trouble and expense. Three neighborhood boys assisted me and were equally responsible for the mischief which consisted in changing the corner-stones of a number of adjoining farms, including those on my father's land. The alterations were not discovered until some time after and several years passed before the trouble was remedied by repeated surveys of the tracts involved. They each had the same area of land because we had measured off a certain width and added it to the next adjacent, consequently it was necessary to start at an established corner and re-survey all the subdivisions of the 640-acre tract which, when located according to the field notes, identified the corners correctly.

The land in controversy was then in Bexar County, and I think the differences in their claims were settled without litigation. I am sure that my father arbitrated his claim in a friendly manner because he never had a suit in court, although he frequently served as a grand juror and on petty juries in the district court.

My parents had become more prosperous as a recompense for their hard labor and strict economy, and their children were old enough to assist in performing the routine duties of the farm. The settlement in the meantime had been extended and the population in the country was greatly augmented, therefore, the opportunities for securing a living had increased. A stage route had also been established between San Antonio and Eagle Pass, which passed by my father's door. It was under the management of Alex David, who had secured a contract to carry the United States mail between those points, and at the same time he was granted a similar contract to transport the mail between San Antonio and Bandera. As the latter was tributary to the main line it was open to a sub-contractor and my father applied for and secured the route. It extended from his house, four miles east of Castroville, to Bandera and back, a distance of thirty-two miles, each way, and it was stipulated that it should be ridden every Monday, and back the next day, for which my father was to receive $300 per annum.

I was then about fourteen years old and the duty of carrying the mail was assigned to me, whereby I became the youngest mail-carrier in the United States. The Bandera mail sack that was brought by stage to my father's house every Monday, about noon, was conveyed by me to Bandera, on horse-back, and I returned the next day in time to meet the Eagle Pass mail-hack which took it on to San Antonio.

The country along my route was sparsely settled then, as the following facts will show. After leaving my father's house it was eight miles to the ranch owned jointly by Dr. Bohm and Richard Tuerpe. The last served fifteen years as commissioner in Medina County, and now resides in San Antonio. Twelve miles further on was Mitchell's ranch, that was in charge of John Green, the father of Will Green, who is now a mounted policeman in San Antonio. Six miles beyond, the ranch of August and Celeste Begno was located, who now own a large ranch on Turkey Creek, and Ed. Montel, an attorney in Hondo City, is their nephew. The next settlement was the beautifully located town of Bandera which is widely known as a health resort on account of the salubrious climate.

These were frontier settlements and about that period the wild Indians made frequent incursions through the country, but I was lucky enough to avoid coming in contact with them, nor did I see any signs of them on any of my journeys. On one occasion, though, I was badly frightened by a party of Mexicans, who were mistaken for Indians, and I made a record run when making my escape. As I am giving my experiences I may as well relate the circumstances.

The trip under consideration was made in company with a boy then on a visit to Castroville, whose home was in Bandera, and as he wished to return I allowed him to ride behind me on my horse. He was about my age, and though his name is forgotten, I remember that John Adamadez, now a horse-dealer in San Antonio, was his cousin. Nothing happened until we got into the Medina mountains, where I took a wrong trail that led us into the Medina valley, about six miles below Mitchell's ranch. About the time I realized my mistake a scattered body of men suddenly appeared in sight among the trees, who we supposed were Indians. We were very much alarmed and I quickly turned my horse without waiting to make a close investigation, but the movement was not fast enough to satisfy my companion, who, in a panic, jumped to the ground and ran in the brush. It was done so quickly I thought he was killed, and under that impression my horse was urged to his best speed until I arrived at Mitchell's ranch and excitedly related all that had happened.

Mr. Green tried to quiet my fears, and promised that when his men came in he would send one with me to Bandera for assistance. While we were waiting a party of Mexicans came up to the ranch and with them was the boy who I supposed was dead. They proved to be those we had assumed were Indians, and I knew I had given a false alarm when they explained that they had been engaged in thrashing pecan trees and gathering the nuts. They were near enough to witness our fright and hastily quit their work to overtake the boy, who, when found, was undeceived. Knowing that an alarm of Indians being in the vicinity would create excitement, they hurried to the ranch with a view to relieve the anxiety of his friends. Of course I was glad that no serious results were attached to the adventure, but my Indian scare became a standing joke among my acquaintances and it was a sore subject until I lived it down.

Nothing else happened to me while I carried the mail that was of any consequence, except once, when I was thrown from a wild mule I was riding, which, incidentally, caused considerable excitement. He was a skittish beast, and so easily frightened he would frequently snort and jump suddenly to one side when nothing was in sight but his shadow. Generally I was on my guard, but that evening I was careless, and when he made a quick bound sideways I was thrown out of the saddle to the ground. Before I could recover my feet he darted away at the top of his speed with my mail-bag and I had to walk to Bandera, a mile or two distant. When I related what had happened, my story enlisted the services of all the men in the town, but their search was unsuccessful until late the following evening, when the brute was brought in and I was glad to know that the mail-bag was safe.

The next morning I started for home, feeling badly at the thought that I was a day behind because it was the first time such a thing had happened. When within twelve miles from home I was surprised to meet my father with a party of neighbors on their way to look for me. Among them was Dan Adams, Sam Etter, John Bippert, Tab Woodward, Jim Brown and others. They were all very much relieved when they saw me, because they thought I had either been killed or captured by Indians.

The mail route was in existence one year and ten months, and in that time I made about one hundred round trips, each averaging sixty-four miles, without failing to be on time except on the occasion to which I have referred, and that was not my fault. When my youth is considered, in connection with the fact that the country was infested by roving bands of Indians who were continually depredating upon the people and committing many murders, I have a right to flatter myself on the record I made. It is evident that I escaped numerous dangers and I feel grateful for my good fortune. Although I carried a six-shooter as long and heavy as that worn by Big-foot Wallace, or any other Indian fighter, it is an open question whether I would have used it, in case of an encounter with Indians, or would have trusted, instead, to the speed of my good horse, Sam, who carried me on nearly all of my journeys.

All mail contracts granted by the United States government in Texas were canceled in 1861, at the commencement of the Civil War, and of course Alex David discontinued his services. When my father's sub-contract was annulled a sum amounting to about five hundred dollars was due him for carrying the mail; but neither he nor his heirs have been able to recover a cent from the government on the account; consequently all my services in that connection were performed for nothing unless the claim still pending in Washington City should be favorably considered in the future.

The great Civil War was initiated and Texas became involved in that lamentable struggle, but I do not intend to discuss the subject. I will only say that my father, like many other good citizens, voted against secession, but, after the measure was carried, he submitted to the laws of the land and directed his attention to his legitimate business. Partly with a view to giving me employment, he engaged in freighting cotton from Columbus to Eagle Pass, and I drove an ox-team between those points until September, 1862, but the occupation was not such as I fancied. I was then nearly seventeen years of age, and in December of that year I visited Eagle Pass on my personal account, with the intention of making my own way in the world. I entertained no political prejudices, nor was there any necessity for me to take sides in the war, on account of my age, consequently it had nothing to do with my visit to the Mexican border. Afterwards I passed over the Rio Grande, and did not again return to Texas for several years, but my experiences until then will be related in the following chapter.

Chapter Three:

Employments in Mexico—Silver Mines

I felt no misgivings regarding my future prospects when I left home in September, 1862, with the determination to seek my fortune in the world that I believed was waiting for me somewhere. I was young, healthy, and vigorous, with a mind strengthened by independent thoughts that had sustained me in many responsible positions and I felt that I could earn a competency by my own exertions. With such confidence in myself, a good horse, and a few dollars in my pocket, I parted from the loved ones at home with no definite idea with reference to the date of my return.

My route on horse-back to Eagle Pass took me through the town of D'Hanis, where I was joined by Joe Carle, the father of Carle Bros., who now conduct a mercantile establishment on West Commerce Street, in San Antonio. He was a merchant in D'Hanis and we had previously arranged to go to Mexico together, where he had business to attend to, but as he was engaged to his present wife he returned home after an absence of a few weeks.

In the meantime I became acquainted with Billy Egg, a young man who had fled from east Texas to avoid serving in the army. He was stopping with his brother, Thomas Egg, a married man, who lived in Piedras Negras, and I secured board with the family.

A few days afterwards I, and two other men, accompanied Thomas Egg thirty miles up the Rio Grande to a bottom where there was a growth of willow trees, which he proposed to cut into lengths suitable for rafters, called _vieges_ in Spanish. They were used by the Mexicans as a sub-structure for the flat roofs of their houses, which were built of adobies or sun-dried brick, 4 x 10 x 18 inches, made of mud. The rafters most in demand were twenty-five feet long, with a diameter of twelve inches at the butt and six inches at the small end. These could be readily sold in Piedras Negras at one dollar and a half each, on account of their scarcity because of the difficulty in hauling them.

When constructing a roof for a house the Mexicans placed these rafters on top of the adobe walls, about two feet apart, and the entire space was then closely covered over with split boards, about two feet long, that reached from one rafter to the next. A mortar of mud, made from a particular kind of dirt, was thoroughly mixed with dry grass until it could be handled. This was spread in a continuous layer about four inches thick near the eaves and much thicker in the middle, so as to give a slope to the roof. After becoming thoroughly dry a second layer of about the same thickness was put on, and it was followed by a third when ready to receive it. The finishing course was a layer of cement about four inches thick, composed of earth and lime, which only the Mexicans know how to mix, and the roof with its slope from the center was made smooth by dragging over it the edge of a board. Such roofs last a long time, and I remember one that was shown me in Paras, Mexico, which had received no repairs in thirty years, that was then in perfect condition.

Our party cut about one hundred and eighty of such rafters, and as we had planned to secure them in a raft and float them down the river, we carried them to the nearest point on our shoulders, a distance of three hundred yards. When we were about ready to start our raft the Mexican authorities interfered, under the impression that it could be used for smuggling purposes, and they prohibited its completion. We then changed our plans, and were compelled to employ Mexican carts to haul our rafters to Piedras Negras, which was expensive, consequently we realized only a small sum above our outlay.

I was next employed under a contract to make two dozen American ox-yokes at one dollar and a half apiece, for Semon de la Penia, who had a wagon-shop in Piedras Negras. He had removed recently from San Antonio, to which place his family afterwards returned. I worked in his shop and used his tools until I finished the yokes, and perhaps they were the first that had ever been made in that town.

Soon after completing my job, in November, 1862, I visited Matamoras on horse-back, in company with Thomas B. McManus, John Heinemann and Billy Egg. We traveled down the Mexican side of the Rio Grande a distance of four hundred and fifty miles. My only object in going was to see the country, but my trip was not satisfactory, because after spending all my money I was compelled to work in a cotton-yard, and after a short stay I was ready to return to Piedras Negras. I was without means, but fortunately I fell in with a theatrical troop, and secured employment with them as door-keeper. We left Matamoras in December, 1862, and on the way up the river the company gave performances at Camargo, Renosa, Renosa San Antonio, Roma, Mier, Laredo, and finally at Piedras Negras, where I left them.

With a part of my earnings I purchased a mule and cart, paying seventy-five dollars for the outfit, and engaged in hauling water from the Rio Grande, which I sold at 25 cents a barrel. Considering the amount of capital invested it was the best paying business in which I ever engaged, and it was my constant occupation until I was offered employment that gave me an opportunity to see the country, then I hired a man to drive the cart during my absence.

Messrs. Herman and Gilbeau, cotton-brokers in Piedras Negras, wanted to visit San Luis Potosi on business.

As the distance was five hundred and fifty miles over an unsafe road an escort was necessary, and they hired me and a Mexican to serve in that capacity. They traveled in an ambulance with four mules driven by a Mexican and the escort accompanied them on horse-back all the way.

A brief sketch of our route and the prominent places of interest is worthy of notice in a section of country where the greater part was a desolate wilderness, but as it is described elsewhere as far as Monterey in another connection, the reader's attention will be directed to a few places of importance beyond that city:

The city of Saltillo is situated in the State of Coahuila, seventy-five miles southwest of Monterey, on the north slope of a ridge that crosses the whole valley, and it is in sight after passing the hacienda of San Gregario. It was then a well-built town of substantial houses, with good paved streets, and a beautiful Alameda. A number of factories were established there, and they contributed greatly to the prosperity of the place by giving employment to the inhabitants. Several of them manufactured unbleached cotton goods exclusively, and others turned out woolen goods. They also had the reputation of turning out the finest of the well-known hand-made Mexican blankets that were admired for their excellent quality and workmanship, not only in the republic but in Europe and the United States, where they were sold for from thirty to fifty dollars apiece.

The road from Saltillo to San Luis Potosi passed through San Cristobal, and the Hacienda de Guadalupe, to the right of the Catorce mountain, which rises two thousand feet above the surrounding plain. When within twenty-five miles of San Luis Potosi the beautiful city appears and distance adds enchantment to the view which becomes more attractive the nearer it is approached. Stately domes and numerous lofty towers give prominence to the substantial buildings that crowd upon its narrow streets. These, when entered, are found to be interesting on account of the way they are laid out and because of their superior construction and cleanliness. Among its public buildings is a splendid city hall and five or six magnificent churches adorned with carvings and sculpture that rival any in Mexico, the most superb of which is the cathedral.

In 1862 San Luis Potosi was one of the most enterprising cities in the republic, independent of its mining interests, that at one time attracted great attention. The San Pedro mine was once the most prominent in Mexico, on account of the single piece of pure gold taken out of it, that is said to have been the largest solid lump of gold ever found in Mexico or any part of the world. It was sent to Spain as a present to the King, and in return for that act of generosity, the King contributed a beautiful and costly clock to the city as a gift for its cathedral, which I suppose strikes the hours now as it did in 1862 when I was there. The noted San Pedro mine, which was near the city, was abandoned many years before my visit on account of water that flooded the interior and caused it to cave. So far the evil has not been remedied, but perhaps scientific skill will overcome the difficulties eventually and make its wealth accessible.

After reaching our destination my employers ascertained that a lot of silver bullion that was due them had not been delivered. The treasure was expected from the mines of Real de Catorce, distant about one hundred and forty miles, and it was essential that it should be secured with as little delay as possible. For that purpose I and the two Mexicans of our party were sent with four packmules, under the orders of Angel Hernandez, a resident of San Luis Potosi. We arrived at the smelting works of the Catorce mines about eight o'clock in the evening.

The city of Real de Catorce is situated on top of a high range of mountains, and the only approach was up a narrow winding path cut in the side of the ragged acclivity that could only be ascended on foot or the back of mules.

This and another similar trail were dug out of the perpendicular face of the precipice, and each with its windings was about two miles in length. Its name Catorce, "fourteen," was given it because this cañon was first inhabited by a band of fourteen robbers.

The population of the town then numbered in the neighborhood of six thousand people. The public buildings and houses were substantially built of stone, and the streets, though narrow, were paved, and cleanliness was enforced. No vehicles of any kind could be seen in the place, and it was said that none had ever been introduced, but the deficiency was supplied by pack animals. The inhabitants derived their support from the rich mines situated in a cañon of the mountains which rise above the plateau on which the city is built. The ore was very rich and the mines were owned by Santos de la Masa, who worked them according to very primitive methods.

The ore was conveyed from the mines to the foot of the mountain in hampers on the backs of burros. Each burden weighed one hundred and fifty pounds, and they traveled in a slow pace, as they wound down the trail leading from the mine, in a continuous line, and returned unloaded, in a snail-like pace, along an equally narrow trail up another route.

The reducing works of the Catorce mines were situated near a stream that ran along the base of the mountain where the ore was worked both by smelting and by patio, or cold amalgamation process. The first method was used for the hard, and the last for the soft ores that were taken from the mine. There were several circular depressions, each about two feet in depth and seventy-five feet in circumference, with its bottom sloping from the center to the outer rim. These were cut in the solid rock and cemented, and each was enclosed around the edges by a strong fence about eight feet in height.

The soft ore was first ground on steel mills to the fineness of sand; and the powder was then placed in one of the circular excavations to the thickness of eighteen inches. It was then saturated with water, and a quantity of quick-silver was added. A number of wild mules was then turned into the enclosure until there was not enough room for them to turn round and the gate was closed. The mules were then driven around the circle as rapidly as possible by men with whips who were stationed at intervals on the fence. When the animals were completely fagged out others equally wild relieved them and each time more water was added. When the pulverized ore was reduced to the consistency of mud, it was washed clean, and nothing but the silver amalgam remained that was deposited in grooves, made for that purpose in the cement floor. This was gathered and smelted in a furnace from which the silver was run into bars.

The process was similar to the common practice in olden times, when grain was tramped out by horses on a barn floor, and it was equally successful. The owner of the mine raised large numbers of mules on his ranch expressly for the purpose, and when sufficiently tamed they were placed on the market. This description is given with the belief that the methods then in use have been discarded since the introduction of stamp mills and other improved machinery.

A much harder ore was taken from the same mine, called milling ore, which was carried direct to a furnace. The furnace was built in the side of a hill and resembled a lime-kiln, with an opening in the top to receive the ore. A peculiar kind of wood was used for smelting the ore that produced an intense heat which was kept up until a sluggish stream of silver flowed out below into molds that turned out bars of uniform size.

We remained at the smelting works three days, during which time I made several visits to the town of Catorce. I rode up the mountain on a donkey and the round trip cost me twenty-five cents. I had a good time frolicing, dancing, and seeing everything that was worth the trouble. Felix Barrera, of San Antonio, who was known to me, was working in the mine, but I did not see him, although I became acquainted with his brother who lived in the town.

We loaded our pack-mules with eight bars of silver bullion, valued at eight thousand dollars, and returned safely to San Luis Potosi with our valuable cargo, but I do not know what disposition was made of it, although I am confident that it was left there. Before our departure the Mexican ambulance driver was discharged on account of drunkenness, and his duties were assigned to me. I knew all about driving oxen and a pair of horses, and I assumed the task without hesitation. Though it was my first attempt at driving four-in-hand, I succeeded admirably and my employers complimented my skill when we arrived at Piedras Negras, about the latter part of February, 1863, after an absence of twenty-five days.

I next offered my services to Messrs. Rinehold Becker and George Enderle, merchants of Piedras Negras, who were preparing to visit Monterey for the purpose of replenishing their stock of goods. My recent experience was a sufficient recommendation and they employed me to drive their ambulance.

My expertness in handling horses was not put to a test on the journey until we passed over a stretch of road that was full of stumps. Although I exerted all my skill I gave my passengers frequent jolts and they were rather free with their criticism when commenting on my carelessness. Finally they concluded to take a more conservative view of the situation by turning their mishaps to some account, and decided that every time a wheel struck a stump they would console themselves by taking a drink. As we had a long jaunt ahead of us the encounters with stumps and the bottle were frequent, consequently my employers were well loaded when we reached an open country. We returned from Monterey in March and I was again out of a job. Mr. Enderle has been dead a number of years; he was a brother-in-law of Mr. John Fries, who for many years was a merchant in San Antonio, where his son, Fred Fries, is now City Clerk. Mr. Becker is now living in said city, where, until a few years ago, he was in active business.

I was not disposed to remain idle and I undertook to dig a well for John Heinemann, in April, for a stipulated price. I had never had any experience in that line of work, and my ignorance was perceptible when I struck water because of its crookedness the mouth of the well was hid from view when at the bottom. After it was finished it answered every purpose on account of its abundant supply of water. It was the first well that was ever dug in Piedras Negras, and the owner made it pay by selling water at the well for twelve and a half cents per barrel. It did not interfere with my water business, which had been prosecuted during my absence, and it was continued by hired help for some time afterwards.

I was again free, but in May I found employment with the firm of Messrs. F. Groos & Co., in Piedras Negras, who placed me in charge of their cotton yard under Gustave Groos, a brother of Mr. F. Groos, now a banker in San Antonio. I commenced working for them at a salary of seventy-five dollars per month, and held the position until the following October. Strong influences were then brought to bear which made me give up my situation and dispose of my water business, but when doing so I acted contrary to my inclinations. I was led away from all my former occupations, and was influenced to engage in the trade of war, which was repulsive to me.

Chapter Four:

Service in the Civil War

I was not much concerned on account of the Civil War that was raging in the United States, and I was content so long as Texas was free from its ravages. I did not know much about it, but before that time many men from the Southern States had entered Mexico on account of the troubles there. Some were refugees who fled from the country because of their opposition to secession and sympathy for the Union cause, but many were skulkers seeking to avoid military service, and a large number were deserters from the Confederate army. Among the former was Joe Christ, who was devoted to the Union cause. He was a good old friend of my father's, and he, more than any one else, persuaded me to close up my business and go with him to Brownsville.

The country along the west side of the Rio Grande was then infested by outlaws, and one of the most notorious was Abram Garcia, who first appeared there in 1860. He was personally known to Louis Hastings, now living in San Antonio, who is acquainted with his career, but through other sources I became familiar with the many depredations he committed between Laredo and Matamoras.

He was commonly known as "Caballero Blanco," or the White-horseman, on account of the white horse he always rode, and the people in that region feared him very much, particularly in the towns of Mier, Roma, Renosa Vico, Renosa San Antonio and Camargo. He had the reputation of being a very brave man, but the cru-

elties he perpetrated on those who fell into his hands
indicated that he was influenced by a brutal nature. He
took special delight in humiliating the victims that were
overpowered by his gang and robbed, by forcing them to
dance at the muzzle of a six-shooter and then maltreated
them by whipping them cruelly with a quirt before they
were finally dismissed.

When passing through the territory in which he operated, Mr. Christ and myself observed a continual watchfulness, but nothing was seen that excited suspicion,
though we came in contact with a party of unfortunate
Mexicans who had been subjected to his unmerciful
treatment. They had come from Saltillo or Monterey
with a lot of superior horses, some fine Mexican blankets, saddles, and other things that were intended for the
Texas market, when they encountered Caballero Blanco
near the river, at Roma. The property, which was valuable, was all taken from them, and the entire party of six
men, after being forced to dance, were horribly beaten,
but one more severely than the others. Their condition
was such that it was necessary to convey them to Renosa San Antonio for medical treatment, and Mr. Sanders,
a merchant of Roma, a particular friend of theirs, was
summoned to their bed-side.

After seeing the evidence of his deviltry, our party, like
every one else, was fearful of meeting Caballero Blanco,
and we kept constantly on the watch until our destination was reached. As I left Mexico a few months later
and did not return for several years, I heard no mention
of him, nor do I know what became of him.

Persons who violate the law in Mexico are quickly arrested, and generally the penalties are impartially enforced; but some people think otherwise, and many
stories have been published which convey a different
impression.

I recall an unusual incident which came to my knowledge that happened at Mier, near the Rio Grande, when

I and my three companions, Tom Egg, John Heinemann, and Bill McFarland, were stopping there. The third day after our arrival four other Texans put up at the little meson where we were quartered. The next morning the newcomers led their horses to water and when returning from the river they observed a Mexican woman moving slowly in the trail before them. A large jar that held about four gallons was gracefully poised on her head, without any support from her hands, which contained water that she had procured at the river and she was carrying it to her home half a mile distant.

One of the young men in the party was an excellent marksman with a pistol, and he wanted to show his skill by breaking the jar with a bullet. His aim was accurate, the vessel was broken, and the poor woman received an unexpected shower-bath. It was a mean thing for him to do, and perhaps he feared the consequences or else his offer to compensate the woman for her loss by paying her a dollar, showed that he regretted his thoughtless act.

She communicated the circumstances to her friends, who complained to the Alcalde of the place, and in a short time eight armed men appeared before the meson and conveyed the young gentleman to jail. Until then no one in my party knew what had happened, and then Messrs. Heinemann, Egg, and McFarland, accompanied by the prisoner's three friends, followed him and the guard, but I remained in camp.

Heinemann, who had married in a prominent Mexican family in Laredo, could speak Spanish fluently and he undertook to defend the young Texan. He proved by the testimony of his friends that the prisoner was an expert with a pistol, who could shoot an egg off a man's head at any reasonable distance, and that the woman's life was in no danger when he fired at the jar. But for Heineman's influence it is probable that some sort of punishment would have been meted out to the young man, and he was fortunate in escaping so easily, because then Americans were looked upon with less favor than now. Possibly when he returned to Texas he made himself a hero by telling incredible stories about Mexico, like others have done, but they only deceive the ignorant.

After arriving in Brownsville, Mr. Christ exerted his influence over me and in compliance with his earnest solicitations I enlisted in the United States army, in December, 1863, as a private in Captain Braubach's company of scouts. The company was an independent organization, raised for service on the Rio Grande, and it was composed of white Americans exclusively. I was then in my seventeenth year and when the officers were elected I was made second corporal. The First Texas Cavalry was then in camp at Brownsville, under the command of Colonel Davis, who was afterwards governor of Texas, and my company was embodied with it and was known as Company H. During the six months that the command remained in that region it was constantly engaged in scouting along the Texas border.

On one occasion a detachment of the regiment, consisting of twenty men, was sent to Padre Island with orders to collect a lot of beeves under the protection of a vessel that was to sail a mile or so from shore and warn us of the enemy's presence should any appear. After proceeding some distance we came in sight of a herd of cattle and soon headed them toward our lines. We did not make much progress before the enemy appeared with a larger force that compelled us to retreat and the beeves were recaptured. The vessel off shore promptly came to our rescue and shelled our opponents, but they could not be prevented from driving off the cattle to a place of safety.

A large Federal force, represented by all branches of the service, was then concentrated in the vicinity of Brownsville, and the commodious buildings at Fort Brown, on the banks of the Rio Grande, opposite Matamoras, were occupied by them. An invasion of Texas was in contemplation that was to be conducted on a large scale by two armies, one on Red River and the other on the Rio Grande, both acting in concert, but the battles of Mansfield and Pleasant Hill changed these plans and Texas was spared from witnessing the havoc incident to the ravages of war.

After Banks' army was defeated on Red River and driven back to Morganza, on the Mississippi River, the western division, that was to have participated in the invasion of Texas from the west, was ordered to rendezvous at that point in Louisiana. Only five companies of the First Texas Cavalry were included in the order, and Companies A, B and C remained in Brownsville under the command of Captain Zoeller until the close of the war, when they were reunited with the regiment.

When we arrived at Morganza the encampment of General Banks' army of 80,000 men extended along the river a distance of about ten miles and the line of outposts was, necessarily, about twenty miles long. A reorganization of the army was in progress and it was understood that preparations were being made for another advance into Texas. During that period the picket line was constantly harassed by the enemy's scouts and they sustained many losses, although they had a strong support and were always on the alert. Every day a dozen or more of the poor fellows were either killed, wounded, or captured, and it seemed as if it was impossible to restrain the Rebs, who seemed to be always ready to attack our front. These fatalities do not figure in history, but it is an actual fact that the Confederates caused more losses to the Union army in that encampment than was sustained by the American forces in the recent Spanish war.

The Confederates occupied a fortification on Bayou Atchafalaya, about twenty-five miles distant and west of our position, which gave them a strong support. When the attacks became insufferable it was determined to drive them from that location, and, if possible, force them to abandon the country east of that stream. For that purpose a force numbering about three thousand infantry, with four or five batteries and one thousand cavalry, was sent against them with orders to treat all Confederate scouts as guerrillas and show no mercy to those who should fall in their hands.

The excuse for vigorous action and the adoption of harsh penalties was justified by the report that the Confederates had hung several Federal soldiers; but the reason for doing so was unknown, and if it was a fact the circumstances did not warrant such extremely harsh measures, though many acts are perpetrated in time of war which are unjustifiable. Possibly they were executed as spies or deserters, but it is more probable that they were foragers who were depredating on the citizens, and hanging was too good for them.

A detachment of sixty men from the First Texas Cavalry was placed under the command of Lieutenant Lilly of Company A, and eight of them were selected from Company H. My disappointment because I was not one of them led me to offer my services as a volunteer and they were accepted. I was anxious to go because we all thought that it was the first movement towards the invasion of Texas and my confidence led me to believe that we would march direct to San Antonio. Fearing that there would be no more fighting, I was anxious to participate in one engagement so that I could tell my friends in Texas that I took part in a battle. When I was chosen in another man's place I was delighted and I considered it a very great favor.

We left our encampment about three o'clock in the morning and our detachment led the advance with a part of a New York regiment of cavalry in our rear. We were chosen for the post of honor because the First Texas Cavalry had the reputation of being very good horsemen. We rode about twenty miles before we came in contact with the enemy's pickets. They gave us a warm reception, and held us in check for half an hour, in which time about thirty of our men were killed and many wounded. After the first attack reinforcements of infantry rapidly advanced and a charge was made which routed the enemy. We pursued them about five miles, or until we were under the fire of the fort, and we then skirmished until our entire force was concentrated.

Our troops were sheltered behind a levee and the enemy was strongly fortified on the opposite side of the Atchafalaya with their cannon commanding the bridge. The fight lasted about four hours, during which time a heavy infantry and artillery fire was maintained on both sides. The Federal loss in killed and wounded was considerable, and I saw enough fighting to satisfy me, but I did my part without making myself conspicuous. My first shock was received when I saw Major Black, a gallant officer, who commanded a battalion of Illinois infantry, shot from the top of the levee and roll down the embankment. The retreat was ordered none too soon for me, and I never afterwards was foolish enough to volunteer when a detail was needed, on which occasions I was always glad when my name did not appear.

After the invasion of Texas was abandoned, the encampment at Morganza was broken up and the five companies of the First Texas Cavalry were stationed successively at Natchez, Brookhaven and Baton Rouge. Subsequently, when the war was brought to a close, they were ordered to New Orleans, where they were joined by Companies A, B, and C that had been left in Brownsville. They had performed efficient service on the western borders of Texas under the command of Captain Zoeller, and they participated in the last battle that was fought for the Union. The engagement took place the 13th day of May, 1865, below Brownsville, at Palo Alto, which is now known as the "White Ranch." It was not much of a fight, but it is worthy of notice because it happened sev-

en days after the Trans-Mississippi Department of the
Confederacy was surrendered by General Kirby Smith,
consequently it was the last battle of the war.

After the companies of the regiment were reunited,
Company H, which until then was known as an independent organization, was disbanded and the men enrolled
in the companies of their choice, otherwise they would
not have been entitled to pensions and other emolu-
ments of the service. I became a member of Company C,
commanded by Captain Zoeller, who now is a prosperous farmer and ranchman and resides at Waring, Texas.
The regiment marched over-land to San Antonio, Texas,
where on the 28th of October, 1865, the men were honorably discharged from the army.

Before dismissing the subject, I wish to pay a just trib-
ute to the character and services of my commander, and
it will be appropriate to do so in this connection.

Captain Zoeller claims a long list of ancestors who were
prominently connected with military life in Germany,
therefore, he was instinctively a soldier and the profession of arms was not repulsive to him. He was conscien-
tious in his views with reference to the political troubles
that arose in 1861, and he not only opposed secession at
the ballot box, but he entered the army and was active in
defense of the Union during the great Civil War.

His talents and qualifications recommended him for
promotion, and as a captain of cavalry his superior
horsemanship and gallantry made him conspicuous on
all occasions where his services could be made effective.
As an officer he recognized the fact that obedience was
the first duty of a soldier, and he exerted himself to in-
still his principles into the minds of his men. As a disci-
plinarian he was strict but kind and considerate to those
who served under him, consequently he won their respect and confidence. The estimation in which his abilities and services were held by those in authority was
expressed when he was offered a position in the regu-

lar army of the United States. When he returned to the peaceful pursuits of private life he not only retained the affections of his comrades in arms, but he won the good will of all men and he commanded an influence that was felt wherever he was known. No man is perfect, but my friendship for Captain Zoeller has placed a high estimate on his character, and I believe that when his life's record is closed few blemishes will appear to mar the purity of his existence.

I returned immediately to my father's farm, where I received an affectionate welcome from my people and neighbors. I had been absent from home nearly three years, and many changes had occurred during that period, but none had taken place in my father's family. After spending two pleasant months among my old associations, I became restless and anxious for some active employment. As mail contracts were then being let in Texas, I filed an application for the route from San Antonio to Eagle Pass and from there to Fort Clark. My bid was accepted by the Post Office Department and in January, 1866, a contract was awarded me.

Chapter Five:

Indian Depredations—Mexican Highwaymen

I was not quite twenty-one years of age when I secured a contract to carry the United States mail from San Antonio to Eagle Pass and that from Eagle Pass to Fort Clark. The length of the first route was one hundred and sixty-two miles, and I was required to make the round trip once every six days. The post offices were Castroville, New Fountain, D'Hanis, Sabinal, Uvalde and Eagle Pass, from which place the mail was carried to Fort Clark, a distance of fifty miles, by George Swanda, whom I hired for that purpose.

My outfit consisted of a three-seated hack, capable of carrying six persons, that was drawn by a pair of mules, which I drove myself. Stations were established at suitable distances, where I changed teams; and as I had sublet the route to Fort Clark, Eagle Pass became the terminus of that under my immediate control.

My regular charge per seat, for a through passage, was twenty dollars, but it was seldom that all seats were occupied.

The road was always beset by many dangers, and I considered myself extremely fortunate after passing through them. The frontier was practically unprotected against the Indians who were then plentiful, and they made raids with impunity through Medina, Uvalde and Atascosa Counties, where they killed and plundered the people. The Eagle Pass and El Paso roads were continually infested by them, and those who traveled those routes always tempted Providence unless they were strong enough in numbers to resist an attack.

I often saw the trails of marauding parties of Indians where they crossed the road and have found the mutilated bodies of many men lying where they had been murdered. I frequently traveled the route alone, and it is remarkable that on such occasions I was never molested, and the exceptions were when I had one or more passengers in my coach. The risks were so great that business men would rarely travel the route alone, but formed parties of several who were well supplied with arms and ammunition.

On one of my trips in 1866, I was traveling westward entirely alone, and when about eighteen miles from Eagle Pass I drove into a camp, about three o'clock in the afternoon, where nine Mexican carts were standing by the roadside. The bodies of the drivers were scattered around where they had been killed and some of them scalped by Indians. Evidently the murders were committed not more than three hours before and apparently when the men stopped for dinner.

I did not waste much time making investigations after seeing that they were all dead, but hurried onward as fast as possible under a dread of the barbarians who might have lingered in that vicinity. I reported the tragedy to the authorities immediately after my arrival at Eagle Pass. The bodies were brought in that night and buried the following day in the public graveyard. One of the unfortunates was Felipe Calabera, a nephew of Jesus Calabera, who now lives on South Laredo Street in front of Emil Oppermann's store. If the Indians were followed I cannot recall the fact, but as such murders were frequent, and as it was not troublesome to find the perpetrators at any time, it is probable that no action was taken to have them punished.

The Indians sometimes were very bold, and on one of my trips to Eagle Pass, in 1866, they exhibited their adroitness as thieves in the vicinity, and the performance caused the good people of that town considerable inconvenience. It happened in connection with a patriotic occasion, on the 4th of July, when the citizens were enjoying themselves at a ball, that was given in honor of our national anniversary, to which everybody was invited.

The abandoned United States post, situated about half a mile south of town, that is known in history as Fort Duncan, was selected as a suitable place for the celebration, and the hospital, with a floor space measuring about 30 x 100 feet, was chosen for dancing purposes. The arrangements were all perfected by Thomas B. McManus, the customs-house officer at Eagle Pass, with the assistance of Henry Bruhn, of San Antonio, the father-in-law of Otto Evert and Ed Galm of said city.

The Mexican customs-house officers from Piedras Negras, with their families, all the best people from Eagle Pass, and the settlements along the river were in attendance. Those who rode horseback secured the animals to the buildings or surrounding trees and gave them no further attention after joining in the dancing or other pleasures of the occasion. No apprehension of danger was entertained, and nothing occurred to mar the happiness of the evening that gave life to the old fort which caused it to resound with joyous mirth until the early tints of dawn admonished the participants to close their revels.

Those who first departed returned hastily and caused a scene of excitement by announcing that all the horses had disappeared except a few that were tied to the gallery posts of the building. The evidence was clear that the revelers had been made the victims of an Indian raid, and the impudent enterprise was shrewdly executed. The skulking savages only took advantage of the distracting incidents of the occasion, and without interrupting the festivities quietly left them to return to their homes on foot. They were less merciful to two poor Mexicans who left Eagle Pass that morning on an ox-cart with the intention of hauling wood, who were killed by them below town.

Such audacity was exasperating, and Henry Bruhn immediately organized a party which started in pursuit of the Indians with a view to their chastisement. They were overtaken at El Canado, near the river, about eight miles above town, and a fight occurred in which two Mexicans were killed before the Indians retreated.

Another time, when returning from Eagle Pass in the early spring of 1867, Mr. Black, of Uvalde, and Angel Torres, of San Antonio, accompanied me as passengers, and Pablo Castro drove the hack. We were all well armed and had plenty of ammunition, but our journey was not interrupted until we reached a point about four miles west of Turkey Creek on the Eagle Pass road. We were in an open prairie, about four o'clock in the afternoon, when we saw a party of eleven Indians, whose movements indicated that we were in for a fight, and we prepared for trouble.

Perhaps they thought it would be an easy thing to take our scalps, and they charged toward us, uttering their terrific war-whoops, but their yells only frightened the mules, and Pablo had all he could do to keep them from running away. Black and myself took a position in front of the animals, but Torres stood alone near a crooked mesquite tree, and we waited until we could shoot with accuracy.

The Indians saw that the mules were frightened, and with the intention of stampeding them, they strung out in a circle, about two hundred and fifty yards distant from us, in which they rode singly about fifty yards apart. The movement was one in which they were well trained, because the distances were kept remarkably well. Their actions reminded me of a circus, but I did not look at them with the same sensations of pleasure. The continual series of war-whoops and yells which accompanied their performances failed to make the mules break away before they were well secured, and our uneasiness was removed on that account.

In the meantime we were not idle, although we found it was impossible to do any effective work at that distance, because the Indians clung to the opposite side of their horses, out of sight, and the rapidly moving animals were exposed to an uncertain aim. Finally one of the horses dropped in his tracks, and the dismounted Indian hastened to shelter behind a tree in his vicinity. The range was open before him, and he fired several shots at Torres without effect before that gentleman realized that he was being used as a target, and when a bullet threw bark in his face from a limb that served as a rest for his rifle, he abandoned his exposed position and joined Black and myself in front of the mules.

The instant the horse fell one of the Indians uttered a peculiar whoop which made Torres think one of them was wounded, but it was explained when they gathered near the animal and proceeded to rescue the Indian. After he was mounted behind one of them they sped away, uttering a series of war-whoops until they disappeared over a neighboring hill.

The fight only lasted about fifteen minutes, in which time about seventy-five shots were fired, and the only trophy of the battle was a dead horse! The carcass was examined and a hole was found, about two inches below the base of the left ear, where the bullet had entered that caused his death. The investigation decided a question with reference to who fired the fatal shot by awarding the honor to Black and his five-shot Colts rifle, because it was evident that the wound was not made by a Henry rifle, the weapon carried by Torres and myself. The only thing left by the owner that might have served as a memorial of our victory was a piece of rope around the beast's neck, and that we did not remove.

Torres conducted an established business in both Piedras Negras and San Antonio, and it was necessary for him to visit those places frequently, consequently he was often on the road, and generally he traveled with me. When Henry rifles, that chambered eighteen cartridges, were first put on the market they cost $95 apiece, and Torres and myself probably owned the first that were brought to Texas. We ordered them through Mr. Hummel, of San Antonio, the father of Charles Hummel, now City Treasurer of said city, who still keeps up the business of Hummel & Son. This was our first opportunity to test them in battle, and perhaps the Indians, who knew nothing about them, were disconcerted by our rapid fire. We were much pleased with them, although we could not brag on our marksmanship on that occasion, but it was no proof that Mr. Black's rifle was superior because it was the only weapon that drew blood, or that Pablo's Spencer carbine, which he did not have an opportunity to use, was not just as good.

The Indians we encountered belonged to the same tribe that killed John Sanders three days before. He resided on the Rio Frio, below the Eagle Pass road, and he was a good friend of mine. They would have made a good haul by capturing my hack, as I had ten thousand dollars in Mexican silver that was consigned to Goldfrank, Frank & Co., wholesale dry-goods merchants in San Antonio.

Mr. Black was afterwards killed by Tom Wall, in Uvalde, and Angel Torres, who was an uncle of Modesto Torres, of San Antonio, is also dead. Pablo Castro afterwards joined a band of cattle thieves and was killed near the Rio Grande.

On another trip, in the spring of 1867, Thomas B. McManus and Sam White, of Eagle Pass, and Herman Schleuning, now in Austin, accompanied me to San Antonio. We proceeded as far as Ranchera Creek, about four miles east of the present site of Sabinal station, without meeting with another adventure of any kind. At that point, where we suspected no danger, we were very much surprised, about nine o'clock at night, when a party of Indians charged out of the darkness in our direction. Their frightful war-whoops, which they uttered with the intention of scaring our mules, were startling, and we expected an attack, but, much to our relief, they passed some distance in front of us, after changing their course, and soon disappeared. No shots were fired on either side, partly because they were too far away, but really their movements were so rapid there was no chance for a fight and we were very well satisfied to see them go.

I had another and worse fright when on my way to Eagle Pass, that also occurred in 1867. I was traveling alone on that trip, and after changing mules at Chichon station, twenty-seven miles east of Eagle Pass, had proceeded about six miles, when I saw a dust rising about two miles away, to the left of the road, beyond a hill that obstructed my view. The time was about two o'clock in the afternoon, and I knew that the cloud of dust was raised by something moving in my direction under cover of the hill. My impression was that they were Indians, and I waited until they appeared on the brow of the naked elevation more than a mile distant. I then saw ten men driving a herd of loose horses and mules, and my fears convinced me that my first impressions were correct.

I realized the danger of my situation and could see no chance for me to get out of their way. With the determination to defend myself as best I could, I hurried my team to a lone mesquite tree, that stood about one hundred yards from the road, and tied them to it with a heavy rope that I always carried for emergencies. As the mules were skittish when anyone got in front of them, it was necessary to approach them with a great deal of care, and I could ill afford to spare the time it took to secure them. I then prepared to protect myself against the approaching enemy with my Henry rifle and an abundant supply of cartridges.

The herd and its drivers were then much nearer and could be seen more distinctly. Much to my gratification I perceived that the herd was driven by Mexicans, and as they crossed the road about five hundred yards behind me they passed without noticing me. Perhaps the animals had been stolen and evidently they were smuggled across the Rio Grande somewhere between Laredo and Eagle Pass.

Rattlesnakes were found in great numbers in west Texas and they were enemies that had to be guarded against at all times. Wild turkeys always show a great antipathy to them and never fail to make a deadly and persistent attack until the reptile is destroyed. An opportunity to witness such conflicts is seldom offered, therefore, I will notice one instance of the kind that came under my observation.

I was traveling the road near Uvalde when I saw a large flock of wild turkeys in an open glade near the highway. I stopped when I saw the gobblers had congregated in a circle where they seemed to be fighting, but I soon perceived that they were killing a large rattlesnake. One after the other would spring into the air in rapid succession and come down on the reptile, which they struck a hard blow with one wing that might have been heard quite a distance. Apparently all the gobblers took part in the fracas, and they appeared to be greatly excited, but the hens fed quietly in the vicinity and seemed to be indifferent to what was going on.

I watched them about ten minutes before they observed my presence and became alarmed. After they disappeared in the brush I approached the place and found the snake coiled up and almost dead. Evidently the gobblers had been engaged in killing him for some time before I appeared on the scene, and if they had not been disturbed the victim would have provided a feast for the whole flock, because it was their custom to eat the snakes killed in that way.

Deer are equally prejudiced against rattlesnakes and invariably attack them in favorable localities. Nature has made them enemies, and it is said that when an encounter is unavoidable, with no available means of escape, the snake appreciates the danger; also that it makes no effort to strike, but suffers a collapse under an instinctive fear which prompts it to submit to its fate with its head hid beneath the coils of its body, which are closely drawn together.

The deer springs from a safe distance into the air with its four feet brought together, and it comes down on the snake with its sharp pointed hoofs which cut like a knife. The movements are rapid and often repeated until the rattler is mangled into a shapeless mass. I have seen places where snakes had been killed by deer, but have never witnessed the performance. The marks of their sharp hoofs showed in the hard beaten ground and the bones of their victims were in evidence.

Highwaymen in Mexico are called *ladrones*, or robbers. They usually frequented the frontier, but other parts of the country were often infested by them before they were finally suppressed by the government. Generally they were a select body of men of good appearance, who wore broad-brimmed felt hats elaborately embroidered with silver and gold thread, and dressed in the regular riding costume that was profusely ornamented with silver buttons in front, on the sleeves, and down the trousers. Their horses were the best that the country afforded, and silver mountings were lavishly displayed on their saddles and bridles.

When a band of ladrones decided to hold up a stage, after ascertaining that it was conveying a large sum of money or on other occasions, they selected an uninhabited region at a point where it was necessary for the vehicle to ascend a steep hill, and concealed themselves on both sides of the road until it approached. The first intimation of their presence was given by one of the gang, who ordered the driver to stop, when the others showed themselves and the spokesman made known his intentions to the passengers. Pointing to his companions, who silently awaited the result of the conference, he explained that it would be folly to offer resistance, as they were ready to enforce his demands. With the greatest politeness he requested them to pass out their money, and when they complied he placed it all together on the roadside. Force was rarely used in such cases, and I never heard of an instance when the pockets of passengers were searched. The money wanted was in sacks and generally amounted to large sums in silver that could not be concealed.

When Major Porter's brother was robbed by ladrones on the national stage line near Monterey, in 1868, no resistance was offered; the passengers delivered ten thousand dollars to one man, who was in a short distance of his companions. After securing his treasure he ordered the driver to proceed on his journey.

I was never molested by ladrones when staging in that country, and only know of one occasion when I believed they intended to hold me up. It happened near Palo Blanco ranch, twenty-five miles northeast of Salinas. Victoria, where ten or twelve men were lined up on both sides of the road. I was riding on the outside with my driver and escort when I saw them. The speed of the team was checked and I called the attention of my passengers inside the stage to the suspicious circumstance. We all recognized them as regular ladrones by their dress, etc., which corresponded with the general description I have given, and no time was lost in getting our weapons ready to meet them. The team was in a walk when we passed between them, but evidently, seeing that we were prepared to offer resistance, they were content to extend to us their friendly greetings. My passengers were Daniel Wueste of Eagle Pass, Carlos Sada of Monterey, Pedro Morales, customs-house officer at Piedras Negras, and two Mexican army officers.

I only know of three stage robberies that occurred in Mexico when I was in the business. One took place within five and another in less than ten miles of Monterey, on the road leading from Saltillo; and the other was forty miles from Monterey, on the Matamoras road near Lenares. The money thus obtained, when added together, amounted to a large sum, and it was all secured without a drop of blood being shed.

Chapter Six:

Smugglers— Emperor Maximilian

The fact is well known that smuggling has always been conducted along the borders between the two republics, but in earlier times it was practiced with greater impunity than at present. There were two classes of smugglers then, as there are now, who operated according to their means and influence. Those who could command both met with no difficulty in advancing their measures with the aid of friendly officials who boldly passed large transactions through the doors of the customs-house at a small expense. On the other hand, persons without means or patronage and with only a bold and enterprising spirit to sustain them were compelled to resort to secret methods when conducting the same kind of business on a small scale. Much trading was done in that way with goods and animals that were acquired in legitimate transactions and the tariff due the governments was the only loss sustained; but a much more extensive smuggling business was done by unscrupulous persons with property that was feloniously acquired. This class of thieves generally were organized to operate in gangs on both sides of the river and acted in collusion with each other by exchanging stolen property brought from Mexico for other property acquired in a like manner in Texas. In that way a large number of animals of all kinds were transferred from one side of the Rio Grande to the other with little risk of detection.

One of the most notorious characters that was ever engaged in such practices was Manuel Telamantes, a Mexican, whose home was in Eagle Pass. At one time his character was held in the highest estimation and he exerted a great influence among Americans. I was well acquainted with him, and at that time, in 1866, he was generally liked by all who knew him. He was also looked upon as a good and honest citizen until it was discovered that he was a leader of an organized gang of thieves and smugglers that had been in existence for years.

He was a young and handsome fellow who dressed well and made a respectable appearance; he was also liberal with his means and conducted himself properly; although at frequent intervals he absented himself for a short time and always returned with large sums of money, his business was not suspected, but after his character was exposed it became known that his secret expeditions were made to meet his confederates and to receive his share of the spoils.

His career was prolonged until 1879, when it was made unsafe to engage in such enterprises, and his, like many others under similar circumstances, was closed by a violent death. The particulars relating to the case, as they were represented to me, show that he entered Texas with a large herd of horses and mules, which were stolen in Mexico, and they were traded for beeves that had been stolen from ranchmen by associates in Texas. The thieves who received the horses and mules made good their escape, but Telamantes and his men with the cattle were pursued until overtaken between Fort Clark and the Rio Grande. The beeves were recovered, and Telamantes and his men were captured and hung.

I do not doubt but that he had earned his fate, but when I recalled his many good qualities I could not help feeling regret that he had come to such an end. I saw him last in 1877, in San Antonio, when he offered to sell me one hundred and fifty choice mules, which were concealed somewhere in the mountains near Devil's River. He pro-posed to let me have the entire lot at a bargain, but I declined his offer. He was a bold fellow, and if he was a thief he took desperate chances in enterprises that re-quired brains that gave him control over men. He would have scorned the methods practiced by common thieves and highwaymen like that once attempted against me.

The incident occurred in 1867, when I was returning from Eagle Pass and after I had delivered the Castroville mail-sack to Mr. John Vanze, the postmaster. A few min-utes later he returned with the mail-pouch for San Anto-nio, and I paid him a twenty-dollar gold piece that John Kenedy, of Sabinal, had requested me to give him. I had taken it from a sack that contained about fifty dollars in Mexican silver, which I returned to its proper place un-der the seat during his absence.

I was about to continue my journey when two men ad-vanced and engaged two seats in my hack to San Anto-nio, for which they paid me five dollars. I had noticed them at the post office when I exposed my money bag, and, doubtless, they supposed the coin was all in gold, when I took the gold piece from it, which they saw. There was nothing suspicious in their appearance, and I was pleased to have their company.

The distance from Castroville to my father's house, where I changed my team, was only four miles, and we passed an unusual number of people on the way. Soon after starting an unaccountable feeling caused me to form an unfavorable opinion of my passengers and made me suspect that they were not all right, and the sequel will show that my impressions were correct.

While the horses were being changed I greased the axles of my hack as usual, and when through the four-pound monkey-wrench which I used was returned to the toolbox in front. When ready to start I noticed that the cushion of the rear seat, which my passengers were waiting to occupy, did not fit properly, and I reached over to straighten it. As I raised the right-hand end I saw under it the monkey-wrench that I had replaced in its proper receptacle a half-hour before.

In the meantime no one but the two men had been near the vehicle, and I was convinced that they had placed the wrench in that place with murderous intentions. Evidently they designed using it as a weapon in a plan to kill and rob me, and I did not hesitate to charge them with the cowardly scheme. They denied having had anything to do with it, but I entertained contrary convictions and ordered them to leave the yard. They obeyed me without uttering another word, but my father, who was holding my team, called them back and insisted that I should return them the five dollars they had paid me. He said the poor fellows might need it, and I obeyed him, perhaps reluctantly, because, naturally, I felt no sympathy for them. Later I was told that they returned immediately to Castroville, and I afterwards learned that they were deserters from the United States army.

The dangers I confronted in my travels were often compensated by pleasant entertainments at the end of my journey; and I recall one in which I took part that had no Indians or robbers connected with it, like those I have noticed. The occasion was a grand ball that was given about the latter part of June, 1867, in the customs-house at Piedras Negras, to celebrate the termination of the war that closed the reign of the Emperor Maximilian in Mexico. All foreigners in Eagle Pass were invited, and many, including Thomas B. McManus, Charley Groos and myself, were in attendance, together with all the best people in that part of the country. My impression is that the news of Maximilian's executon, which took place on the 19th of June, had not been received, and the ball was an expression of joy on account of the restoration of the republic.

My information with reference to that tragic event was acquired, principally, from individuals who participated in the war, and I will relate a few facts connected with the subject that were communicated by Colonel Morales of the Mexican army. He spoke of the great sympathy of the people for Maximilian, after he was condemned to death, and particularly of its manifestation by five hundred of the most respectable ladies in the City of Mexico, who drew up an appeal for clemency. Dressed in black robes, the long procession presented themselves before the military tribunal with the petition for the emperor's pardon; but it was useless; his fate was sealed and he was beyond the hope of mercy.

He witnessed the execution of Maximilian, Mejia, and Miramon, and his relation of the facts was very impressive. They were taken to a hill outside of the city of Queretaro by the platoons of soldiers that were detailed to execute them. When drawn up in line Maximilian advanced and presented each of the firing party a gold doubloon, with the request that they would take good aim until he gave them the signal to fire by removing his hand from his breast. After resuming his position he eulogized his generals and resigned to them the honor of dying first. After they fell he calmly confronted the death that awaited him and met it with a fearlessness that became him. In after years I saw the spot in the Cathedral of Mexico where the emperor and empress stood in all their pride and glory when crowned, and, as I thought of their sad fate I could see the chapel that marks the place where he and his generals were executed.

Generals Mejia and Miramon were gallant and competent officers in whom the emperor placed implicit confidence and they proved themselves worthy of his trust, but another, in whom he confided to an equal extent, betrayed him. The "foreign legion," to whom was entrusted the duty of sustaining his throne, was composed of criminals taken from the prisons of Europe with the design of getting rid of them and were utterly unreliable as soldiers. I was told by responsible Mexican officers of both armies that the legion was a band of robbers who plundered indiscriminately and that the regulars of the French army would have nothing to do with them. All the facts show that Maximilian was the victim of a conspiracy and his fate was regretted all over the civilized world.

I only met with one accident during the eighteen months of travel while conducting my mail route, and that was not serious. It happened at Chichon, where I stopped for dinner with my three passengers, and to change my team. I had agreed to break a pair of wild mules for Domingo, the ranchman, and had been working them for about three months, from one station to the next, but every time they would try to run away, though I always got the best of them by allowing them to run, after getting them in the road, until they tired themselves down. I had them hitched up on this trip, and a man held them until we were all seated in the ambulance. When he turned loose the unmanageable brutes, they headed for a high and strongly built picket fence, and before I could turn them, the hack came in violent collision with the posts. In my efforts to hold them I was badly hurt by being pulled from the seat, and as the vehicle was smashed, it was necessary to procure another conveyance before we could proceed. The nearest place where one could be had was Eagle Pass, but as the Indians were raiding in that part of the country, no one at the station would undertake the chances of making the ride for love or money.

When troubles accumulate to a certain point something generally happens that improves the situation, and in our case the emergency was met by Henry Shane, a friend of mine, who lived in that vicinity. His offer of assistance was accepted, and he started for Eagle Pass about one o'clock on his favorite saddle horse. The distance of twenty-seven miles was ridden and the return trip with an ambulance and two horses, that he got from Albert Tuerpe, was made in about eleven hours.

Immediately after his arrival we hitched up the same wild mules, and without further mishap arrived at Eagle Pass about daylight. I started back the same morning, in the borrowed vehicle, about eight o'clock, as usual, and after driving about fifteen miles I met Mr. Shane with the broken ambulance, driving the horses he had gotten from Albert Tuerpe. He had added to my obligations by following me with it, and it was taken to the government post, at Fort Duncan, which had been established a short time before, where it was repaired in the shop there, in a most suitable manner, without one cent of charges.

The following week when I returned from San Antonio I met Mr. Shane and asked him what I owed him for his services and trouble, but he disposed of the subject by saying, "Nothing; I was very glad that I was able to help you when you were in need." His generosity had been displayed by traveling fifty-four miles over a dangerous road at the risk of his life when no one else would take the chances. He had left his horse in Eagle Pass and assumed the responsibility of taking the conveyance through and his return, making a total distance of one hundred and eight miles, together with all the incidental troubles and expenses attached, all on my account and with no expectation of reward.

There is an old and true saying that "a friend in need is a friend indeed," and Mr. Shane's practical illustration of the fact was demonstrated in a manner that was a test which few persons have an opportunity to apply. I have always felt grateful towards him for his act of kindness and will never cease to entertain the warmest friendship for him while I live, because I know he is an honest and worthy man.

I was under other obligations to him afterwards, and at one time especially when he assisted in recovering my stage mules that were driven off by the Indians, with John Kennedy's horses from the ranch. He went with John and Ross Kennedy and their men in pursuit until they overtook them on the Rio Frio, eight miles east of Uvalde, near General Knox's ranch.

Henry Shane is now about seventy-three years of age and he resides on his ranch five miles below Sabinal Station, on Sabinal Creek, with pleasant surroundings and in good circumstances. He is highly esteemed by all who are acquainted with his generous nature and have knowledge of his general character. He is well known throughout west Texas, where his life has been spent, and also in San Antonio, where he has many friends, and among them Colonel C. C. Gibbs is one of long standing.

His early life was spent on the frontier of Texas, where he had many experiences, and the stories he could relate about his encounters with wild Indians would be interesting; but he rarely speaks of them, and he had one that he never talks about. It occurred in a fight when in pursuit of Indian raiders, on Sabinal Creek, after his ammunition was exhausted. When the fact was discovered he was close to an Indian who was also without ammunition, but both were equally brave, and they rushed at each other with clubbed guns. Those who witnessed the fight say that Mr. Shane was worsted in the fight by a lick on one side of his head which brought him to the ground, and he rolled down the creek bank. Other particulars are forgotten, but Mr. Shane confesses that it was the hardest fight he ever had in his life. In later years he served during the Civil War as a soldier in the Confederate Army, and in that connection he sustained his reputation for courage and fidelity to duty that distinguished his previous career as a worthy citizen on the borders of civilization, but not more honorably than he has since done in private life.

Chapter Seven:

First U.S.-Mexico Stage— Valley of Death

Captain Adolph Muenzenberger and myself established the first stage line between the United States and Mexico, in August, 1867, under the firm name of A. Santleben & Company. The corporation was organized on August 1, as a private enterprise, for the purpose of transporting passengers, and, incidentally, to convey letters, money, and other packages suitable for the capacity of the stage. The institution was licensed under the general laws of the State of Texas and those of Mexico, but no subsidies were granted, and the business was conducted at the risk and expense of the company. The facts to be given will show that, throughout its continuance, the line was liberally patronized and was highly appreciated by the public because of its great convenience.

The success of the enterprise was assured beforehand through special privileges granted by the Mexican government, which would not, or could not, be allowed under existing laws. The most important of these concessions was an exemption from tariff charges on everything except money, on which a municipal duty of two per cent, was collected in Monterey and an export duty of ten per cent, was exacted by the customs officials at Piedras Negras. During the two years that the line was operated the contents of the coach was never investigated nor was it ever delayed on any occasion by government officials on either side of the Rio Grande. Thomas B. McManus, who was in charge of the United States customs-house in Eagle Pass, and the Mexican customs officials in Piedras Negras, Nicholas Gresanta, and his assistant, Pedro Morales, were all my intimate friends whose personal influence and official powers were exercised in the interest of the line whenever an opportunity offered.

Our stage as a mail carrier was guaranteed the same privileges and protection as those granted the general mail lines in Mexico; but otherwise it had no connection with the postal department, as the right to levy our own postage and collect it in advance, for the company's benefit, was conceded to us. Our company used a metal stamp that was furnished by the Mexican government, on which were the numerals "&5," with the words "Republica Mexicana" in a circle around them, which the postal department used until stamps were introduced in 1870; but no account of our mail transactions was required. The only agreement we had with the government stipulated that all letters handled by us might be weighed, and after a payment of twenty-five cents an ounce was exacted, the stamp should be applied once for each ounce. No other government stamp was placed on letters brought by us from Mexico, but it was necessary for all letters sent to the United States to carry stamps of that government, at the rate of five cents for each ounce after crossing the border. Frequently two dollars for postage was paid on one letter, and these carried eight impressions of our stamp, in addition to the United States postage. Messrs. Weber and Ulrich were one of several firms in Monterey, who paid as much or more on letters sent through us to the United States. On many of our trips as much as fifty dollars was realized on mail matter alone, that was collected at points along the route.

Besides passengers and their baggage, we carried all kinds of paying freight, but mostly money, and occasionally we transported live-stock, such as game chickens and blooded sheep. The games were known as *Guieo de Seguin*, and they had a great reputation on account of their fighting qualities, in which respect they resembled the people in that region. They were raised mostly in Seguin, and some of them were billed over our route to the City of Mexico, where they were highly prized by chicken fighters. Two were placed in a coop divided into two apartments, and our freight charge was twenty-five dollars. One pair of Merino lambs was conveyed on the stage to Monterey, that Charles Griesenbeck consigned to Governor Maduro, ex-governor of Coahuila. They were crated, and the charges amounted to fifty dollars.

When not too heavily loaded, we imported as many as two thousand choice oranges, which brought us one hundred dollars per thousand in San Antonio at wholesale; also, chili pepper, that we sold at one dollar per pound wholesale, and other things of equal value. Our return freight to Mexico consisted mostly of eatables, which we also sold at wholesale prices. We often took as much as two hundred and fifty pounds of hams, and sold them at one dollar a pound; and twice a month we bought from Joe Ney, at D'Hanis, two hundred pounds of butter, in four cans, that was placed under the driver's seat, for which our customers paid us one dollar a pound; they retailed it at one dollar and fifty cents. One of our customers was Mrs. Russel, now Mrs. Cloudon, the mother-in-law of Mr. Socia, the cotton-buyer, who conducted a bakery and confectionery store in Monterey. Our stage fare from San Antonio to Monterey was $75.00.

We often carried large sums of Mexican money out of the country, and charged three per cent, for freighting it to San Antonio, which, when added to the twelve per cent, export duties, increased the expense to fifteen per cent. Our charge was less than those formerly prevailing and they were reduced by the premium allowed on Mexican silver on account of its purity. New York drafts then commanded a premium, ranging as high as twenty per cent, and there was always a demand for them in Monterey. The Texas firms that transacted the largest business with merchants in Mexico, at that period, were Messrs. Halff & Bro., Goldfrank, Frank & Co., and F. Groos & Co., all of San Antonio, and our stage often brought for them as much as twenty thousand dollars from that country. Not one cent was ever lost that was entrusted to our care, and we established a confidence that was upheld by our company throughout its career.

After the close of the French war, we contracted with Philipe Naranjo, a brother of General Naranjo of the Mexican army, to deliver two thousand Minea rifles to the national government. We found a lot of secondhand guns in New Orleans that had been used in the Civil War, and we bought the required number at auction, for eighteen hundred dollars, or less than a dollar apiece. They were brought to San Antonio and placed in Captain Muenzenberger's store, on West Commerce Street, where the Washington Theater now stands. Only five hundred were delivered before the building, including the other rifles, was destroyed by fire, and we suffered a total loss because we carried no insurance, but the profit on those that were sold more than covered our entire outlay.

We drove six animals to the coach in Texas, and in Mexico eight, on account of the heavy traffic. The coach weighed about three thousand pounds, and was substantially built, with a capacity for carrying about four thousand pounds. The wood used in its construction was the choicest hickory, and all the iron work was the best quality of steel. The spindles of the steel axles were two and a half inches thick and about fourteen inches long. The cushions were upholstered on coiled steel springs, with horse-hair filling, and covered with the best quality of brown calf-skin leather, consequently they were very expensive. The body was swung on leather braces and it was capable of seating eighteen average sized persons very comfortably, as it had three seats inside, each large enough for three people, and three others on the roof, capable of accommodating a like number. One of the outside seats was close behind that occupied by the driver, similar to those used on transfer buses in large cities. The third seat was on the hind end of the coach, above the *boot* where trunks and other bulky baggage was usually carried, which faced toward the rear, and it had a top attached to it like those used on buggies, that could be raised or lowered. The flat top of the coach was covered with heavy ducking that was impervious to water, and it had an iron railing two feet in height around its outer edge. The two seats on top, in the rear of that occupied by the driver and guard, were rarely used except in Mexico, where there was more traveling, when they, and the floor of the roof, were often crowded. Once the coach entered Lampazos with twenty-three passengers, but that was an exceptional occasion, though generally we received a liberal patronage.

The coach was manufactured by Abbott, Downing & Co., in Concord, New Hampshire, and it was imported by Mr. A. Staacke, their agent for such vehicles and Concord buggies in west Texas. He was also agent for Wilson & Childs, of Philadelphia, and introduced the first wagons, called "prairie schooners," that were used for overland freighting, and the first Studebaker farm wagons, which have since become so popular. He suggested to this firm the manufacture of large cart wheels with heavy iron axles for freighting purposes, that were first introduced through him into Mexico, where they came into general use. In addition to his large stock of vehicles, in his establishment on West Commerce Street he kept an extensive assortment of supplies necessary for teamsters and train owners, and nearly all of them purchased their outfits from him.

I note these facts, with reference to Mr. Staacke's extensive business in early times, with pleasure, and it is necessary for me to do so because I will be compelled to notice him frequently in connection with my affairs. Mr. Staacke is still alive, but he retired from business about fifteen years ago, and his establishment has since been successfully conducted by his sons in San Antonio under the firm name of Staacke Bros.

We paid Mr. Staacke nine hundred dollars for the first coach we bought from him in 1867, when we started our line, and we purchased later the coach which has been described, for which we paid $1250, without the harness. The set of harness that was made for it was intended for six horses, to weigh twelve hundred pounds, but it was useless to us because our animals were much smaller.

Our stage line extended from San Antonio along my old mail route to Eagle Pass, on the east bank of the Rio Grande. The distance to that point was one hundred and sixty-two miles, and the road was good in dry weather. I crossed the river there to Piedras Negras, now known as Ciudad Porfirio Diaz, situated on the high banks of the west side, in the State of Coahuila, Mexico. From there it continued southward three hundred and sixty-two miles to Monterey.

We had, at first, very few stations, and lost entirely too much time on account of wet weather that often prolonged the trip to seven or eight days because of insufficient teams. To remedy the defect, suitable stations were selected, where the animals could be protected in the wild country through which it was necessary for us to pass, and we stocked the route with seventy-two good mules. We were satisfied, before these changes were made, that the line would pay if run to advantage, and afterwards an experimental drive was made over the route in five days, but the average time thereafter never exceeded six days.

The road between Santa Monica and Paso de la Laza was an unoccupied desert except by the stage-stand on the banks of the Rio Sabinas, which was abandoned later, on account of the Indians, and thereafter we were obliged to make a ninety-mile drive between Santa Monica and Lampazos with one team and without water, after crossing the Rio Sabinas.

The town of Lampazos had about three thousand inhabitants who were sustained by some irrigated land, and it was also a great sheep, goat and cattle country. The people of the town manufactured by hand good Mexican blankets, and they seemed to be industrious, as they were always at work. Northeast of the town is the Mesa de los Cartuhanas, that was then known as the Mesa de Vedura.

From Lampazos to Villaldama, by the way of Sierra Colorado Pass and Golondrinas, is fifty miles. The town had about four thousand inhabitants in 1868, and the silver, copper, and lead mines in that vicinity gave constant employment to the people. The leading men in the place at that time were Mariano and Machor Sanchez, who were mostly engaged in the mining business.

From Villaldama to Palo Blanco it is thirty-two miles and the road is good; and from there to Morales the distance is eighteen miles. This stretch of fifty miles was considered the most dangerous for travelers on the frontier of Mexico. From Villaldama the road passed through a valley near the base of the Sierra Madre and another range of mountains enclosed it on the east side. The valley was from ten to fifteen miles in width, and thirty miles of the distance was through a palm-tree forest with a thick undergrowth of brush that in some places grew so close to the road it was impossible for two vehicles to pass each other.

The heights of the Sierra Madre were constantly infested by Indians, and the road that lay below them could be observed for miles. When travelers were seen approaching from either direction, they would descend to some suitable place in the valley and waylay them in ambush. The most dangerous place was about six miles from the

Palo Blanco Ranch, where the road was confined to a narrow pass, between hills that rose from twenty to thirty feet high for a distance of about one hundred and fifty yards. Here and at other places they would make a sudden attack, with the result that the travelers were murdered generally before they could offer the slightest resistance. I was told by the people at the ranch that more than seventy-five people had been killed in the pass in about twenty years, and I had personal knowledge of a family with their children, and several other persons that were killed there at different times. After perpetrating their murderous work, the Indians would flee to the mountains, where they were safe from pursuit, and it is doubtful if large bodies of soldiers could have dislodged them from their place of refuge.

One of our stations, where we changed horses, was Palo Blanco Ranch until it was removed elsewhere. On one of my trips westward, in 1867, when I reached that point the people informed me that the Indians had come out of the mountains and were depredating in the country along my route. They begged me to stay with them, as they thought it probable that the Indians would attack the ranch; but as I was not looking for Indians, and did not wish to have trouble with them, I only delayed long enough to change my team.

When I returned I learned that, after my departure, about five o'clock in the evening, the Indians appeared and took three children into captivity, after killing two men and one woman who were traveling the road I had passed over, on their way to the ranch for protection, but those at the ranch were not molested. My good friend Jose Sanches was in charge of it at the time, and I believe he is still alive.

The custom of showing respect for the last resting place of the dead prevails in Mexico, where it has been observed for ages. Wherever a murdered person has been interred near the roadside, a cross is erected, and many travelers stop there to pray, but before leaving they always deposit some token, even if it is a stone, at the foot of the cross, though many cast a stone on the accumulated pile as they pass. In the valley referred to, at one of the places I passed, I counted as many as twenty crosses, some of them showing the marking of age, but many, and sometimes ten near together, were secured to palm trees and others to bushes. An appropriate name for it would be, the Valley of Death, and I always felt relieved after passing through it. On such occasions I usually adopted every precaution to guard against surprises, and when passing the most dangerous places I and my armed passengers rode on top of the coach.

Chapter Eight:
Mexico City—The Mexican War

From Morales to the beautiful town of Selinas Victoria, on the Victoria River, is seven miles over a less dangerous road. The town has a neat appearance, the streets are well paved, and it has a fine church. There are rich mines in the vicinity that give the people employment, and in the country many horses are raised on ranches that are devoted to that business. From Selinas to Monterey it is twenty-five miles. The capital city of Nuevo Leon is situated on the Rio de Santa Catarina, and it is about six hundred and twenty-five miles from the City of Mexico. Many beautiful buildings of cut stone adorned the city, and the streets and squares were well paved. The principal plaza was the most general place of resort, and it was provided with stone benches for the accommodation of the public, who congregated there for social purposes and to listen to the music. The cathedral is one of the attractions of the city, and the theater and Plaza de Toro are the most popular places of resort. About that time the city had about forty thousand inhabitants, and its citizens were esteemed for their enterprising spirit which kept them abreast with the times.

The climate of that region is justly extolled on account of its temperature, which is rarely cold enough in winter for frost, and as fire is seldom needed for warmth, the majority of houses have no fire-places, but in summer it is sometimes quite warm, though the nights are cooled by the refreshing breeze that passes through the valley from between the Sierra de la Sileria or Saddle Mountains and the Sierra Madre. Vegetation grows to perfection under irrigation, and the products of the soil are raised in abundance. Tropical fruit, especially orange trees, need no protection and give large returns for the little attention they receive, and I realized many dollars from the sale of oranges brought from there to San Antonio.

There are many places of historic interest near the city and the most prominent is the Bishop's Palace, which is situated on one of the foot-hills of the mountain, beyond its southern limits, that was the residence of the Catholic bishops of Monterey a long time after it became a diocese, but it has been abandoned for years. When the American army invested the city in 1847, the place was occupied by a detachment of Mexican troops until they were forced to surrender by a battery on Independent Hill that commanded the position from the opposite side of the valley. The battery is said to have been in charge of Lieutenant W. T. Sherman, who was afterwards a general in the United States army.

The mother of Peter Bass, my station-keeper at Villaldama, gave me some information relative to the siege and capture of Monterey by General Taylor, and I will relate a few facts in this connection. She had resided in the city from early childhood and was about twenty years old when the operations of the American army occurred in that section of the country. She pointed out the place, on the east side of the city, where the Americans gained their first success in the fight of Casa Blanca, and the site is now occupied by the Monterey brewery, one of the largest establishments of the kind in Mexico. She related what her father had told her about Mexican horsemen lassoing straggling soldiers from the American army and dragging them to death. She showed me the place where Captain Gillespie was killed, on the street called Mar Prieto, or Black Sea, when the Americans were entering Monterey; also the place where he was buried after the battle; but his remains had been removed some time before and were carried to San Antonio, Texas, where they repose in the Odd Fellows' Cemetery. She was present when the body was disinterred and heard a Mexican remark to one of the party of Americans who were performing the duty assigned them, that very few men were killed in the capture of Monterey, compared to the number engaged on both sides; and also the American's reply that, "If those who were killed could be estimated at their actual worth all of their virtues combined would not equal those once possessed by the man who lies before us." A monument was erected over his last resting-place; and, unless I am mistaken, Texas has perpetuated his memory by naming a county in his honor.

A national prejudice against Americans was entertained in Mexico long after the termination of that war, and the feeling was not only justified by its results but it was aggravated by the threatening schemes of filibusters in the United States for the conquest of that country prior to the Civil War. The friendly attitude of the northern republic through that period, and its more recent position with reference to the empire under Maximilian, quieted all apprehensions in official circles, although, perhaps, it lingered to some extent among the people; but it was never manifested in my case, because I was always treated with uniform courtesy in all my travels among them, and every facility was extended to me, both by the government and the people, to insure the success of my business.

The interest manifested by the Mexican government in our stage line through its employees was never as great as that displayed by the citizens along the route, who neglected no opportunity to express their appreciation of our services. The most conspicuous among them was Joe Maria Perez, of Piedras Negras; Santiago Tomas, of Santa Monica, who is the father-in-law of Dr. Serna, of San Buenaventura; Philipe Naranjo of Lampazos, and Mariano and Machor Sanchez of Villaldama. Wherever the stage appeared a greater sensation was created than is usually expressed in a new railroad town when visited by the road's officials in their private car. Frequently the natives, with their primitive flutes, made of burnt clay and of cane, would serenade the passengers at the stations where we stopped, and very often a dance was arranged for them at night, to which the respectable class of people were invited. As I was fond of dancing, these events afforded me pleasant recreation and I never failed to attend them.

On one occasion General Wardwell, the general inspector of United States custom-houses along the Rio Grande from its mouth to El Paso, participated in one of such entertainments. He was on his way to Brownsville, and as there was no public means of conveyance to that place, other than on my stage to Monterey, where connection was made with the Mexican stage line to Matamoras, he accompanied me to the end of my route. At Lampazos the general and other passengers, including myself, were invited to attend a select dance gotten up for our benefit by the best people of the town, and as many of them were present it proved to be a swell affair.

The general was a close observer, and he noticed particularly, that several ladies present wore a silver ornament of beautiful workmanship attached to their belts by two chains, that had the handle and sheath of a dagger. He took advantage of the first opportunity that offered to express his interest in the subject by remarking to his companion that he had always discredited the statement made about Mexican women carrying daggers about their persons, but with the evidence then before his eyes he was forced to believe it was true.

His criticism was circulated among the ladies and it gave rise to many pleasantries at his expense. One of them approached him in a spirit of raillery, and suddenly but gracefully drawing from its sheath one of the deceptive daggers it spread into a beautiful fan which she fluttered before his face in an elegant manner while merrily laughing at his confusion. The outer folds of the fan were two flexible springs that were secured with the folds at the lower end to a delicate rod which, when drawn outward to the mouth of the sheath, unfolded in the shape of a half circle. The novelty was imported from France and they became very popular. Some of them were expensively ornamented with precious stones and displayed the highest grade of workmanship, but those most commonly in use were supplied at a reasonable price.

The Republican government of Mexico had been fully reinstated, and before this time a law was passed to forbid the circulation of money bearing the stamp of the empire, with a view to eliminate every evidence of Maximilian's reign. The law also authorized its being sent out of the country free of export or other duties with the intention of ridding the country of it as soon as possible. As it was not a legal tender in the republic the money became greatly depreciated, but it commanded a premium in the United States and we bought all we could afford with the means at our command through Messrs. Weber & Ulrich, our agents in Monterey, who secured all that was offered. We never cleared less than thirty-five per cent, by the speculation, consequently so long as any could be had, we made it a profitable business.

We transported many thousands of dollars from Monterey and other points along my route that was consigned to merchants in San Antonio, compared to which our own, in the above noted speculation, was insignificant. As it was known that we carried money, and sometimes large amounts, it is remarkable that we were never molested except on one occasion in Texas, and that time the attempt was a failure. It happened about thirty-seven miles east of Eagle Pass on my way to San Antonio, but I had been forewarned and the designs of the highway-men were frustrated.

When I arrived at Eagle Pass I found a letter awaiting me from my partner, Captain Muenzenberger, written at San Antonio, and dated February 10, 1868. He stated that he had received information of a scheme to rob me, and that a party of men had left that city with the inten-tion to waylay me. He advised me to be on my guard and not travel at night, as it was probable that they would make their attack under the cover of darkness. I also re-ceived a letter from John Kenedy, of Sabinal, at the same time, in which he communicated the fact that a party of eight men of questionable appearance had spent the night at his ranch, and the next morning, as it was nec-essary for him to go to Fort Clark, he accompanied them to Uvalde, a distance of twenty miles, where they took the Eagle Pass road. When on the way they asked him if he was acquainted with my schedule time between Chi-chon and Turkey Creek; also if I carried much money over the route, and many other questions which excited his suspicions. He also warned me to be on my guard be-cause he was convinced that the men intended to attack me somewhere between the points designated.

These warnings of my friends made me cautious and I took their advice by changing my usual programme. It was my custom to drive the twenty-seven miles between Eagle Pass and Chichon before dark, stopped there un-til two o'clock the following morning, and generally, I arrived at Turkey Creek about five o'clock A. M.; but on that trip I did not start from Chichon until seven o'clock, and we resumed our journey with the expectation of having an exciting time. I took my seat on the outside of the stage with my extra man and driver, where I could look out for the robbers and be prepared for anything that might happen. On the inside of the coach were my four passengers, Mr. Gilbeau, the father of Mrs. Bryan Callaghan, who is the wife of the present Mayor of San Antonio; Mr. Fernando Garza, also of San Antonio, and Messrs. Nicholas Burke and Jim Riddle, of Eagle Pass. We were all well armed with Winchester rifles, which were placed where they would be ready for use at a moment's notice.

We were all determined to give the highwaymen a warm reception in the event of an encounter, and a strict watch was kept ahead, but nothing occurred to excite suspicion until we started down a long grade when we saw a party of men in the distance on the north side of the road. Evidently they were the expected robbers, but we agreed to let them start the fight, after deciding to "run the gauntlet" as the best means of avoiding the attack.

I ordered the driver to lash the mules and at the crack of the whip the half-wild animals dashed forward at full speed. We approached the men under full headway, and nothing but a volley of bullets could have stopped the team on that incline. When passing the party we noticed that only six men were in sight, but when they saw our strength and that we were prepared, they abstained from making any threatening movement. Those inside the stage greeted them, saying, "We are behind time. We are in a hurry. We can't stop." But the baffled outlaws made no response and we dashed onward until they were lost to view.

The faces of the six men were fully exposed, but we passed so quickly none of them could be recognized. Later they were all identified, but it is wrong to circulate harmful reports about the dead by naming them and equally cruel to their families. It is sufficient that I eluded them through the aid of friends and I shall never cease to be grateful for their interest in my welfare on that occasion. If they had not forewarned me of the danger I would not have been on my guard when the would-be thieves waylaid me, and as all my passengers were brave men they would not have submitted quietly to being robbed, consequently the incident might have had a tragic ending instead of terminating as it did in a farce.

Mr. Gilbeau once had an experience with highwaymen in the Paso de la Laza, near the Sabinas River, in Mexico, and his cool, determined action on that occasion brought about decisive results. The ambulance he was on was stopped by ladrones and they surrounded it, but before they could commence their depredations Mr. Gilbeau dropped two of them in rapid succession, with a double-barrel shot-gun, and the others ran away.

Mr. Garza was credited with an equally resolute character and his bravery was never questioned. He was the youngest of three brothers that were members of a prominent family in San Antonio. They possessed equally fearless natures and all, at one time, held commissions in the Mexican army, but when Major Adolph Garza was killed in a duel by Colonel Henrico Mejia in 1867, Captain Juan Garza and Lieutenant Fernando Garza resigned.

It fell to my lot to bear the sad news of Major Garza's death to his family, and I became acquainted with the following pathetic incident that preceded the tragedy. Under the influence of a presentiment that the encounter would result fatally to himself he was impressed to write letters to his mother and relatives containing his last messages. These he enclosed in a mourning envelope, which he addressed and placed in his desk with a note expressing an earnest entreaty that the package should be delivered to his people in San Antonio, Texas. The package was given to me in Monterey, with the request that I would deliver it to the grief-stricken mother, and I performed the duty with a sorrowful heart.

Mr. Fernando Garza married after he resigned from the army, and died a few years later, but his widow survives and she still conducts a respectable restaurant in San Antonio which she opened twenty-five years ago. Captain Juan Garza also returned to Texas after resigning from the army, and was appointed assistant city marshal of San Antonio in 1868, which position he has since filled, almost continuously, to the satisfaction of the public up to the present time.

Santleben

Chapter Nine:

Robbers—Horse Breeding

The only time that I came in actual contact with robbers in Mexico was in 1868, on one of my trips when returning from Monterey. It was brought about by a favor I extended to a man I found on foot in an uninhabited country, by inviting him to take a seat in the stage. The only passengers with me in the coach were Dr. Felix, of Monterey, and Antonio Rivas, of San Antonio, the father-in-law of Dr. Chapa, the druggist, and I was accompanied by my usual guard and the driver. As day was breaking we were at the foot of the table mountain known as Mesa de Vidaurri, about twenty miles northeast of Lampazos, that is also called Mesa de los Cartuhanes.

The country in that vicinity was a sterile region, and I was surprised when Alex Gross, my driver from Lampazos to Santa Monica, called my attention to the form of a solitary man on foot a short distance ahead of us. The presence of a lonely human being in that locality was unusual, and it was very remarkable to find one there at any time, in his condition. Thinking that the man was in distress I stopped the stage and got out to speak to him. He was a well-dressed Mexican, his form was manly, and I was favorably impressed by his appearance. I inquired if any misfortune had happened to him and offered my services.

He seemed to be pleased at the interest I manifested, and very politely informed me that he was there because his horse had broken loose and run away, also that his men were in pursuit of him on the road leading to the Rio Grande. I inquired if the men would return to that place the way they had gone. He answered, "Yes, because there is no other road they could travel." As our route lay in that direction and we would be sure to meet the men, I invited him to take a seat in the coach and ride with us. He accepted my invitation with seeming pleasure, and after he, with his belongings, together with those of his six men, were stored on the stage, we resumed our journey.

We entered into sociable conversation with our passenger and he was equally friendly and polite, but he never gave me a chance to question him about himself. We all talked freely to him, but he had very little to say, and evidently he did not know much about the country or what was going on in Lampazos and other small towns near the frontier. His reticence with reference to himself was noticed, but our conversation was agreeable and we traveled very pleasantly about eighteen miles before we saw the horse-hunters approaching in the distance.

The stage was stopped and I got out my field-glass, and after adjusting it to the proper focus, passed it to our traveling companion. He did not know how to use it, but after I showed him, he identified his men and the horse they were leading. The fact that his horse had been secured was most gratifying to him, and when the men met us he begged the driver to stop the coach. After stepping out he walked forward to where his men were and talked to them, but we could not distinguish what was said. Evidently he told them of our kindness to him, because they advanced and returned thanks for all we had done. They received their property and after bidding us goodbye they remained there when we resumed our journey.

A few minutes after starting, Alex Gross turned his head and said, "Say, Boss, that fellow isn't all right." I readily agreed with him because I entertained the same impression and had sized my friend up during the few hours I was in his company; but Dr. Felix and Rivas differed with us and believed the man was only a prosperous ranchman.

On my return trip to Monterey I was told by Santiago Tomas, of Santa Monica, that I had made a warm and constant friend of Castro the highway robber and outlaw. He said that Castro had related the particulars of how I had befriended him, and stated that he could not feel grateful enough to me, and was ready to serve me in any way that offered. Of course I knew that Castro was in existence, and I was also acquainted with his origin and some of his exploits; but I did not know, until then, that he was the gentleman I had hauled several hours in my stage. Subsequently the fact became generally known, because Castro never missed an opportunity to relate the adventure, and to every one he expressed his gratitude for the assistance I had rendered him in the wilderness.

He was evidently sincere, although he magnified my services. Some of my friends on the contrary, entertained an opposite belief, and thought that the presence of Castro, at the place I found him, was planned with a view to gain information and afterwards lay a trap for me; but his conduct when I met him about four months later proved that they entertained an unjust opinion of him.

The meeting took place about twelve miles east of the Sabinas River when returning from Monterey, and it was entirely unexpected. I saw a bunch of men lying under the shade of a huisache grove, about two hundred yards from the road in the direction we were traveling. The stage was moving slowly up a hill, and when nearly opposite them one of the party we had been watching walked towards us, at the same time making motions for us to stop. I recognized Castro immediately after leaving the coach, and when we met about half way he greeted me cordially with a hearty hand-shake. To his inquiry, if I remembered him, I answered yes and that I was pleased to meet him again. I asked if I could render him assistance, and if so to let me know. He said he would like to get from me some cartridges suitable for a Spencer carbine if I could spare them. I replied that I could and returned to the coach to get them. When I gave them to him, he offered to pay me, but I insisted on his accepting them as a present and assured him that I had an ample supply. He thanked me very earnestly and urged me to go with him to his camp. I knew I would be safe in his company and did not hesitate to accompany him. His men rose to their feet as we approached and I was introduced to them as his friend "Augustin el Correo," or August the stage man. They all shook hands with me, and among them I recognized several of the party who met us with Castro's horse.

They numbered about fifteen men and all were armed with Spencer carbines and six-shooters. That pattern of rifle was the first breech loaders, using metallic cartridges, introduced into Mexico. Castro was a well-preserved man about fifty years old, and the ages of his men, apparently, ranged from thirty to forty years. They were all fairly well dressed, were decent looking and made a good appearance. They did not resemble the regular ladrones, who wore fancy clothes, which, like their saddles and bridles, were trimmed with silver. They also rode good horses which seemed to be in fair condition.

We talked about many things, but I carefully avoided any allusion to their occupation; nor did I refer to Santiago Tomas, the father-in-law of Dr. Serna, of San Buenaventura, or the information he gave me with reference to Castro's gratitude, because it would have led him to infer that I knew his reputation. Castro did not call my attention to the subject, although he assured me that I could rely on the friendship and services of himself and men at any time. Of course I thanked them for their good will and promised to assist them in any way that I could.

Indians were plentiful along my route at that time, and Castro inquired if I was not afraid of them. I replied that I was not, but that I was afraid of ladrones (robbers). He asked me if I had ever met any of them, and I said yes, but fortunately they never molested me. He then questioned me about my business and wanted to know if my stage line was a paying investment. I replied that it was because the Mexican Government had granted me many concessions and ample protection. One of the men suggested that I ought not to place too much confidence in the government of Mexico, because it had ruined and oppressed the people; but I knew why he talked that way and was not inclined to discuss the subject.

When I was ready to leave I repeated that I was willing to serve them if possible, and asked if I could do anything for them. They said no, and thanked me with many kind expressions. The men all embraced me, but before Castro did so, he unfastened a pair of silver buttons from the side of his hat and presented them to me, with the request that I would keep them as a remembrance. They were shaped like a bell and fastened to silver plates an inch square. I kept them many years, but finally lost one of them, and the other I presented to Judge Spooner of the United States Court of Claims, when he was a visitor in San Antonio, in 1904.

I never met Castro or his band on any other occasion, but shortly after I last saw him, I was told that he held up a stage-coach on the international stage line between the City of Mexico and Matamoras, nine miles west of Monterey, near Santa Catarina, and secured about ten thousand dollars. One of the passengers was Mr. Porter, who was returning from a business trip to the capital on account of a consignment of arms he sold to the Mexican Government during the war with France. He was a brother of Major Porter of the United States army, then stationed at Brownsville, and also an intimate friend of Theodore Lamberson, of El Paso, who at one time had charge of my wagon train, and afterwards was Sheriff of Duval County. This was the last robbery that Castro committed in Nuevo Leon or Tamalipas on account of the vigilance of the Mexican authorities, who pursued him continuously until he was driven out of the states.

Castro was not a common robber who took from the people indiscriminately, but only those who had an abundance were made to contribute to his demands, and he was lavish in his distributions to the poor. Consequently the rich feared him and he always found a friend and protector among the needy. Evidently he was grateful as well as generous, and he had many friends. I rather liked him myself after our first meeting near the base of the table mountain called Mesa de Vidaurri.

The strangeness of that encounter in connection with the interesting features of the mountain are impressed distinctly on my memory, and as it is a conspicuous landmark on my route I am constrained to give it further consideration. My description is based on information gathered from others, because I was never on the mountain, but have passed around its towering walls of solid stone on the north and south sides. The interpreted meaning of the name is Table of Vidaurri, that was suggested possibly by its appearance. It is an isolated mountain that is situated in the State of Nuevo Leon, about two hundred miles north of Monterey, about twenty miles west of the International and Great Northern Railroad, and its precipitous sides that rise to the height of 1,000 or more feet can be seen from passing trains.

Perhaps, in ages past, when the country was a wilderness, the natives knew it as a place of safety, when their merciless conquerors were reducing their captives to slavery. Its inaccessible walls, rising perpendicularly from the surrounding plains, could only be scaled at a few points, and doubtless they found a secure place of refuge on its summit.

Some time in the last century its value for ranch purposes was appreciated by Governor Vidaurri, of Nuevo Leon, and he became its owner. He stocked it with the necessary animals and for many years the top of the mountain was devoted to the raising of horses and mules exclusively. The large herds raised on its summit were not molested, because the only accessible point was up a winding road, cut in the side of the declivity. The opening at the top was constantly guarded by a detachment of soldiers to guard against intruders and to protect the surrounding country. A small settlement of peones occupied a village in the vicinity, who performed the labors of the ranch. These defenses, together with the natural obstructions, made the mesa or table of Vedura one of the strongest places in the country, and it was always safe from the depredations of horse-thieves and Indian raiders.

The top of the mountain covered an area exceeding three hundred and fifty thousand acres, as it was about twenty-five miles square. The surface is generally level, with occasional elevations, and it is partially covered by forests, but the pasture land is extensive. Much of the land is fertile and suitable for cultivation, especially in the low lands near the numerous water-courses.

When the mountain was first occupied it was infested by a number of native wild animals. Cinnamon and the common black bears, tigers, panthers, and Mexican lions were common and dangerous; other animals also were numerous, including the mountain sheep of Mexico that have immense horns that serve to protect them when forced by danger to jump down precipices. On such occasions their bodies and limbs are drawn into a lump and they fall without injury on their enormous curved horns, which throw them a somersault before landing them on their feet.

In order to protect his domestic animals Governor Vidaurri found that it was necessary to destroy the carnivorous animals, and he paid a bounty of twenty-five dollars for each tiger, panther and lion that was killed on the mountain, with the result that, perhaps, they were exterminated. At one time, too, he had trouble with a party of Indians who discovered a trail and ascended the mountain on foot. After remaining there some time they were seen by ranchmen, who notified the soldiers and an immediate attack was made. The Indians were cut off from the trail and driven over the bluff. Those not killed by the fall were too badly crippled to escape, and the Mexicans dispatched them all.

The mountain top was afterwards developed and much of the land was put under cultivation. Governor Vidaurri sold the ranch, ultimately, to his son-in-law, Pat Milmo, the father of the Milmo bankers of Laredo, who, I think, are the present owners.

Such ranches in those days were extremely desirable because of the perfect security against loss when property of all kinds received very little protection. The country was constantly exposed to inroads of wild Indians, but in 1868 they were unusually bold and more frequent in northern Mexico, also in Texas, where they were sometimes extended. The murders and thefts committed on such occasions have never been estimated, consequently the savages were held in considerable dread. I seemed to be under the protection of Providence, because I never saw wild Indians but once in Mexico while running the stage to Monterey, and then they did not bother me.

Equestrianism was carried to the highest point of excellence in Mexico during the period to which my writings refer, and every horseman in that country was ambitious to own a beautiful, well-trained horse with expensive trappings. The outlay necessary to gratify his desires in that connection was never considered, and it was a luxury that was indulged in to extravagance. It was not uncommon to see riding horses that cost $1,000 with silver mounted saddles and bridles for which $500 was paid. The fashionable riding costume of a wealthy Mexican, embroidered with silver and gold thread and ornamented with silver buttons, involved an outlay of from $75 to $100, and his felt hat, with its broad brim, similarly embroidered, cost from $100 to $250. They made an attractive appearance on their well-trained horses, and others besides Mexicans indulged themselves in the same way. A well-known citizen, who now resides in San Antonio, was then engaged in business in Mexico and he invested not less than $1,000 in a riding costume, saddle and bridle.

The horses that were in demand were the hardy, active, native-bred horses of the country which trace their origin to the time of the Conquest. They were susceptible to thorough training and became submissive to the will of the rider through a pressure of the knee, a touch of the heel, or a twitch of the bridle. In that way a horse could be made to spring suddenly to the right or left, a distance of ten feet, or rear on his hind feet and walk several steps forward, and perform many graceful acts that displayed his intelligence in which the rider showed his horsemanship. I once saw a Mexican ride a very fine horse into a room in which a crowd had gathered, where the animal was made to rear and place his front feet on the counter. It was not an unusual occurrence and the act was applauded.

These trained horses were also used to run races, and on such occasions a rope was stretched along the ground across the track at the starting point. The two horses were then placed in position with their front feet even with the rope, where they stood quietly until their riders made a motion with bridles and heels, when the signal to go was given, and then they leaped forward a distance of twelve or more feet. All the race tracks were straight and another rope was stretched across the furthest end in front of the judges' stand. The race was decided in favor of the horse that first put his front foot over the rope.

Chapter Ten:

1868—Fording the Sabinas—Mesmeric Encounter

On one of my return trips from Monterey, in 1868, I came upon a band of Indians at Santiago Creek, which is about twenty miles southwest of Santa Monica, where the battle of Cinco del Mayo was fought, in 1865, that resulted in a defeat of the French army by the Mexican forces under the command of General Trevino, the man who afterwards married a daughter of General Ord of the United States army.

The Indians were encamped about three hundred yards south of the road when I drove in sight of them about two o'clock in the evening. They seemed to be resting and evidently the rattle of the coach on the rocky road roused them from sleep, because we could see them spring to their feet as if alarmed. Their hasty movements indicated that they were preparing for trouble, but they made no effort to intercept us nor did they show any disposition to attack us. Perhaps they were startled by the interruption, not having noticed the road and believing themselves in a place of safety, because their horses together with a large herd were grazing along near where we passed and all the animals seemed to be exhausted by fatigue from hard service. They may have concluded that we were capable of giving them a warm reception after seeing that we numbered eight men, including passengers, driver, and escort, and all were well armed. As our wish was to avoid an encounter we passed through them as quickly as possible, but not fast enough to prevent me from recognizing several well-known brands of Texas ranchmen on the horses.

We were informed later that this band of Indians, numbering twenty-five bucks, had recently made a raid into Medina and Atascosa Counties, where they stole about one hundred head of horses from Judge Noonan and others. They also killed Rumanas Gross and his son, near where La Coste station is now. They crossed the Rio Grande somewhere between Eagle Pass and Laredo when returning to Mexico, and, probably, they reached the place where we saw them that morning and were resting after the fatigues of the journey.

Another trip, in 1868, when I arrived at Lampazos, on my way to Monterey, the people informed me that the country was swarming with Indians on the war-path, and they advised me not to proceed further until news could be had from the soldiers who were in pursuit of them. I was told that a body of about sixty Indians were holding a position on the west side of the Sierra Colorado Pass, and that a small detachment of Mexican troops had advanced to the east side of the pass, about twenty-two miles distant, but were unable to drive the savages from the point they occupied.

The pass was on my route and after determining to proceed I started as usual between two and three o'clock in the morning and drove to the place held by the soldiers. They told me that the Indians were still on the other side of the pass, and it would be unsafe for me to go on, so I took their advice and returned to Lampazos. Later in the day the soldiers were reinforced, and an attack was made, in which many Indians were killed and the others were driven into the mountains.

I did not like the idea of turning back, but the lives of my passengers would have been jeopardized if I had done otherwise, and as I had women and children under my care I could not afford to take any chances. One was the wife of Jose Brosic, with his three children, her mother, and her sister, all of whom took the stage at Piedras Negras; another was Pedro Morales, the assistant customs-house officer at that place.

Mr. Brosic, of Villaldama, who was then paymaster of the Mexican army on the frontier, was at the ranch of Golondrinas, west of Sierra Colorado Pass, with an escort of ten men waiting to meet his family, and he was overjoyed when he saw them safely arrive the second day after we left Lampazos. He had good reason to be uneasy, because, it was said that, during the time the Indians were on that raid, they killed thirty or forty people.

These few Indian alarms are about all that I experienced when staging to Monterey. They were of little consequence in comparison with the thrilling adventures of others on the frontier, but the excitement they occasioned gave variety to a journey that would otherwise have been monotonous. We met with few accidents on our route during the two years of its continuance, and I can only recall one of a serious nature, that happened in 1868. As it was one in which the lives of many passengers were involved, the circumstances are vividly impressed on my mind, but fortunately my foresight averted a fatal disaster.

I was on my way to Monterey, but knowing the Sabinas River was flooded, I turned from my usual route and went to a ferry at the Paso del Cocha, a short distance above. I arrived there about daybreak, but found that the channel of the river was about one hundred feet wide and about fifteen feet in depth. It was full of water to the top of the banks, from recent rains, and it was a raging torrent. The current of the river, at its natural stage, was always rapid, though at such times it was fordable; but a ferry was maintained at the crossing for the convenience of travelers when the river was swollen.

I was not deterred by the swiftness or turbulence of the water, but determined to encounter the risks and made immediate preparations for passing over the river. The little ferry-boat was only about 8 ft. wide and 25 ft. long, consequently its capacity was limited, and it was necessary to make three trips across. One of them, in which the mules and harness were transported, consumed two hours, but when the coach with all its luggage was loaded on the boat, preparatory to making the second trip, the ferry-man insisted that the passengers should go with it, but I protested against the arrangement, because the craft was loaded to its full capacity, and the swiftness of the current made it dangerous. We finally compromised the matter by an agreement on my part to pay the charges he demanded for a third trip.

The first trip was made without the slightest difficulty and unloaded at the usual landing place, but the second was less fortunate. Each time, before crossing, the boat was pulled by a rope up the river, near the bank, where the water formed an eddy, to a point about one hundred and fifty yards above. When the oars turned it toward the opposite shore the rope was cast loose with the expectation that the force of the water would carry it across.

I was on the boat with two of my men, and it was guided by four ferry-men with oars in front and rear, but it rocked badly, partly because the luggage on the coach made it top-heavy. When about the middle of the raging torrent the surging waters capsized the flat-bottomed craft and emptied its load in the river. Those on board had prepared for casualties by stripping to their underclothing and we plunged into the water. When relieved of its freight, the boat rose again to the surface with many loose articles, including the cushions, and the current carried them onwards, but the coach and its load rested on the bottom of the Sabinas.

When the lady passengers and children, who had been left until the last, saw the boat sink they thought we were all drowned, and I could hear their piercing shrieks as I swam toward the eastern shore. We landed about fifty yards below the crossing place and relieved their anxiety as soon as possible by joining them. They had given way to despair, under the impression that they were left in a desolate wilderness; but before night closed around us all of them were safely transported in a rowboat to the western shore where our party was reunited.

Our situation was rather deplorable, especially for women and children, because we were without bedding or shelter, but afterwards we were able to buy sufficient food from Mexicans, who, with their carts, camped that night at the ferry. The country on either side was without habitations of any kind, and the nearest, on the river, was fifty miles above where the boatmen lived. They only visited the ferry on horseback when the water was high, and generally made it profitable on account of their exorbitant charges, which were never less than two dollars and a half for each trip, and they always made me pay ten dollars for my coach and mules.

We made no attempt to recover the coach the first day, because we had no appliances for taking it out of the river, even if we could have located it in the deep water; but that evening fortune favored us when two trains of Mexican carts, numbering thirty in all, appeared upon the scene, and camped in our vicinity. I approached the drivers immediately, and offered to pay them seventy-five dollars if they would find my coach and take it on the west side of the river where we then were. They accepted my proposition and nearly all the men engaged in the search the following morning, but they were unsuccessful until the third day. They found it lying on its side about four hundred yards below where it sank, in water about ten feet in depth. Chains and ropes were fastened to the wheels and axles, by which it was dragged into shallow water, from where, after setting it on its wheels, it was pulled out to the shore.

Nothing about the coach was broken, but everything that was not secured was missing, including many articles belonging to the ladies. The trunks and other baggage in the boat and on top of the coach that were bound by heavy straps were all safe. Of course everything was wet, dirty, and more or less damaged by water and mud, but we were glad to recover them even in that condition. The lost stage cushions I afterwards replaced with new ones that cost me one hundred and fifty dollars, but in the meantime I supplied the deficiency by substituting straw and sheepskins, which I purchased from the men of the cart train, that answered the purpose. We did not take time to unpack the luggage before starting, and delayed our journey no longer than was necessary to hitch the team.

The following passengers were on the stage: Mrs. Buss and her two children; Mrs. Dressal, a sister of ex-Congressman Schleicher, and her child; three Robin children, of San Antonio; Charles Sada, Dr. Felix and Henry Rice, all citizens of Monterey; Colonel Morales, of the Mexican army, and several others whose names I cannot recall. I am happy to say that not one of them experienced any serious inconvenience on account of the accident, and they bore the discomforts to which they were obliged to submit, with becoming fortitude. I was heartily thankful that it was no worse, although I was put to considerable expense on account of it.

The list will convey an idea of the patronage I received on account of the care and attention I always bestowed on my passengers. My thoughtfulness made me many friends along the route and also in Monterey where there was a large foreign population. Among them were Messrs. Weber and Ulrich, who did a large commission business, and Mr. Ulrich, who now lives in San Antonio, was then United States Consul; Mr. A. Buss, who conducted a large lumber business; Mr. Dressal, a large hardware merchant; Mr. Lickhart, Mr. Cartwright, Theodore Lamberton, and Mr. George Paschal, ex-mayor of San Antonio, a brother of Dr. Frank Paschal. These were all my friends, and they always took a great interest in the line because of the facility it gave them to communicate with their friends in Texas.

On account of the amicable feeling expressed for me I never lacked attention and was welcome wherever I went, consequently I entertained a good opinion of myself, until on one occasion my self-conceit was lowered considerably. This incident occurred at a mesmeric entertainment which I attended through the persuasion of my friend, George Paschal.

I had never seen an exhibition of the kind and knew nothing about the subject. The claim that one man could exercise such power over another, as was represented by Mr. Paschal, who told me all about it, seemed to be absurd. I could not doubt the sincerity of his information, because he was evidently in earnest; but it appeared more rational when he explained that some persons were more susceptible to the influence than others.

When I entered the room I felt that I was exempt from mesmeric powers and that it would be foolish for any man to attempt to bring me under his control against my will. The gentleman was from California, and he appeared to be about forty years of age. I was introduced to him and we entered into conversation. He inquired if I had any belief in mesmerism; and I answered, "None at all, nor do I think that any person could control my thoughts and actions contrary to my will, or that I would submit to another's power except by the exercise of superior force," and then closed by saying that I was open to conviction.

I met his gaze as he looked intently into my eyes and said, "You are about the weakest subject I have had in the house." I was so much disconcerted by his opinion that I did not know what to say and remained silent. He then placed both of his hands on my head, and immediately after I yielded to a drowsy feeling that over-came me. I knew nothing more until I was restored to consciousness and found myself undressed to my under-clothing. Evidently I had been made to perform all sorts of antics for the amusement of the company, and their mirthful humor indicated that they had been witnessing a regular monkey show.

My over-confidence in my mental powers was consid-erably weakened on that occasion, and perhaps it was a good lesson, because I was more conservative after-wards. I was convinced that the human mind is amena-ble to mysterious powers that are beyond our compre-hension, and that under certain conditions it must yield to a superior control.

I might relate many other reminiscences connected with Monterey during the continuance of our stage busi-ness, and some of them are pleasant to recall, but per-haps they would not interest the reader. Many customs prevailed there among the natives that would, perhaps, attract only a casual notice, but some of them are quite interesting. One of the strangest sights to me was the facility with which the *cargadores* or carriers of Mexico convey enormous weights on their backs. The dexterity displayed in handling their burdens and the perfect ease with which they transport them have always created as-tonishment in the mind of the observer. The fact that a man weighing not exceeding one hundred and sixty pounds, will place five hundred pounds, or more, on his back and trot off with it, seemingly, without the slight-est inconvenience, is certainly remarkable, consequently the custom is worthy of a more extended notice.

The truth of the axiom that "there is a trick in all trades," is not questioned, and the cargador, who is al-ways an expert in his business, has brought his to perfec-tion. His secret lies in the use of a cushion that removes the direct pressure and friction of the weight from his body. It rests against the lower part of the back, between the hips, where it helps to give a swing to his burden corresponding with the movements of the body and legs of the carrier when traveling in a jog-trot. The pad is called a *muelle*, and usually it is about six inches thick, ten inches wide, and fourteen inches long. The muelle is suspended to a strap about four inches wide, after it is secured to a corner at each end, then the loop passes behind the shoulders and rests against the forehead.

The cargador, when about to receive his load, turns his bent back to it and instantly begins to lift his feet up and down, similar to soldiers when marking time. The movement gives a swing to the body and the same rhythmical motions are observed in the hips and knees, with which the two or more assistants, who hold the load, keep time, after the weight is received by the hooks of the carrier, until it is in the proper position. He grasps his burden with a hook in each hand and the instant it is correctly placed on his back the carrier trots off and it adapts itself to his preliminary movements. Another secret is the necessity of maintaining the same rate of speed without stopping until relieved of their load; because if they should halt even for a moment or even check their gait, their burden would tumble to the ground or they would be crushed by its weight.

I have often seen a continuous line of such carriers moving bales of cotton on their backs almost in double-quick time, in Matamoras and Monterey, a distance of four hundred yards, and I never saw one of them use the least exertion. It is said that they can carry a piano, that weighs more than a bale of cotton, in like manner, and with the same ease. Many times when I was hauling money from Chihuahua to other places I would employ cargadores to help me load it on my wagons, by carrying it nearly a mile to the Meson. A load for one of them was four thousand dollars in silver in two boxes, which together weighed two hundred and eighty pounds, and they would move off with them without an effort. The usual charge for such services was twenty-five cents for each trip, and they handled for me in that way at various times many hundred thousand dollars.

The cargador everywhere in Mexico is entirely trustworthy, and no one is liable to suffer loss on account of his carelessness or dishonesty. Those who are eligible for such employment are men hardened by labor, and the applicant must be recommended by one or more responsible persons who have known him a number of years, and can testify to his honesty and integrity of character, before his petition is presented at the Palacio Municipal. If its endorsements are satisfactory a license is issued to the applicant, for which he deposits about fifty dollars as security, and a badge is given him on which is a number that is entered before his name in a book kept for that purpose.

When a cargador approaches a person and offers his services he politely calls attention to his number and solicits employment. Strangers need not concern themselves about the safety of baggage entrusted to their care, but it is always proper to make a memorandum of his number to guard against accidents. No transfer company in the United States could assure greater safety or more prompt delivery of property than these humble carriers in Mexico, who never strike for higher wages and are always ready to work.

Our stage line to Monterey was discontinued in August, 1869, on account of sudden changes in the custom-house officers at Eagle Pass and Piedras Negras by both governments, because the removal of our friends naturally affected our business. During the two years the line was in operation I was constantly on the road, nor did I ever miss accompanying our stage on any one of the forty-eight trips we made from San Antonio to Monterey and back, and I had sole charge of the business. Our net profits were large and we hated to give up the line, but were compelled to do so.

The following list contains the names of all the passengers that I can recall who traveled on our stage to and from San Antonio, Texas, and Monterey, Mexico:

Colonel Bliss and Colonel Shatter of the United States army.

Mrs. Eliza Noll and Mrs. Schenk, of Austin, Texas.

Nicholas Burke, Mr. Dolch and family, Mr. Dresch and family, George and Fred Enderle, Mr. Grober, James Riddle, A. Salinas and family, Mr. Stone and family, Sam White and Daniel Wueste, of Eagle Pass, Texas.

Wolfgang Kapp, of Germany.

Pedro Lastro, of Indianola, Texas.

General Naranjo, Filipe Naranjo, and Mrs. Carnales, of Lampazos, Mexico.

General Escobedo and Colonel Morales of the City of Mexico.

Mrs. Buss, Mr. Degetau, Mr. Doese, A. Douglas and family, Mr. Drissil and family, Henry Dreiss, Dr. Felix, Henry Rice, Charles Sada, Gonzales Trevino, John Weber, and Charles Ziegler, of Monterey, Mexico.

Frank and Mrs. Coreth, and Julius Mauraux, of New Braunfels, Texas.

Mr. Labenburg and Major Magirdy, of New York city.

Nicholas Gresanto and family, of Piedras Negras, Mexico.

Mr. Koenig, of Paras, Mexico.

Ex-Governor Abristo Madero, of Saltillo, Mexico.

Dan Bonnett, Henry Brown, Lorenzo Castro, Mr. Elmendorf, A. B. Frank, John Fries, Mr. Frittilier, Ferdinand and Captain Juan Garza, Francisco Gilbeau, H. Grenett, Charles Griesenbeck, Carl Groos, F. Groos and family, and Gustave Groos, John Guerguin, Meyer and Saul Halff, Mr. Herman, Mr. Koenigheim, Ernest Kramer, Mrs. Lottie Muenzenberger, Russell Norton, George Paschal, Mr. Pentenrieder, Antonio Rivas, August and Martin Robin, ex-Congressman Schleicher, Herman Schleuning, Angelo Torres, Mr. Ulrich, and R. Wolfing, of San Antonio.

Santiago Tomas, of San Domingo, Mexico.

Carlos Brosic and family and Machor Sanchez, of Villaldama.

Thomas B. McManus, of Washington, D. C.

I could tell many things that would be interesting concerning other people, but my information must necessarily be confined to my own experiences and this sketch must suffice, though I will add that they were the hardest two years' work I ever did in my life.

After settling up the business, we dissolved partnership, and Captain Muenzenberger moved to Santa Rosa, Mexico, with his family, where he engaged in mining and the milling business. I retained the mules and bought others with which I started a train of wagons on my own account.

Chapter Eleven:

1869—Freighting From Indianola to Chihuahua—
Clubbing Jackrabbits

The discontinuance of our stage line practically cut off all regular communication between Texas and Mexico until other means was established. But for the interruption to our business, it is probable that we would have increased our service to a weekly line in each direction and made it permanent through concessions we had in prospect. My individual efforts had made it remunerative, and I gained a large amount of practical experience that was valuable in my later enterprises. I had encountered all the dangers and difficulties on the route successfully, and learned to rely largely on my own judgment, therefore, I felt competent to grapple with larger undertakings. I became acquainted with numerous people and claim to have gained the confidence of many business men through my transactions with them which gave me a commercial standing.

With these advantages in my favor I did not hesitate to invest my hard-earned profits in my new business of freighting, with which I was familiar. My former experiments served as a guide and I secured six large, strongly built wagons, called "prairie schooners," and ten mules for each of them, besides a few extra animals for emergencies. I then employed competent drivers and placed my train in charge of Theodore Lamberson, who came with me from Mexico. My wagons made their first trip to Indianola, in September, 1869, a distance of one hundred and fifty miles, with a cargo of wool that belonged to Mr. Lockwood, the banker in San Antonio, and others. On account of constant rains and high water the wool got wet and I was held responsible for the damage it sustained, consequently I had to pay Lockwood's losses to the amount of about twelve hundred dollars and six hundred dollars on other claims. This drain on my resources in the very beginning of my new enterprise only stimulated me to greater exertions and I determined to enlarge the scope of my business by extending my route to the city of Chihuahua, in Mexico, for which purpose I increased the number of wagons in my train.

Goods were then moved through Texas from Indianola to Mexico under bond. The guarantee was exacted by the Federal custom-house officials to insure prompt transportation through the United States to the Mexican border where the duties were paid, and all bonded freight for Mexico was shipped from that point until 1877. In that year the Galveston, Harrisburg and San Antonio railroad was completed to Luling, and I persuaded Colonel C. C. Gibbs to use his influence to have the road bonded. It was done, and my wagon train hauled the first bonded freight that was consigned to that point through Messrs. Heicke & Helfrisch, of Galveston, Texas.

I commenced my first trip from Indianola to Chihuahua and Parral, Mexico, on a journey of eleven hundred and fifty miles, in December, 1869. The goods I received were loaded out of the bonded warehouse of Messrs. August and Valentine Heicke, commission merchants in Indianola, after I had given a heavy bond, payable to the United States, to insure their prompt transportation. My supplies for the trip were purchased from the grocery store owned by Mr. Dan Sullivan, now a banker in San Antonio.

I was personally unacquainted with the route beyond Fort Clark, but as I traveled with Mr. Froboese's train to

Fort Stockton I felt no uneasiness on that account because I had men in my employ who were familiar with all the watering places. I knew that the country was infested by Indians, but I did not worry about them after providing an abundant supply of arms and ammunition, and adopting suitable precautions.

The road we traveled from Indianola passed through San Antonio, Castroville, Uvalde, to Fort Clark, a United States military post, one hundred and fifty miles west of San Antonio. It is on a hill on the west side of Las Moras Creek, opposite the town of Brackett. This place was the last settlement on the El Paso road, in 1856, when the fort was first established. Thirty-five miles beyond is San Felipe Springs, where Del Rio is now situated. These beautiful springs and adjoining land were secured by Jim Taylor, Joe Ney and others as early as 1866. Two years later farms were opened and water for irrigating purposes was taken out of San Felipe Creek at a point from which a thousand or more acres could be watered. It was about the first irrigated farm west of San Antonio, and the land could not be bought then for fifty dollars per acre.

The next interesting place is Devil's River, twelve miles beyond, in a northwesterly direction. The first crossing was one of the most beautiful places I ever beheld, and its pure crystal water, in addition to the attractive scenery, excited the admiration of everyone. The stream was fully five hundred feet across, and the water ran from two to three feet deep on a smooth rock bottom. After crossing the river and going four miles west we passed Painted Cave, that was once a favorite resort of the Indians. Its name was conferred on account of numerous Indian paintings on the walls, such as chasing buffalo, scalping white men and stealing white children, war-dances, and many other things that were quite legible until recent years. Twenty miles beyond, in a northwest direction, is the narrow cañon called Dead-man's Pass, where many unfortunate travelers have lost their lives near the south entrance. Fort Hudson is located on the west bank of the second crossing of Devil's River, twenty miles farther in the same direction, but it was abandoned at the commencement of the Civil War and was never reoccupied. Twenty-three miles further, at the eighteenth crossing of Devil's River, is Beaver Lake; and forty-five miles beyond, in a northwest direction, is Howard's Well, that has an abundant flow of delicious water. The site of Fort Lancaster, an early military post, that was abandoned before the Civil War, is forty-eight miles beyond. A more desirable location for a frontier post could not be found in the western country. It is situated near the west base of a high mountain, on the east side of Lancaster Creek, in which flows a constant stream of limpid water, that empties into the Pecos River, a mile below.

We traveled four miles to the lowest ford before crossing the Pecos River, a few miles above the present site of the wonderful steel bridge on the Sunset Railway that spans the river at the height of 321 feet above. From thence we journeyed in a northerly direction to a place called Horsehead crossing, where the Concho road intersects with the route. The next place, forty miles, in a western direction, is Fort Stockton, an important military post, where United States troops were stationed. It may be noted that the entire distance of 230 miles from Del Rio to this point was uninhabited. An open country surrounds the fort on all sides, but there is little to recommend the site and its most objectionable feature is the strong alkali water that can't be surpassed in the country.

Nine miles west of the post is Leon Water-hole, that is also strongly impregnated with alkali, and it is as clear as crystal. The spring is thirty feet in diameter and so deep that the bottom has never been touched. Once, it is said, the depth was tested by a party of over-land travelers who camped there and threw two of their wagon wheels, that had loose tires, into the hole. They spent the next three days dragging for them with long ropes, without being able to recover them, and perhaps the wheels will remain there indefinitely.

We left the El Paso road at Leon Water-hole and followed the route, leading in a southwest direction, to Presidio del Norte, distant 200 miles, that was then without a habitation. The first watering place, forty miles beyond, is Leon Seto, that was settled two years later by Joe Head. Forty miles further is Burges Water-hole. Then we traveled twenty miles to Antelope springs, that is better known as Barando. The next water is at Tinacha San Stevens, thirty miles beyond. Then comes El Alamita at the distance of twenty-five miles, which is forty miles from Presidio del Norte, that was also settled two years later by John Davis. These distances make one hundred and ninety-five miles, and the road is tolerably good excepting the last forty miles, which is hilly, and the sand is heavy, but its principal recommendation is an abundance of grass that affords good pasturage.

Presidio del Norte is situated on the Mexican side of the Rio Grande below the mouth of the Rio Conchas, and Presidio is on the Texas side, where the Cibolo Creek empties. Custom-houses, were established in both these towns by the two republics, and a large quantity of goods passed through them. The river at that point is always fordable, except when the water is high, and then the passage is made on ferry-boats.

After submitting an inventory of my freight for inspection to the United States officials, who approved it, I crossed at the ford into Mexico, and my train was placed under guard until the inspectors verified my manifest and the duties on the bonded goods were paid. I received courteous treatment from the officials of both governments and was not unnecessarily delayed.

I resumed my journey and traveled forty-five miles to El Rancho de la Mula over a tolerably good road. Thence to Chupadero it is sixty miles, and from there to Julimes is ninety miles through a desert country without water, except at Chupadero, where the supply was scarcely sufficient for my teams, but afterwards, when passing over the route, I secured an ample supply by sending two men six hours ahead, with tools to dam up the water below the rock from where the water escaped. From Julimes to Bachamba ranch, that belonged to the McManus family, of Chihuahua, the distance is twenty miles over a road heavy with sand and the country is covered with brush and cactus. From the ranch to Chihuahua is thirty miles, and the road traverses the Hojito Cañon, one of the most dangerous places on account of Indians, in the State. It is only about five miles long where it passes through the Sierra Madre range, and many persons, including large parties, have been killed there by savages, but beyond the mountain pass the road is good and safe to Chihuahua. The entire distance from Presidio may be estimated at about two hundred and fifty miles.

After delivering my freight that was consigned to Chihuahua, it was necessary to retrace my route about thirty miles to the McManus ranch, to avoid the mountains, where the road turned southward to Parral, which is about one hundred and seventy-five miles from Chihuahua. After leaving the ranch the road passes through a farming country about twenty miles, where Augustine and Tomas Cordero, two brothers, owned a large irrigated farm in the Conchas valley that they sold for $250,000 in 1872. We then came to the Rio Conchas and passed through the town of San Pablo that then had a population of about two thousand souls; then through Santa Cruz with about three thousand. The next place was the beautiful town of Santa Rosalia with about seven thousand inhabitants, and then we arrived at the mining town of Parral. The entire road after leaving the McManus ranch was bad and hard on the teams.

I loaded my wagons at Parral with bars of silver and crude copper ore, belonging to F. Stalfort, of Parral, and hauled it to Chihuahua. The silver was coined there into Mexican dollars at the mint belonging to Henry Mutter, who was licensed to coin money for the government under a contract which allowed him twelve and a half per cent, for all the money that was turned out by his mint.

I was detained there ten days, waiting until the money was coined, and one hundred and eighty thousand dollars was delivered to me for transportation to the United States. With it and the copper ore, which was also consigned to parties in Texas, I started towards home over the same route I had recently traveled.

The only incident worth noticing on our homeward journey was observed near Santa Rosalia, one Sabbath afternoon after leaving Parral, where we saw a crowd of between four and five hundred men and boys each with a stout stick, about five feet in length, in their hands. They seemed to have assembled for some definite purpose, but their object was not apparent as they stood in line out in an open country, and the appearance excited my curiosity. I was aware that my wagon-master, Eutimio Migarez, was born and reared in the State of Chihuahua and I asked him what it meant. He informed me that the people had gathered with the intention of exterminating jack-rabbits that had become a pest in the country on account of their numbers; that in farming districts the animals were often very numerous, and if the nuisance was not suppressed the growing crops were entirely destroyed by them; that they only foraged in the fields at night, and waste places in the vicinity sheltered them during the day, consequently the only effective method of getting rid of the nuisance was to surround their resting-places in the daytime with a sufficient number of men and kill them with clubs.

Sunday afternoon was usually chosen for the slaughter, and, as the hunt was exciting, the occasion was one that attracted every man and boy in the vicinity who was active enough to participate in the sport. A valley or plain was selected which the rabbits frequented, and the party placed themselves in a circle at intervals of from fifty to one hundred yards from each other, until the area was surrounded. The hunters then advanced from every direction and roused the animals, which ran before from their resting-places in the brush and openings. The circle was closed as quickly as possible so as to form a continuous line through which it was impossible for the rabbits to escape. Then the timid animals were arrested in their flight at every point by threatening poles and they became distracted with fright. When the space that enclosed them was sufficiently contracted the work of destruction with sticks commenced and it did not cease until the last rabbit was dead.

Large numbers of animals were killed in that way in the neighborhood of cultivated land, and it was necessary to resort to the method repeatedly, otherwise the crops would have been ravaged by other rabbits that came from places more remote. Eutimio said that once, when a boy, he joined a party of hunters who killed between four and five hundred jack-rabbits in one day. The Indians often secured a supply of food by similar means, and probably the custom descended from a remote period. In Kansas, where the animals are numerous, similar methods have been adopted in recent years, but they drive them into nets instead of killing them with sticks.

Chapter Twelve:

The Ox-Wagon in Texas—Prairie Schooners

Before the age of railroads all over-land transportation in Texas and Mexico was done by carts and wagons. For many years ox-teams were generally used for hauling to and from the coast country to the interior, but later, mules were substituted, to some extent, in the business, especially in the West, where the country was rough and mountainous and on account of the scarcity of water.

A history of the ox-wagon and its usefulness in helping to develop the sparsely settled regions of Texas, together with a description of the habits and customs that prevailed among the people engaged in the business, would be entertaining to those who feel an interest in following the progressive steps of civilization. My personal experiences as a driver of an ox-wagon for my father, from San Antonio to Port Lavaca, when I was a boy eleven years of age, and about five years later, when I drove alone, qualifies me to express myself on the subject, but the details would be too lengthy in this connection. It is sufficient to say that teamsters made themselves indispensable to the commercial world, but the services they rendered are not appreciated.

During that period all freighting between Texas and Mexico was done by individual owners of wagons and Mexican carts drawn by oxen, but they were gradually displaced by trains of wagons hauled by mules. Such trains, consisting of ten or more wagons under one management, were common in Mexico long before they were seen in Texas.

The first wagon trains drawn by mules that hauled freight out of San Antonio to Mexico, before the Civil War, were owned and conducted by John Monier, a Frenchman, now residing in San Antonio; but before directing attention to the subject other primitive means of conveyance will be considered.

The ancient Mexican cart was unique in appearance, and as they are still common in that republic, its peculiar construction and importance is worthy of particular notice. The most remarkable feature about them, as originally constructed, was the absence of metal in all of its parts, which were fashioned exclusively out of cottonwood timber and fastened together with wooden pins and thongs of rawhide.

The cart had two wheels, each about seven feet high, and both, separately, were made from three pieces of wood hewn to the proper dimensions. The middle piece was seven feet long, with circular ends, three feet wide, and its thickness was twenty inches at the hub, from which it sloped to ten inches at each end. The other two pieces were in the shape of a half circle, about seven feet long and two feet wide, and they also sloped to ten inches. These circular pieces when fitted to the two sides and secured to the middle piece by four long wooden pins, three by five inches square, that passed through the three pieces from one rim to the other, made a complete circle, and formed the wheel, with a hub twenty inches through and a rim ten inches thick. A round hole that sloped from six inches on one side to eight in diameter on the other, was chiseled through the center for the axle, and the second wheel was made exactly like it.

A live-oak or a pecan tree was selected for the axle and squared to eight inches; then a spindle was shaped at each end that sloped on the upper side from seven inches at the shoulder to five inches at the end; and when the wheels were put on they stood about seven feet apart. The bed, which was about six feet wide and fifteen feet long, was framed out of heavy timbers firmly secured to the axle by wooden pins and rawhide thongs. The tongue, that projected twelve feet in front, formed the centerpiece for the bed, and passed over the axle and both ends of the frame, at which points it was also secured by wooden pins and thongs, and other pieces formed the bed, which was covered by a thatched roof of straw that was supported by heavy standards set in the frame.

These carts are common in many parts of Mexico, where they have been used a long time. In the State of Chihuahua I saw many of them as late as 1877, mostly in San Pablo, Santa Rosalia, and Julimes, but they were also used in other towns in that region where the land was irrigated. The Cordero brothers, whose farm of two thousand acres has been noticed, also those belonging to Frank McManus, Gustav Moye and many others, used such carts to haul corn, wheat, and other products to market. A full load for such carts was thirty-five *fanegas* of corn, that weighed about five thousand pounds, for which five or six yoke of oxen were required as a team, and they used fine animals that were always kept in the best condition.

In Mexico the yoke is lashed behind the oxen's horns with a broad rawhide strap about twelve feet long, and the first yoke is secured to the end of the tongue. Any number of animals may then be attached in couples at certain distances apart to two lengths of a rawhide rope extending from the tongue, that is doubled and twisted together. The load on the cart was always equally distributed so that it would balance on the axle, and a substantial stake, fastened underneath to the hind end of the frame, with its end near the ground, kept the tongue on a level and sustained the weight when the cart was not in motion.

The wheels and axles of such carts, after long use, wore away until the former wobbled considerably, and the screeching they made was awful. A remedy for the noise, when it became excruciating, was prickly-pear leaves, which were shoved in, one at a time, and when crushed on the axle served as an excellent lubricant.

These carts, but of lighter build and drawn by only three yoke of oxen, were often seen in San Antonio in earlier times, when they hauled freight from Mexico; and at one period they entered into competition with Texas freighters until serious disturbances occurred, that are known in Texas history as the "cart war," which were not quelled until the State was forced to exercise its authority. This, and other causes, brought about their gradual disappearance, until it is doubtful if one could now be found in Texas.

When Mexico began to be developed and iron became plentiful, the carts were modernized to some extent, especially in Nuevo Leon and around Monterey, where the wheels were reduced to four feet in diameter, and iron was used in their construction; consequently they were better proportioned, the material was lighter and one yoke of oxen was commonly used to draw them. In the course of time these also were nearly all discarded for heavier cart-wheels with tires six inches wide and an inch thick, which required three yoke of oxen to draw them, that were introduced through the agency of Mr. Staacke, the first large dealer in vehicles in San Antonio, whose business has been noticed.

Mr. Staacke is also justly credited with being the first importer of the heavy freighting wagons, known as "prairie schooners," that were used for commercial purposes in connection with overland transportation to all points west of San Antonio. They were constructed to withstand the wear and tear of the rocky and mountainous roads in western Texas and Mexico, and they could not be used to advantage elsewhere on account of their weight, which was estimated to be about four thousand pounds.

The following dimensions of a few parts will convey an idea of their strength: The hind wheels measured five feet, ten inches in height, and the tire was six inches wide and one inch thick; the front wheels were built like them, but they were twelve inches lower. The axles were of solid iron, with spindles three inches in diameter, and all the running gear was built in proportion for hard service. The wagon-bed was twenty-four feet long, four and a half feet wide and the sides were five and a half feet high. Wagon-bows were attached to each, and over them two heavy tarpaulins were stretched, which hung down around the sides, that thoroughly protected the freight. On these covers the train-owner's name was painted, and beneath, a number, from one upwards, to distinguish the wagons, in which freight was loaded as it was entered on memoranda. The woodwork of these wagons was painted deep blue and the iron-work black.

Every wagon was furnished with a powerful brake which was used to regulate the speed when going down steep hills, and two heavy chains were provided that were attached to the wagon-body for use in cases of necessity. Occasionally accidents happened to a brake and the heavily loaded wagon would become uncontrollable, with the result that mules and driver were often crushed to death under the wheels.

The beam that constituted the brake was seven feet in length, six by eight inches square, and it was made out of choice hickory timber. It was placed beneath the wagon-box, before the hind wheels, in two heavy iron stirrups that were secured to the frame on each side by heavy braces or bolts, and a block of wood was fastened near each end which pressed against the wheels when the lever was manipulated by the driver in his seat. He could control the motion of the wagon according to the grade by forcing the brake against the wheels until they ceased to revolve, when necessary, or check them at will with a motion of his hand as easily as a motorman controls his car.

An average load for such wagons was about seven thousand pounds, but generally, with ten small mules attached, sixteen bales of cotton was a load, because it could be transported with more ease. The great capacity of such wagons may be estimated by comparing them with wagons used by the United States government, which haul an average load of three thousand pounds with six large mules, and thereby prove their superior advantages.

Bulky freight was usually top-heavy and it made the wagon sway from side to side with a regular motion when passing over rough roads, which practically threw the weight alternately on two wheels, consequently it lightened the draft on the team. But when so loaded it was dangerous to pass along the sloping roads high up on the sides of mountains; and it was then necessary to attach ropes to the two axles on the lower side, which, after passing them over the top of the load, were held by a dozen men who moved along the slope above and kept the wagon from toppling over into an abyss where it and the team would be dashed to pieces. There are many such places on the road from San Antonio to El Paso where the country is extremely rough, and the entire distance, with the exception of about two hundred miles, was a constant drag.

The mules used for freighting purposes were small but active, and they had untiring energy, with a constitution that enabled them to endure extreme hardships. The manner in which the ten mules were hitched brought them close to their load and made them almost a unit when a steady pull was necessary. This fact, in association with their good qualities, more than compensated for their size, and their numbers were not out of proportion to the load if the heavy mountain roads are considered.

Before the prairie schooner was adopted as a means of communication between Texas and the northern states of Mexico, commercial energy in that direction was hampered; but after they were introduced it became interested in the subject, and when the benefit to be derived from direct trade, between those regions and the seaports of Texas, was understood, wagon trains of six or more prairie schooners were introduced, with a capacity to move a large quantity of freight in a given time. These were conducted under a systematic management which inspired confidence, and it was not long before both countries realized advantages through the arrangement.

They encouraged San Antonio to extend her business connections with Mexico more than any enterprise that had been started before that period, and they did much towards stimulating a trade between the two countries and Europe, which has continued to grow until it has reached large proportions. They opened a way for the railroads that followed in their trail, which removed all competition in the way of transportation and travel by offering superior advantages. The prairie schooner was a humble pioneer that plodded its way slowly over plain and mountain, through a wilderness peopled by warlike savages, yet it was appreciated in its day, and its arrival at its destination was greeted with far more interest than that manifested when a modern, up-to-date train stops at a station. Their rarity, and because they were the main dependence in the West for the transportation of goods, always insured them a warm welcome; but it cannot be denied that a long train of prairie schooners was always attractive, and they were picturesque; many of them would have commanded a romantic interest if the episodes and tragedies through which they passed could be related.

The Mexican trains could not compare with those of Americans in general appearance, but in many respects they were far superior, and they were managed more successfully, because of the strictness with which they conducted the business. Their wagons were clumsily built, with frames twenty-four feet long, without sides, that rested on a heavy running-gear with three and a half-inch axles and enormous wheels with six-inch tires an inch thick. They were capable of carrying very heavy loads, and to illustrate the fact, a train of twelve wagons, each drawn by fourteen mules, distributed in three sets of four working abreast and two to the tongue, would transport one hundred and twenty thousand pounds of freight with ease over the roads in Mexico. Many of such trains were operated there, and the largest were owned by Rocke Garady, David and Daniel Sada, of Monterey, and John Gargin, of San Antonio.

Their mules were superior to ours because they were raised on their home ranches, and they had the advantage of being able to select the best. They did not depend for feed on grass alone, as the Americans were compelled to do, but always carried a sufficient supply of corn and wheat straw that kept their animals in the finest condition. On the contrary, all the teams belonging to Americans showed hard service because of their long journeys, when they were frequently exposed to great privations on drives of ninety miles in length without water and often went without corn or grass. The finest lot of mules I ever saw belonged to Rocke Garady, who owned and ran a train of twelve wagons, with fourteen mules to each, that was known as the finest outfit in Mexico, and I am sure that their equal could not be found in the United States.

The same drivers were employed continuously by train-owners in Mexico, who were subject to strict obedience as peons, and discipline was rigorously enforced. The mules, too, on account of long service, were easily controlled and became trained to routine movements. This was seen when it was time to hitch up, after the caporal walked to the center of the corral among the loose mules, where he cracked his whip and ordered them to their places. Inside of five minutes every mule, sometimes as many as two hundred, would stand in their proper position, backed up against the wagon with their heads towards the caporal, ready for the bridles which the drivers placed on them.

The Gonzales brothers, of Saltillo, owned a train of twenty-five carts, with five mules for each. They had shafts in which a mule was hitched, with one on each side and two in front. They passed through San Antonio, in 1867, on their way to New Braunfels, where they loaded each cart with eight bales of cotton, that was bought from Julius Morron for the Mexican market. The one hundred and twenty-five mules in this train knew their own carts, and would back up to them with their heads toward the center of the corral when the caporal gave the signal. I saw them go through the performance without making a mistake, and John Monier will confirm the truth of my statement.

This historical sketch of overland freighting in Texas is necessarily brief and therefore imperfect, but it will serve as an introduction to the business in which I became engaged. I will also anticipate my experiences by explaining some of the customs and regulations that I observed when on the road, and also refer to a few of the hardships and tell how we guarded against Indian attacks and other dangers that constantly confronted us during the time that I was freighting between San Antonio and the city of Chihuahua in Mexico.

The scarcity of water and grass on the route frequently made it necessary for me to divide my daily journeys into three drives or camps, especially where the watering places were about fifty miles apart. Generally, when making a long drive from one watering-place to the next, we started about one o'clock in the afternoon and drove until about six, when we stopped to eat supper and graze the teams; we started again at ten P. M., and drove until three A. M., when we camped without water; at seven we were again under way, and at ten o'clock we arrived at the watering-place, where the teams were watered and turned loose to graze for about four hours, then watered again before being hitched. Sometimes, when the distance between the watering-places was less than thirty miles, only one drive was made that day, but they did not occur often. Our longest was a distance of ninety miles, between Julimes and Chupadero in Mexico, and the road was so bad it usually required forty-eight hours, including stoppages, without water for my teams, though sometimes it was made in thirty-six hours.

The inconveniences we experienced on account of a scarcity of water could not compare to the discomforts occasioned by the necessity of protecting my mules and ourselves against Indians. Knowing that they were constantly watching for an opportunity to overpower us, we were compelled to be alert at all times to guard against surprises. When in camp at noon, while the herd was grazing in charge of the caporal, or chief herdsman, and his assistants, two teamsters stood guard on a prominent elevation in the vicinity, when in the mountains, where they could view the surrounding country, and they were relieved from time to time by others until the caporal brought the mules into the corral to be hitched.

Arms used in my train were short needle guns of 50 caliber that were ordered by Elmendorf & Co., of San Antonio, for me, at a cost of three hundred dollars a dozen. The gun was carried in a scabbard that was fastened to the driver's saddle mule, and when in camp, as a rule, it was placed against the left wheel of his wagon. The forty-five caliber six-shooter was carried in a scabbard on his cartridge belt, and if not, it always was in reach of his hand. The belt carried fifty rounds of cartridges for the needle gun and twelve rounds for the pistol.

The guns ranged about eight thousand feet, and the pistols about one thousand feet. I always carried about two thousand rounds of cartridges for the guns and about five hundred for the pistols.

When camped at night in a region known to be infested by Indians, or if the danger was imminent, a detail of four men always stood guard over the animals when grazing, who were relieved every two hours, and on such occasions the caporal, the wagon-master and all the teamsters slept in a group near the train with their arms ready for use at a moment's notice.

My wagon-train averaged about twelve wagons, sometimes more and sometimes less; and twenty-three men was about the average number that accompanied it, including drivers and others in my employ. As I worked ten mules to a wagon and took along about twenty loose mules for emergencies, the herd consisted of about one hundred and fifty animals.

Mexicans made the most expert drivers, and those of other nationalities whom I employed never gave equal satisfaction. The most remarkable thing in their duties was the facility with which they picked out their teams in the darkest night, when colors were not distinguishable, and they rarely made a mistake, but it took a little more time to hitch up, or about forty minutes, against thirty minutes in daylight. This talent is confined to teamsters of that race, but I never understood how it was done. I seldom found one that was unreliable, and they were always ready, night or day, to attend to any duty that was required of them.

Every wagon-train was under the general supervision of a wagon-master, who was responsible for its management at all times, and directed its movements on a journey. The next important person was the caporal, who was constantly in charge of the herd of extra mules when moving and of all the animals after making a camp. His duties required him to look out for watering-places and good grass, and also to see that the mules were not mistreated by the drivers.

A train, say of twelve wagons, was always divided into two sections, and each section of six wagons was in charge of a captain who was held accountable for the performance of certain duties and the accuracy with which his wagons were placed when forming a corral, which was provided for by dividing the train into sections. The captains generally were expert drivers who understood their business, and when making a corral errors seldom occurred even in cases of emergency.

The captain of the first section drove wagon No. 1 in the lead the first day's journey, and the captain of the second section led the train the following day, consequently they were experienced in the duties required of them. These changes in the positions of the sections were absolutely necessary on a long journey, otherwise the teams in the rear sections would have been strained entirely too much, on account of frequent stoppages, if they had traveled continuously in the same order. The corral to which I have referred was an important institution in the freighting business when the train consisted of a number of wagons, because it was indispensable for the security of the animals wherever the train was encamped, and it served also as a fortification which afforded ample protection for man and beast when attacked by Indians or other enemies.

When forming a corral with twelve wagons on a highway, the captain of the first section drove wagon No. 1 out of his line of travel in a curve to the left, until his team returned to the roadside at an angle where it was stopped with its rear end outwards. Wagon No. 2 followed, making a similar curve, and stopped when the rim of its front wheel was even with and four feet distant from the rear rim of the left wheel of No. 1, with its body at the same angle. The driver of No. 3 did likewise, under the guidance of the others, and his wagon was stopped in the same relative position, also, at the same angle as that occupied by the other two wagons. Then wagons Nos. 4, 5 and 6 were turned out of the road and driven straight to their proper stations, where they stood at the same distance with reference to each other and the first three wagons, but the angle was reversed so as to throw the rear wheels inwards, consequently they formed a half circle, with No. 6, like No. 1, close to the road, and all the teams were on the outside.

The same maneuvers were made on the right of the road by the captain of the second section, who drove wagon No. 7 in a curve to within twelve feet of No. 1, where it was stopped at the same angle as that in which the last three wagons in the first section were placed, with its rear end in the same direction. The others followed in rotation and formed upon the first wagon and occupied the same relative positions to each other as those in the first section on the left, with No. 2 standing within twelve feet of No. 6.

These two lines of wagons completed the corral and enclosed an oval space about 75 feet wide by 10 feet in length, with two main openings in the front and rear about twelve feet wide, and five others between the wagons, in both sections, each four feet in width, that were made for the mules to pass through, as a matter of convenience, when preparing to harness the teams. All these openings were provided with heavy ropes that were stretched across them when the mules were in the corral.

A corral could be formed as readily in any open space where there were no roads or other guides, and they were always a necessity on account of their convenience, which no other arrangement could have supplied, because the mules were always taken from the wagons and unharnessed on the outside, and there was no place in which they could have been secured so well. When turned loose they passed through the rear opening into the corral, where they were fed in long canvas troughs that were stretched from the wagons, and from there they were driven in a herd through one of the large openings to a watering place or to pasture by the herders in charge of the caporal.

After the mules were returned to the enclosure, the caporal gave the first intimation that it was time to move by cracking his whip in the corral and ordered the mules to take their places, as noticed elsewhere; they were then bridled, the ropes were removed, and every mule walked through the gap nearest the wagon to which he belonged. They knew their places as well as a well-trained horse of a fire-engine when the signal is given, and they took them with the same certainty, though not as quickly. A company of soldiers could not have moved more orderly to the places where they belonged, and when harnessed and the train was ready to start, every animal was prepared to resume his journey.

Frequently, when the herd was driven from the pasture, some of the train mules did not wait for the signal, but took their places at once, with their rumps against the wagon, and avoided the jam caused by the commotion into which the herd was thrown when ordered to their places. This evidence will suffice to show that the mules were familiar with every movement in the train. The corral was his home where he was broken in, and he never forgot his training, nor the wagon or place where he worked in harness.

When traveling through the western country in olden times a train was occasionally attacked by Indians, and it became necessary to form a corral immediately for the protection of the men and mules. On such occasions the wagons were placed in the same order as in a corral for an ordinary camp, except that no openings were left between them, but the plan was reversed with reference to the teams, because the wagons fronted inwards instead of outwards and the mules were all inside when the corral was completed, except the two teams of wagons No. 1 and No. 7, that were in the front opening, which were detached and driven in the enclosure. When thus protected the train men were able to repel any savage attack that might have been made unless overwhelmed by numbers. Usually there was no delay after the danger passed, because none but the two teams were unhitched, and the train was soon ready to move forward again in its usual order.

Sometimes we were caught out in awful blizzards, and many times I was alone with my wagons, while the men were in neighboring cedar-brakes with the mules, where they were driven for protection during such freezing weather. On one of my trips from Chihuahua, when I crossed the Pecos River at the Horse-head crossing, and traveled by way of Fort Concho, my train encountered a ten-days' spell of sleet and snow, and at one place, at the head of the Concho, the grass was covered for days where the buffalo had eaten off the small limbs from the trees as far as they could reach. Once a long train of wagons that was in charge of Captain Edgar, of San Antonio, was exposed to one of such blizzards, and he had the misfortune to lose about sixty mules. They had bunched together for protection against the cold, but were frozen to death, and the place was known many years after as "Edgar's bone-yard."

Chapter Thirteen:

1870—Sister St. Stephens—Chihuahua Mines—
Indian Fights

My second visit to Chihuahua was in the early spring of 1870, but I can recall nothing of interest connected with the trip except that a young man, about whom I have something to say, traveled with me to my destination. I remember meeting Colonel Terrell, a pay-master in the United States army, the father of Dr. Fred and Henry Terrell of San Antonio, who overtook me in the Limpia Cañon when on his way to the frontier posts with money to pay the troops. His ambulance and two government wagons were guarded by a detachment of twenty-five soldiers. Sister St. Stephens, of San Antonio, who was visiting the forts in his company in the interest of the orphans, traveled with the party under his protection.

The next time I met Sister St. Stephens was at Fort Concho, where she took the westbound stage as a passenger for Fort Stockton, which was also my destination, as I expected to overtake my train there that had been sent on ahead from San Antonio, where I took the stage, and she was again visiting the forts in the interest of the orphans as on the first occasion. I felt an interest in her work and inquired if she had been successful in collecting for her charities, and she told me that she had been amply rewarded for her trouble. The other passengers were Mr. Head and Mr. Gallagher, who resided at Fort Stockton, and our escort was two soldiers, furnished by the government as a protection for the mail, who rode outside with the driver, but as we were all well armed no uneasiness was felt on account of Indians.

Sister St. Stephens was an entertaining traveling companion, and she made herself agreeable throughout the trip. We sometimes presumed on her sociability by making jolly remarks, but she did not resent the liberty and was always in a pleasant humor. Once I ventured to say that she could be of no service in case we were attacked by Indians. She laughed and replied that if such an event should happen her part would be attended to equally as well as ours; that we should do the fighting and she would do the praying.

I have often reminded the good sister of our journey together, and I always sent her a token of remembrance every month during the many years I transacted business in San Antonio. Her life has been devoted to charitable enterprises and all contributions she receives are worthily distributed. I think, and have always expressed the belief, that Sister St. Stephens, who now resides at Brackenridge Villa, is one of the noblest of women, and I hope that she will be spared many years for the helpful work she is doing in behalf of humanity. Many helpless orphans have been sheltered, nourished, and trained partly through her efforts in the forty years since I first became acquainted with her.

The young man that accompanied my train, to whom I have referred, was a professional clock-maker, and his name was Lurman. He had been sent from Europe for the special purpose of repairing a large clock in the cathedral, that was bought in Germany by Carlos Moye, a wealthy citizen of Chihuahua, who was commissioned by the city to make the purchase when on a visit to that country.

The clock was a splendid piece of workmanship and it cost a considerable sum of money, but it did not give satisfaction with respect to keeping time, perhaps because it was not put together by one who was familiar with its mechanism. An appeal was made to the manufacturers to send an expert to remedy the defect, and they responded by dispatching Lurman for that purpose. His long journey of several thousand miles was made under a contract that stipulated he was to receive seven hundred and fifty dollars in addition to his traveling expenses. After overhauling the clock and remedying the trouble it was unsurpassed as a timepiece, and it served as an ornament for one of the finest churches in Mexico.

According to the estimation of many competent judges, the structural work and graceful outlines of the Cathedral in Chihuahua will compare favorably with any in the republic. I was greatly impressed by its beauty when I first saw it, because I had never seen its equal, but afterwards I visited others that surpassed it in size and decorations.

The cost of the building involved an outlay of many thousands of dollars, and it was all contributed from the earnings of the Santa Eulalia silver mines. The representatives of the Catholic Church in Mexico received an endowment of fifty cents from every mark of silver, valued at $8.50, that was taken from the mines. Under Spanish rule the total yield from the Santa Eulalia mines was $111,000,000, which is equivalent to 13,058,821 silver marks, consequently the tax levied on them for the benefit of the Christian religion amounted to $6,529,411, and the beautiful cathedral was built with a part of the money. I do not know if this is in history, but I am sure it is true, though I am not conversant with all of the facts bearing upon the subject, nor do I know when the foundation of the church was laid or when it was completed.

The State of Chihuahua is considered among the richest mineral regions in Mexico, and the statement about the Santa Eulalia mines is not exaggerated. They are situated about sixteen miles east of Chihuahua. They are reputed to be among the most extensive deposit mines discovered up to that time, and were then considered among the most valuable in Mexico.

The Cosihuiriachic mines are ninety miles southwest of Chihuahua. Their former wealth is known to have been great and they are still very rich. Veins of solid metal 600 feet in depth and fifteen feet wide have been tested that average $100 per ton. I entered the mines in 1871 with Mr. Emil Schedlich; their dimensions only sloped 600 feet to the vein, but it seemed to be about six miles, and I was glad to get out of them. They were sold in 1876 to a San Francisco mining company for $500,000.

The Corralitos mines, that were sold to an American mining company for $400,000, are located about 180 miles north of Chihuahua.

The Botopilas mines, in the southwestern part of the State of Chihuahua, were bought by Wells, Fargo & Co. for a large sum of money. They have produced enormously, and their wealth is said to be inexhaustible.

The rich mine of La Gabilana, situated about 78 miles south of Chihuahua, had not been worked for many years before it was sold to the Chihuahua Silver Mining Company of Logansport, Indiana.

The Knox Dry Mountain Mining Company, in which I have owned twenty-five shares since 1877, is situated four miles from Parral, and the consolidated mines of Parral, owned by the Knox company of Chicago, are under the city of Parral. When I visited them last, the greater part of the city had been undermined, but precautions were used to prevent the mine from caving by introducing heavy timbers and substantial masonry. When San Antonio first became the terminus of the Galveston, Harrisburg & San Antonio Railroad, in 1877-1878, the firm of Froboese & Santleben freighted over 500,000 pounds of machinery to the Knox Mining Company, of Parral, to the Santa Eulalia mines, and to the mines of Cosihuiriachic. Since that date modern methods of mining have been introduced in connection with improved machinery and the business in that region has been greatly improved.

On my return trip the place was shown me in Texas where the San Miguel brothers met with a serious misfortune a short time before, similar to one I afterwards experienced. I knew them when they came to San Antonio from Mexico, in 1868, with ten carts, each drawn by five mules, and subsequently they were employed by the government to haul freight to the frontier posts. Two years later, when on their way to Fort Davis with supplies, the Indians attacked their camp, eighteen miles east of Johnson's Run, and captured the entire herd of mules belonging to the train that was grazing in the vicinity. The cart-men retreated to an elevation and with loose rock built a circular breast-work behind which they defended themselves until the enemy retired with the herd. Two Mexicans were killed in the engagement and they were buried at the foot of the hill on which the rude fortification was situated, where, perhaps, it remains as it was when last seen by me.

I always felt a peculiar interest in such places and many locations along my route where Indian fights occurred are familiar to me. One of them was near Fort Lancaster, that took place after the post was abandoned, where a party of Indians attacked the United States mail coach that was guarded by Mr. Cook and ten men besides the driver. The white men were greatly outnumbered and they had a thrilling experience as it was told to me.

The Indians drove the men from the coach and surrounded them, but the little squad kept the enemy at bay as they retreated and fought their way on foot to Fort Stockton. The savages captured the mules and after appropriating the contents of the coach it was burnt.

When the fight took place I was carrying the mail between San Antonio and Eagle Pass, and the route between Fort Clark and Fort Stockton was controlled by Sawyer, Richie and Hall. A weekly mail, guarded by an escort of ten men under a boss, was carried each way by stage between those points. Mr. Cook was in charge of one coach and Mr. Holiday of the other; but there were other connecting lines, and mail facilities were established between all the frontier posts through to El Paso. George, a son of Mr. Holiday, pointed out the place where the stage was burnt, and recalled some of the particulars of the fight. Mr. George Holiday was once in charge of my train, and since I have mentioned him I may as well relate here an incident that occurred on Sabinal Creek when he was serving in that capacity. A young man from East Texas, who was looking for trouble, rode into his camp with a pistol in his hand, swearing that he intended to kill a Mexican and dared them to show themselves. Holiday did not want to see his men killed, and they obeyed him when he advised them to open fire on the foolish fellow. One bullet struck him in the neck, and another that passed through his clothes, left a mark on his skin. These wounds demoralized him, and he retreated rapidly to the store, a short distance away, crying out that he was shot and was afraid that he would die. Unless I am mistaken Louis and Charles Peters, who live in Uvalde County, kept the store and perhaps they may be able to recall the incident.

I have noticed elsewhere that Captain Muenzenberger moved to Santa Rosa and became engaged in the mining and milling business. In 1870 he contracted with me to haul a lot of machinery for his mill, which I loaded on my train in San Antonio. I met with no interruptions until I arrived at the regular Santa Rosa crossing, on the Sabinas River, where I was delayed fifteen days on account of high water that made the stream impassable. I then became impatient and decided that I would go to the headwaters of the river, where I was assured by several reliable Mexicans that I would find a ford which was always passable.

After ordering my wagons to remain at that place I started out alone and following the directions I found a dim road which I traveled several miles until I arrived at the place that was described to me. To assure myself that it was fordable I rode to the opposite side of the stream and the crossing proved to be satisfactory; but I was somewhat disconcerted when I found myself close to a camp of about twenty Kickapoo Indians, because I knew they were bitter enemies of the white race. Seeing that I was entirely alone they gathered around me, with arms in their hands in a threatening manner, and showed their unfriendly disposition by their insolent behavior. They abused Americans outrageously, in Spanish, and sometimes in English, but they did not seem to care what I had to say because when I talked back small squads walked off a few yards and jabbered in their own language. Their actions showed that they were discussing violent measures with reference to my person, and my uneasiness increased every moment, but I assumed an indifferent attitude that concealed my anxiety.

About that time a one-legged Indian made his appearance and I conversed with him in mixed English and Spanish until he called me a liar in plain English, which I resented by remaining silent. He told me about a fight, on Hondo Creek, in which he was engaged, where his companion was killed and he was wounded in the leg "by a bald-faced-white-man who rode a bay horse." After making his escape he returned to Santa Rosa, but when he arrived his leg was in such a condition that amputation was necessary. This was interesting to me because I knew all about the fight, and in his description of the man who wounded him I recognized Xavier Wanz, who is now a prosperous ranchman on the Hondo, a life-time friend who was a comrade of mine in the Civil War.

The situation became more strained every moment and it was evident that a serious catastrophe would happen to me unless I could say or do something to prevent it. I had left my wagons at the crossing twenty-five miles below and no assistance could be expected from them,

consequently I was entirely at their mercy. Finally I decided to play a game of bluff and told them that I must
go, as I had thirty men coming on behind, and that we
were on our way to Santa Rosa Mountains. This information had a perceptible effect, because they thought I was
alone, and when I turned my head in that direction in a
listening attitude and said, "I hear them coming," they
did not attempt to detain me.

I was only with them about twenty minutes, but the
time seemed to be about two hours, and when I rode
away I not only felt much relieved, but my satisfaction
increased in proportion to the distance I put between
them and myself. I hurriedly proceeded to the town of
Santa Rosa, about fifteen miles distant, but was fearful
all the way, because it was not unusual to meet bands
of Kickapoo Indians at any time near the foot of the
mountains. The Mexican Government had granted them
a reservation in that region and gave them protection,
consequently they were friendly to the citizens of that
country. But they were bitter enemies of the Americans,
and when in Texas, where they made frequent raids,
they recognized no racial distinctions, as many of their
victims were Mexicans.

The Kickapoo Indian reservation was formerly on the
Kaw River, in Kansas, and they were inoffensive and
tractable until an effort was made to compel them to
take sides in the Civil War. This they refused to do, and,
in 1864, about four hundred warriors determined to remove to Mexico. They carried with them their few belongings and their women and children accompanied
them. They proceeded without opposition until after
crossing Red River into Texas, where they were attacked
by Confederate troops that were guarding the frontier,
under the belief that they intended to raid the settlements. In the battle that took place many were killed and
wounded on both sides before the Indians were defeated and fled. But this interruption did not prevent them

from passing through Texas, and they finally settled on the lands granted to them by the Mexican Government near the Santa Rosa Mountains. From these strongholds they made predatory incursions into Texas, and harassed the settlements west and southwest of San Antonio until they were suppressed.

These facts were ascertained from the Indians and others during my stay in Santa Rosa with Captain Muenzenberger, who entertained me at his residence in town. My visit was brief and I returned to my wagons under the guidance of a Mexican in the captain's employ, who was known to the Indians. We crossed the river at a ford twelve miles above my camp, and my train was conveyed safely to Santa Rosa over the road I had explored. The machinery was delivered in good condition and two days after we commenced our return trip to San Antonio over the usual route. We found that the flood in the Rio Sabinas had subsided, but it was necessary to pull my wagons across to the opposite side with a cable drawn by mules. One of them was torn loose and swept down stream a considerable distance by the swift current that was a natural torrent, but it was recovered after spending much time in exhaustive labor. All these delays were expensive, consequently my profits from this trip did not amount to much because my wagons returned empty, and under such circumstances the hauling of special freight was not always remunerative, but the next the compensation I received was unusually large; it was paid on a contract made with the city of San Antonio in 1871, during the administration of Mayor James French, in which I agreed to haul from Indianola the first iron bridge that was bought by the city.

Some of the material was forty feet long and so heavy that it could only be transported on the largest wagons. Fourteen wagons were required to haul it, and I received a total of thirty-two hundred and fifty dollars for freighting it.

The bridge was placed across the river on Houston Street, and Gustave Schleicher, who was afterwards a member of the United States Congress from this district, superintended its construction. After serving the public at that point for twenty years, the bridge was replaced by the present structure on account of the necessities of the street-car line and the demands of an increased traffic. The original bridge was removed to the ancient ford across the river, known as the "Passo de los Tejas," on Grand Avenue, near the Lone Star Brewery, where it is now in use and there is no reason why it should cease to be of service in the next 100 years.

An iron bridge was then a novelty in Texas that attracted considerable attention, but now, since they have become so numerous, especially in San Antonio, they are seldom noticed. The public is convinced that they are an economical investment, and in the course of time all wooden structures in Texas will be replaced by them.

Chapter Fourteen:

Murder in San Antonio—Comanche Attack—
Mule Calamities

A few days before I left San Antonio, and started westward on my third trip to Chihuahua, in the spring of
1871, a Mexican woman was cruelly assassinated in the
city, and one of her countrymen was suspected of having
committed the crime after he disappeared. All the circumstances pointed to his guilt and considerable interest was felt in the case, but the officers of the law failed
to trace him, although they made strenuous efforts to
bring about his arrest.

In the meantime the murderer was cautiously making
his way towards the Mexican border until Providence arranged that I should effect his capture, and I became an
involuntary instrument of the law without having given
previous thought to the subject.

The house in which the murder took place was immediately in the rear of the Kunkel building, that fronted
the old Cassiano homestead on Houston Street, in the
block that is bounded on the west by North Flores Street,
which was then occupied as a mercantile establishment
by my brother-in-law, Henry Wagner, the father of Henry Wagner, Jr., who now resides in San Antonio.

The murdered woman was a poor widow whose re-
spectability was not questioned, and she had labored
hard to provide for two small children who were depen-

dent on her daily efforts for a support. The man who took her life was a stranger in the city who had recently come from East Texas, and it was supposed that she became acquainted with him only a short time previous to her death. He was often seen in her company by persons who noted his appearance, and after the cowardly deed was perpetrated they were able to give an accurate description of him.

The evidence showed that the assassin stealthily entered the woman's home at night, after she had retired, and brutally stabbed her through the heart while sleeping. She died instantly, and it was done so quietly that the children were not awakened. The provocation that led to the killing was never revealed, but evidently it was a cold-blooded deed that nothing could justify, and one from which the murderer hastily fled to avoid detection.

When the crime was discovered the following morning the stranger was instantly suspected, and after all the circumstances became known public opinion centered on him as the criminal. This information and a full description of his dress and personal appearance, his dun horse and equipments was given to the sheriff, Thomas B. McCall, before he and his deputy started in pursuit towards the Rio Grande.

My train left San Antonio before the tragedy occurred, but I was detained by business and they had been gone seven days when I took my seat in the stage with the expectation of overtaking the wagons at Fort Clark. When I arrived there I learned that the train had passed onwards the day before, but I had instructed my wagonmaster to leave my saddle-horse at James Connell's, who was a merchant in the town, and I found him there. About three o'clock that afternoon I continued my journey, and after riding six miles I saw a man in front of me near Pedro Pinto Creek, whose appearance and the dun horse he was riding suggested that he was the murderer of the

Mexican woman. When I approached nearer he suddenly heard the hoof-beats of my horse, because he turned partly round in his saddle to look at me, and I was then sure that my impressions were correct.

I had been authorized by Sheriff McCall to arrest the man in case I should meet him, and I decided that it was my duty to capture him. With that object in view I rode quietly along until I was near enough to get the advantage, and then with my pistol in hand I urged my horse quickly to his left side. Under the cover of my weapon I ordered him to surrender and charged him with the cowardly murder. At first he refused, denied his guilt, and as he knew who I was, he questioned my right to make the arrest. Evidently he was disposed to offer resistance, but as he had no pistol and was only armed with a Spencer rifle, which was hanging to his saddle in its scabbard on the side next to me, the chances were all in my favor and it would have been unsafe for him to make a demonstration in that direction.

Finally he realized that he was in my power, and when I ordered him to turn his horse and return in the direction of Fort Clark, he sullenly obeyed, but I allowed him to retain possession of his gun, after he refused to give it up, because I did not care to approach near enough to take it from him by force. He manifested his reluctance to proceed by checking his horse to a very slow gait in defiance of my efforts to urge him forward. This was very irritating, partly because my horse was restless and not easily controlled, but I retained my advantage by keeping as near my prisoner as possible and kept a close watch on every movement he made. I wished to avoid violent measures, but let him understand that I would resort to them if he offered the slightest resistance or attempted to escape.

The situation was very unpleasant and we traveled about two miles in a slow walk before it was remedied by the appearance of several wagons belonging to the

Dignowitys, that were returning empty from Fort Clark, where they had delivered a lot of hay for the government. They were driven by Mexicans, and I appealed to them for assistance to help disarm and secure my prisoner. After I related the particulars of the murder and explained the circumstances connected with the arrest they readily complied with my request. In a few minutes he was forcibly deprived of the carbine, after refusing to give it up, and his legs were tied together beneath the horse's body. After he was firmly bound I compensated them for their trouble by allowing them to retain the gun, which was useless to me and it would have been troublesome to carry.

After parting from them I had no more trouble when leading the horse with the murderer on his back and we traveled much faster than before. When I arrived at Fort Clark I delivered my prisoner to the deputy sheriff, John Fries, who kept him closely confined until the authorities sent an officer to convey him to San Antonio. He was tried for murder and convicted on circumstantial evidence, and sentenced to twenty-five years' confinement in the penitentiary. I have forgotten the man's name, but it can be ascertained by referring to the records, and a number of persons are now living who are conversant with the facts, one of whom is James B. McClosky, of San Antonio.

The part I took in the affair was authorized by Sheriff Thomas B. McCall, but I was never compensated by the State for making the arrest, because I did not file a claim for my services. But for me the assassin would have escaped to Mexico and avoided the penalty awarded for his crime, and my conscience was amply rewarded for having confronted the risks. In reality I was not exposed to any great danger because he had no chance to offer a successful resistance, and it was only necessary to guard him carefully until he was secured. Perhaps, if I had not met the Mexican teamsters, who made him helpless, he might have tried to escape before we reached Fort Clark and I was thankful that he did not make the attempt.

After getting rid of my prisoner I resumed my journey through an uninhabited region until I overtook my train. The excitement I had passed through would have sufficed for that trip, but I was destined to meet with another adventure a few days later, and it was the most unpleasant that I ever experienced. We were in the vicinity of Johnson's Run, which is about eighteen miles northwest of Beaver Lake and about fifteen miles from a watering place, in rainy seasons, called El Padron, where, we were told by travelers, rain had recently fallen, and we expected to stop there for dinner and water the teams.

The train was under way and I was asleep in my ambulance when one of the herders rode up and roused me by saying that several deer were near the road close by. He was leading my favorite riding mule, that was always kept saddled for immediate use, and in a few moments I was mounted, with my Winchester rifle in my hand. The herder guided me to the place, but a heavy fog made everything very indistinct and I was almost among the deer when they were discovered. I fired instantly, but the dense fog obscured my aim with the result that I only wounded one of them, though after shooting four or five times I killed one as they ran away. After disemboweling the carcass and tying it behind my saddle I noticed that the wagons had passed out of hearing, but I felt no uneasiness on that account, because I was confident that I would soon overtake them.

When I mounted my mule I noticed that she wanted to go in an opposite direction to that I had decided on as the proper course and the one I persisted in following. The air was heavy with dampness and it was about seven o'clock in the morning. The fog was impenetrable beyond a short distance, but I rode along carelessly until the vapors commenced to rise, and then I began to think it was strange that I had seen no trace of the road nor arrived in hearing of the jolting wagons or the tingling bell that led the herd. I began to feel uneasy, and was soon convinced that I was completely lost.

To lose one's reckoning under any circumstances is unpleasant, and only those who have passed through similar experiences will appreciate the sensations I felt when lost in that wilderness which was known to be infested by wild Indians. Fortunately I realized the dangers of my situation and the necessity of preparing for emergencies, though I had no definite idea how I was to get out of my scrape. My first act was to lighten my load by untying the deer and casting it to the ground. I then examined my rifle and when I found only five loaded cartridges in the magazine I was very much disconcerted. In my hurry I had overlooked my six-shooter and belt full of ammunition in the ambulance, but it was then useless to worry because of my carelessness, and I determined to make my limited supply go as far as possible.

I entertained no rational ideas relative to the course I ought to travel and was disposed to trust to the brute instincts of my mule on several occasions by allowing her to go her own way. She would change her course the instant that I ceased to restrain her movements and each time she traveled several miles or until I decided that she was going wrong and guided her in another direction. I did not stop a moment during the entire day, although it was excessively warm about noon. I felt neither hunger nor thirst and my thoughts seemed to be concentrated on the possibility of meeting Indians. Sometimes I imagined that they were concealed in groves of cedar on my route and frequently made detours of half a mile to avoid the possibility of an encounter.

These maneuvers were kept up until nine o'clock at night and then when I was almost distracted I got in the road by allowing my weary mule to travel as she pleased the latter part of the journey. She proved to me that she was right, and if I had not checked her previous efforts to get back to it early in the day I would have had no trouble. Naturally I was greatly relieved because I was satisfied that she recognized the road, though it was unfamiliar to me.

The train did not stop until it arrived at El Padron, and it remained in camp awaiting my return. When night approached, my caporal, Julio Castro, who now lives on Frio Street in San Antonio, concluded that I had been killed, and he started out with six of my men to look for me. Long before we met, my mule heard them approaching and she expressed her joy by braying, but I failed to interpret her meaning because the sound she heard did not reach my ears. I was content to know that I was on a highway that led somewhere, but otherwise my mind was not in a rational condition.

When I saw the men approaching I wanted to run away from them, and would have done so if my mule had been able to make the effort, but the feeling only lasted a moment and I was greatly relieved when one of them hailed me in Spanish, saying, "Who comes there?" I replied quickly to the challenge and we hastened to meet each other. My first desire was to quench my thirst, and it was the first water that I had swallowed since the day before, but I did not suffer on that account. I suppose my bodily cravings were suppressed by my mental anxiety, and when that was relieved nature asserted itself. This experience taught me a good lesson which I carefully observed afterwards by keeping in hearing of my train when in a wild and dangerous country.

These two adventures were the only incidents that happened on the round trip, and I was satisfied because they terminated so successfully; but they were offset by a series of misfortunes, after I returned to San Antonio, that greatly interfered with my business, and otherwise caused me great inconvenience, on account of the accumulated losses I sustained in consequence of the capture, theft, and death of a large number of mules on four different occasions.

Soon after I returned, my wagons were loaded with government freight and suttlers' supplies for Forts Davis and Quitman, and the train was placed in charge of Entimio Mageras, an experienced wagon-master, who now resides at Santa Cruz, near Chihuahua. After delivering the freight according to contract he returned with his empty wagons, and on the 17th of May, 1871, after making a forty-five-mile drive, he made camp, about noon, at Beaver Lake, near the eighteenth crossing on Devil's River. The mules were all tired and they were turned loose to graze on an excellent pasture, in charge of the caporal, Julio Castro, and his herders as usual; but unfortunately no guards were stationed in the vicinity to look out for Indians, although such precautions were always necessary.

Evidently the men were careless, and the proximity of Indians was not suspected until about fifty wild Comanches charged between the wagons and the herd, cutting off the caporal and his four men, who escaped by flight. Their fearful war-whoops raised a commotion in the camp, and a majority of the Indians engaged the teamsters in battle while the remainder, after roping the bell-mare, took charge of the herd. They knew that the mules would follow, and when she was led away in a gallop over the rocky hills they all kept close behind, but in their rear other thieves urged them forward until they disappeared.

The men in camp, though much startled, opened fire upon the Indians from behind the wagons; but the battle could not have lasted many minutes, because when the mules were secured the enemy retreated. Probably it was then that the wagon-master and his men followed them on foot with the hope of recovering the animals. They claimed to have made such an attempt, but under the circumstances it was a useless undertaking.

The caporal and his herders were supposed to have been killed in the first attack, but they managed to conceal themselves in a ravine, and anxiety on their account was removed when they came from their place of refuge. Fortunately none of the men were hurt and if casualties occurred among the Indians the fact was never known. The marks of Indian bullets could be seen on the wagons, and they proved that the men were sheltered behind them, but as I could never get the straight of the story I will let it stand as it is related.

John Kenedy, of Sabinal, arrived at the camp the day after the fight, when on his way to Fort Davis with a herd of beef cattle for the government which he was delivering under a contract. He was the first person that appeared, but he was unable to render my men any assistance, and before I could do anything myself, they and the wagons were brought to San Antonio by Jose Telamantes and Juan Montes with their trains, and they charged me six hundred dollars for the favor.

In July after the disaster, I went to Mexico and bought a herd of perfectly wild animals, except a few that had been handled; but the number was not sufficient and I purchased thirty odd more from Kaneghean & Bro., in San Antonio. One of the last lot, bought in August, 1871, when about four years old, died in Mr. Smelcher's pasture in December, 1905, consequently she was about thirty-eight years old at the date of her death. I entered her in the parade at the Spring Carnival in San Antonio a few months before she died, and she was led by Geronimo Morales, the man who broke her as an off-wheel mule when on a trip to Chihuahua. Her mate was killed on that trip, between Julimes and Chupadero, by a wagon heavily loaded with copper that ran over her when going down a hill.

My next calamity was experienced on the first trip that I made with the mules I brought from Mexico. They were young and freshly broken to harness when I freighted a lot of corn from Austin to Fort Concho for the government. The hardships to which they were exposed, without sufficient grass or other food, was more than they could stand, and forty of them died from actual starvation along the route when returning homeward. I was obliged to replace them with others and the drain on my resources made it necessary to use my credit, but I was not discouraged.

This misfortune was followed by another, near Laredo, when twenty head of mules were stolen from my train, which was in charge of my friend, Fred Miller, and again the loss was supplied by others I purchased in Mexico. I could not afford to give up my business, and I knew that perseverance would make me successful in the end.

The superstition that misfortunes always come in bunches, seemed to be demonstrated in my experiences during that period, but they were exhausted, in January, 1872, when I met with the closing disaster of the series, on the road to San Luis Potosi. I was encamped in a large prairie, about fifteen miles south of Piedras Negras, where a severe blizzard overtook us that caused intense suffering. My mules became uncontrollable, on account of the piercing cold, and the herd scattered in search of protection. Thirty of them could not be found, and it was necessary to secure others at considerable expense before my train could proceed on its journey. Afterwards I lost many animals in various ways, but this closes the catalogue of those that were of a serious character.

Chapter Fifteen:

Pecos Salt Lake—Anastacio Gonzales—
Lost Opportunity

When returning from Fort Davis, in 1872, after delivering a lot of government freight at said fort, I stopped
at the Pecos Salt Lake and loaded my prairie schooners
with salt free of cost from the unlimited quantity that is
found there, and which was in demand among ranchmen
on account of its special qualities.

The lake is situated in a desert region two miles east
of the Pecos River and fifteen miles above Horse-head
crossing. The surrounding country in which it is located
was naturally a level plain before the wind raised upon
it numerous sand-hills, some of them fifty feet in height,
that surround the lake on three sides.

The water of the lake, which covers an area of about
fifty acres of land, was only about eighteen inches in
depth, and its surface was a glittering sheet of white
salt about four inches thick. Evidently the sun's rays had
evaporated it to that depth, and the substance was sustained by the fluid beneath that was densely impregnated with nitrate of soda.

My corral was near the lower end of the lake where no
sand-hills obstructed the view in a southerly direction,
and an open plain extended far in the distance. After
adopting every precaution for the security of my camp,
the mules were side-lined before they were turned
loose to graze on the rich pasture of Gama grass that
was known in the West as Gramer grass, and immediate

preparations were made for getting out the salt because wanted as little delay as possible. All my men, not otherwise employed, were actively engaged in the work of scooping it up near the shore and filling the wagons. As I had no sacks it was bulked in the bodies to the depth of three feet, and three days' labor was necessary to fill them. That taken from the surface crumbled into particles when removed, but that underneath was like wet snow.

The caporal discovered about thirty Indians the second day after our arrival, and the next day they were seen hovering among the sand-hills in the distance. Evidently they were watching for an opportunity to dash in and drive off my herd of mules, but my precautions were carefully arranged and never relaxed, and when they saw that it would be an unsafe and difficult undertaking they did not venture an attack.

The mules were only watered once a day, at the Pecos River, early in the evening, and on such occasions I provided for contingencies by taking all my men along with a sufficient supply of ammunition packed on the saddle mules. The wagons and harness, also corn and other supplies, were left unprotected, but the Indians suspecting a trap, kept aloof and nothing was ever molested. The mules were always side-lined when we returned and then herded on the abundant pasture near camp, under the protection of a strong guard, until driven into the corral at sunset.

We finished loading the third day, and the following morning, after covering my salt with heavy tarpaulins to protect it from the weather, I got my train under way, but I soon discovered that my prairie schooners were loaded beyond the capacity of my teams to haul them. I made slow progress until I reached a point about five miles below the lake, where I took about two thousand pounds of salt from each wagon. Afterwards I saw that the remainder was as much as my teams could haul, but they had been greatly relieved, and the same evening we crossed and camped on the west side of the Pecos.

The next day we proceeded down the river towards Fort Lancaster, and when in camp at noon the caporal reported that he saw Indians on the west side of the Pecos. No doubt they were the same party that had skulked in the sand-hills near our camp at the lake until we left, and then dogged our trail with the expectation of stealing my mules the first opportunity that offered. But my misfortunes had taught me to observe the utmost caution, and I left nothing to chance, consequently we were not disturbed.

My train nooned at Howard's Well the following day and as it was about to move forward Anastacio Gonzales drove into camp with his six wagons. He was a citizen of San Antonio and as I knew him well it was natural that I should stop and talk to him with the intention of putting him on his guard against the dangers that lurked in that vicinity. I told him about the Indians who had constantly watched my camp during my stay at the Salt Lake, and that they had followed my train until the day before. I urged him to be careful and to use every precaution to avoid an attack, because I was satisfied that the same Indians were hovering in the neighborhood, and if they ceased to follow my wagons possibly they would make an assault on his camp if they saw that they could do so with impunity.

In the meantime my train had passed on and when I bade him farewell it was two miles ahead of me. I was the last person that talked to him, exclusive of his immediate associates, because the sequel will show that my warning was unheeded and at that place his negligence brought him and his men to a tragic end.

I did not hear of the disaster that overwhelmed Gonzales until I arrived at Fort Clark. There I learned that Lieutenant Vinson with a detachment of troops was scouting in that country and stopped at Howard's Well soon after

Gonzales and all his men were killed. The wagons were still burning and the charred body of Gonzales was found secured to one of them, where evidently he was bound when still alive. Vinson immediately followed the trail of the Indians until he overtook them, and a fight occurred in which he and several of the soldiers were killed.

Gonzales was a blacksmith by trade and his home was a small but comfortable cottage on the corner of Salinas and Laredo Streets, where his widow now lives. On an adjoining lot, fronting on Laredo Street, he completed the stone-work of a substantial four-room rock house before setting out on his last trip, which he intended to finish when he returned. To-day the bare walls remain in the same condition as when he left them, because the grief-stricken widow will not permit any one to touch the last work of her husband's hands. Possibly, if Gonzales had adopted my suggestions, the Indians would not have attacked him, and it was his carelessness, perhaps, that gave them an opportunity to surprise his camp.

I met with no further trouble from Indians on that trip, and my salt speculation, which cost me little or nothing, turned out profitably. I estimated my cargo at about fifty thousand pounds, and I sold it at wholesale for five cents per pound, part of it at Knox's ranch and the balance to Griner, Wish and Rheiner. All these persons were sheep-men who valued it more than other salt on account of the large proportion of salt-peter it contained. But unfortunately the demand was limited and it would have been easy to glut the market; otherwise a lucrative business might have been conducted by hauling it from the lake, because the sun would have constantly replenished the salt and furnished an inexhaustible supply for an indefinite period; I believe my train was the first that ever hauled salt from the lake and I assumed great risks when doing it.

I had then a fine lot of mules and prairie schooners with which to carry on my business, therefore it was to my interest to extend it as much as possible. My experimental trips to and from Chihuahua had netted me handsome returns and I determined to confine my freighting in the future to that point. My arrangements were soon completed, and I received sufficient assurance that full cargoes of freight in both directions would be consigned to my care at remunerative prices for hauling. These journeys were repeated many times, but as the records have been lost it would be useless to tax my memory by attempting to give an account of each journey, therefore the incidents I will relate are widely distributed.

I have an indistinct recollection of the trips I made in 1872, and I can only recall that on one of them, when returning from Chihuahua, I crossed the Pecos River, at the Horse-head ford, on a pontoon bridge belonging to the United States army. The military authorities had constructed it for temporary use to facilitate the movement of troops and government wagon-trains. The structure was not capable of sustaining heavily loaded prairie schooners like mine, consequently I was compelled to divide my freight, which consisted mostly of copper, and had to carry each lot over separately. The laborious undertaking consumed almost the entire day, and while employed in overseeing the work I made the acquaintance of Mr. Salliway, a prominent and worthy lawyer now in San Antonio, who was then attached to the engineer corps to which was entrusted the building of the western forts, and the bridge was also constructed under their supervision.

I also remember that I brought from Chihuahua a Mexican hoe, called *azada* in that country, that I proposed to submit to manufacturers with a view to having them made in the United States. It was a clumsy, rough and heavy implement, with a blade about ten inches wide on the edge and twelve inches in depth to the handle-socket, from which a projection, one and a half by three inches square, extended above, that served as a clodcrusher. It was considered a necessary tool on irrigated farms, and in the northern part of Mexico they were in general use. All of them were hand-made by native blacksmiths, and at that time they cost five dollars each, partly because of the scarcity of iron and steel.

I delivered the sample to Messrs. Norton and Deutz, who were then the leading hardware merchants in San Antonio, whose business connections extended into Mexico, although their trade was mostly confined to Chihuahua. I stated the facts to them and suggested that they should ascertain from northern manufacturers the cost of an improved hoe similar to the model. Acting on my advice they arranged to have a better and more highly finished hoe made at a price that gave the retailer in Mexico a liberal profit when sold at three dollars each, consequently they supplanted the ruder implement and in a short time were in common use all over that country. Doubtless others made much money out of the improvement, but I received nothing on account of my suggestion except the usual charges for freighting them into the country.

The following year a tempting offer was submitted for my acceptance, and I was influenced by its liberal inducements to give it favorable consideration. Mr. Gustave Moye, who was Consul for the United States in Chihuahua, and a brother-in-law of Governor Tarrasas, offered me a partnership in a large ranch he owned, called El Camado, that is situated eighty miles west of the city. The estate represented contained about sixty thousand acres of land. The property, though only partly improved, was very valuable and the prospect offered great encouragement for the development of its mines and other natural resources.

About one thousand acres were under irrigation, and the same sources of supply were capable of furnishing sufficient water for two thousand more of tillable land. That in cultivation was very productive and the yield of wheat, oats, corn and other crops was enormous. Irish potatoes grew wild in many localities and reproduced abundantly. Apples of good flavor also grew naturally in that region and the trees were generally loaded with fruit in season.

A small village occupied by one hundred and twenty-five persons of all ages was situated on the land, all of whom were peons and belonged to the owner of the premises. These worked the land and performed other duties on the ranch under the supervision of Mr. Moye's brother-in-law, who was his business manager; and a priest attended to their spiritual welfare by preaching at stated periods in the little church. A silver mine had been partially developed on the property from which a large quantity of rich ore had been taken, and subsequently it became very valuable.

Mr. Moye offered me a half interest in the ranch and all of its belongings, in return for my services and a joint interest in my wagon-train. He stipulated that I should reside on the estate with my family and devote my entire time to its management, and that the wagons and teams were to be used exclusively for hauling silver ore and agricultural products to Chihuahua.

His generous proposition was under consideration when I left with my train for Texas, and there is no doubt but that I would have accepted his offer if one of my children had not died soon after my arrival in San Antonio. The sorrow I experienced on that account drove the subject from my thoughts, and I gave it no further attention, although Mr. Moye did not withdraw his offer until two years after it was submitted.

I realized when it was too late that I had made the greatest mistake of my life when I failed to secure the property on such favorable terms. The opportunity to make a fortune was allowed to pass from my grasp without making an effort to secure it, because it would have been possible for me to have purchased the entire property for less than half of the amount that was paid when the country was being developed by American capitalists, at which time the mine was sold for thirty-five thousand dollars and the ranch for forty thousand more. The mine alone is now worth a fortune, the tillable land of the ranch is in cultivation, and the remainder is stocked with cattle.

I afterwards hauled many thousands of pounds of potatoes from the ranch to Texas, which cost me nothing except the outlay for digging them. They were excellent as food, they kept well and were not injured by transportation, but they were small and none were larger than a hen egg. I often sold quantities of them at Forts Davis and Stockton, at retail, for fifteen cents per pound but I once sold Mr. A. Cohen, who now resides on Marshall Street in San Antonio, about twenty thousand pounds for ten cents per pound, when he was the business manager of a suttler's store at Fort Stockton. I also sold at the forts many crates of wild apples that were gathered on the ranch, at from ten to twelve dollars per crate. The fruit was about the size of June apples and resembled the Bell-flower apple in appearance, but they were nicely flavored and the demand for them was greater than I could supply. The fact that apples and Irish potatoes are supposed to be indigenous to the soil in that region is a worthy subject for investigation by scientists; and if the impression is true, the general opinion with reference to the origin of apples and potatoes in America, should be revised.

Chapter Sixteen:

Freighting With My Family—Gen. McKenzie—
Fatal Accident—Mule Fright

My frequent journeys to Chihuahua had made the route familiar to me, and when preparing for a trip I made in February, 1873, I persuaded Mrs. Santleben to go with me and take our child Sophie along. The Indians had caused no trouble in some time and seemed to be perfectly quiet, consequently I apprehended no danger and thought that the journey could be made with safety. The distance was long and the roads were rough, but I provided an ambulance, drawn by two good mules, for my family, also a young girl, now Mrs. Salsman, who resides at Lacoste Station, to travel in, and after making every preparation for their comfort I started about the middle of the month.

When we arrived at Fort Clark I was informed that numerous bands of Indians had been seen in various parts of the country, and it was feared that a general raid was on foot. General McKenzie was at that time in command of the post and he was making the necessary preparations to pursue them.

The news caused me to feel some uneasiness, but I continued my journey with the hope that we would avoid coming in contact with them. I was somewhat relieved at noon the following day, when I met Dr. Livingston and six men at San Felipe (now Del Rio), who were awaiting the arrival of my train, with the intention of traveling with us, for mutual protection, as it was unsafe for his party to travel alone. They were from the Eastern States, on their way to California, with a prospecting outfit, and their appearance made a good impression.

The next morning we crossed Devil's River and nooned at Painted Cave. The following day General McKenzie overtook us at California Springs, where we had stopped for dinner, and he camped there. His command consisted of a regiment of cavalry and one company of Seminole Indians, which was accompanied by ten wagons and a hospital ambulance in charge of a surgeon.

The general advised me to remain and travel under the protection of his troops to Beaver Lake, at the head of Devil's River, where he intended to establish his camp, and promised that from there he would send his scouts towards the head of the Concho, the Pecos and the Rio Grande, to keep the other Indians from coming in, and head off those who had already spread over the country.

I thanked him for his kind intentions and said that I appreciated the interest he took in the safety of my train, but told him that it would be impossible for me to travel with his troops on account of my big wagons and their heavy loads. So we left him there and camped that night at Dead-man's Pass. We nooned next day at Fort Hudson, that was abandoned in 1860 and was then unoccupied, and camped that night between the seventeenth and eighteenth crossing on Devil's River. From there it was only a short distance to Beaver Lake, where at noon the following day General McKenzie overtook us, and made camp. The general was aware that I was compelled to go forward and could not wait for results from his scouting expeditions that he intended to send out next day, and did not urge me to delay, but he cautioned me to be very careful.

We started about one o'clock in the afternoon for Howard's Well, about forty-five miles distant, where there was water. Dr. Livingston and his six men rode ahead of my train, with six pack-mules loaded with provisions and his mining outfit. They were about a mile in front of my wagons and only three miles from McKenzie's camp when a party of about forty Indians attacked them from both sides of the road. They killed Black, a man about thirty years of age, and Jones, about the same age, was wounded in the knee. One mule was killed and all the others were captured, after the survivors hurried by defeat back to the wagons. The wounded man, who was suffering great pain, was sent immediately to McKenzie's camp, where his leg was amputated, but he died that night, and they buried him on the shores of Beaver Lake. Black was buried that evening in a shallow grave among the rocks where he was killed.

The official report of General McKenzie's campaigns in Texas probably refers to this incident, and if so, other particulars relating to the subject may be given in that connection with which I am not conversant. I only know that a detachment of troops was sent in pursuit of the Indians, but I do not know if they succeeded in overtaking them.

Dr. Livingston and his four surviving companions continued their journey with us, and one of them was a boy about eighteen years of age, known as Head Boone, who became greatly attached to Mrs. Santleben and our children. His expressions of discontent indicated that he had grown weary of traveling and was very much disgusted with his trip. He was anxious to return to his home in St. Louis, where his mother resided, and when I told him that he could remain with me, and promised to send him back when we returned to San Antonio, he showed more contentment. Perhaps his despondency was a premonition of the tragedy so near at hand, that prevented me from carrying out my kind intentions.

Four days after the Indian fight, when we were in camp thirty miles southeast of Lost Pond, the unfortunate boy attempted to secure a rope that was attached to his saddle. A heavily loaded, old-fashioned shotgun was also fastened to the saddle, which he overlooked in the darkness, as it was nine o'clock at night. When pulling the rope the gun was accidentally fired, and a load of buckshot entered his stomach just below the breastbone. We all hastened to his assistance, but it could be seen at a glance that his case was hopeless, and he died about an hour afterwards.

The accident was very distressing and we were greatly depressed in spirits after it occurred, because of the friendly feeling we entertained for him. I would not consider the thought of burying him in a desert, and made immediate preparations to move forward to Lost Pond, although it was only a watering-place. We arrived at that place about nine o'clock the following morning and proceeded at once to look for a suitable resting place for the young man's body. We selected a spot on the side of a little hill, about two hundred yards from the road. The grave we quarried through four feet of soft rock, after removing the surface soil, and the corpse, wrapped in a blanket, was placed on a bed of hay in its vault with as much respect as it was possible for us to observe; and above was a covering of boards two inches thick, taken from my wagons. I cut his name on a slab of stone and placed it at the head of his grave, and Mrs. Santleben and the girls planted cactus on the mound, which was enclosed by a rock fence. While these sad rites were being observed, the usual guard was placed on the surrounding hills to protect the camp from a sudden surprise.

In after times when passing the place I would call the attention of my traveling companions to the spot and relate the particulars of the tragedy, and its memories always gave rise to feelings of sorrow. After my return from Chihuahua I narrated the incident, with all of the facts, to James P. Newcomb, who communicated them to a St. Louis paper, but perhaps the article was not seen by his people, because I never heard from them. Possibly some one of his family will read this, who will feel an interest in the fate of the unfortunate youth whose end has remained a mystery so many years, and will be glad to know that strangers gave him a decent burial in the wilds of Texas.

After the funeral was over we resumed our journey from Lost Pond, at four o'clock in the afternoon, and nooned next day at abandoned Fort Lancaster, crossed the Pecos after dinner and drove along the west side of the river until we arrived at the foot of a mountain about three hundred feet high, near Pecos Springs, that rose between the road and the river. From there Livingston and a companion named Williams passed over the mountain towards the river, where they surprised a band of Indians. Both parties were badly frightened and ran in opposite directions, without taking time to note the number on either side. The white men, as they hurried toward me, yelled "Indians!" every jump and showed that they were badly demoralized, consequently they created considerable alarm. Under the impression that an immediate attack would be made, the wagons were corralled in a few moments, with the mules on the inside, and we prepared to meet the enemy, but were not molested.

Our journey was not interrupted afterwards and nothing of importance occurred before reaching Chihuahua. I delivered my freight and remained there fifteen days collecting my cargo of copper and hides with which my wagons were loaded, and in addition I brought one hundred and fifty thousand dollars in Mexican silver coin to Texas, that was consigned to Messrs. Heick & Bros, at Indianola.

Our return trip was devoid of interest until we passed Fort Hudson, when making a night drive, near Dead-Man's Pass, considerable excitement was caused in that desolate region, about three o'clock in the morning, by an alarm that led us to believe that Indians were in our vicinity.

The ambulance in which my wife, with our child, and the girl were traveling, was immediately behind the front wagon that was loaded with money, and in it Mr. E. A. Mills, a brother of W. W. Mills of the El Paso custom-house, Mr. McChalton, a deputy custom-house officer of Presidio del Norte, and myself were riding. The ambulance was driven by Wiley Miller, who was hired for that purpose and to cook, and it was placed in the train where I could be near my family in case of danger.

The scare was caused by the herd of mules, which the caporal and his men were driving in front of the train. Without any perceptible cause they suddenly became frightened and stampeded in every direction, and the caporal and herders instantly followed in pursuit, after warning us by shouting "Indians!" who it was believed caused the terror.

The excitement occasioned by the cry spread rapidly, but none were more panic-stricken than Wiley Miller as he turned loose the lines and jumped from the seat of the ambulance. His team also became wild with fright, and with no one to guide them, they followed in the wake of the scattered herd at full speed.

Mrs. Santleben and child and the girl were in great danger, from which it was impossible for them to escape by their own efforts, because the curtains of the ambulance were all down and fastened on the outside, as was that also in front, behind the driver's seat. But fortunately the team was caught by the men on horse-back, near a steep bluff, about forty feet in depth, towards which they were running, and my family was rescued from a serious or perhaps fatal accident.

The men insisted that the trouble was caused by Indians, but probably it was a false alarm, and the mules may have been scared by a panther, bear, or Mexican lion, because all of these animals were common in that region. Possibly the unusual sight of wagons attracted their curiosity and one may have approached the road nearer than usual before the presence of men was discovered.

This incident caused some delay, but after the excitement subsided and I could think more rationally, I was thankful that my wife and child had been preserved from the tragedy that threatened them. My gratitude influenced me to pardon Wiley Miller, who is now with George Koerner, in San Antonio, where he has been employed continuously during the past fifteen years.

The excitement and dangers of the trip did not deter Mrs. Santleben from undertaking a second journey to Chihuahua, and she accompanied me, with her infant daughter, Charlotta, and the older child, in December the following year. Miss Amelia Stienly, a young lady whose home was in Castroville, traveled with us from there to Fort Stockton, where she stopped to visit her sister, Mrs. Mary Arnold, and her place was filled by Miss Maggie Burns, fifteen years of age, who is now Mrs. Martin of Austin.

My train was about six days ahead of me when we started from San Antonio, and I was anxious to overtake it before the wagons reached Fort Clark, because the Indians were raiding in the country. I drove the ambulance that was occupied by the ladies and children, and my only attendant was a Mexican named Falstina, who rode on horse-back.

We met with no interruptions until we were traveling along the highway near the Nueces River, about nine o'clock at night, when three men suddenly sprang from the side of the road, one in front of the horses and the other two toward the vehicle, one of whom ordered me to halt, and hollered "Hands up!" Acting under the impulse of the moment, I fired at the man in front of the team and a second shot at one of the others on the left side of the ambulance. The two reports and flashes of the pistol, both in rapid succession, frightened the horses, and they dashed forward at the moment the highwaymen commenced shooting. But as they were all on foot, the horses at the gait they traveled, soon removed us from danger after passing the first turn in the road. My wife was cool and collected, but Miss Stienly was badly frightened, as was my Mexican escort, who deserted me.

About twenty shots were fired, but no one was hurt, unless my aim was true, and only one of the robbers' bullets shattered a spoke in a rear wheel of my ambulance. The affair from the beginning to the end only occupied a few moments, and after the danger was over I realized that I had done a very foolish thing when I endangered the lives of my family unnecessarily by resisting the highwaymen's demands, and I reproached myself severely afterwards for my thoughtlessness.

The next day we overtook my train at Turkey Creek, and no other incident occurred that is worthy of notice until we arrived at Fort Stockton, where Miss Stienly was welcomed by her relatives. She had been a pleasant companion and we regretted to part from her, but we did not miss her so much as we would have done, if Miss Maggie Burns had not decided to visit Chihuahua with us.

Our journey from that point was devoid of excitement, and I can only recall one event that was at all remarkable, which happened about fifty miles northeast of Presidio del Norte. Mrs. Santleben walked off a short distance from camp to look for moss-agates, that were abundant in that country, and in the high grass she discovered two complete human skeletons. None of the bones had been disturbed, and they were bleached white. Evidently they had been there a long time, and nothing could be found in the vicinity that suggested the cause of their death; nor could we tell whether the remains were of white men or Indians.

Chapter Seventeen:

Danda, Indian Fighter—Brewing Beer in Chihuahua

On one of my trips with freight consigned to Fort Stockton, I met with an exciting adventure at California Springs, about half way between Painted Cave and Fort Hudson. These two places are situated near the first and at the second crossings of Devil's River, forty-six miles apart, in which distance there is no water except occasionally at California Springs after protracted rains.

We were making a night drive and when within a few miles of the so-called springs I decided to ride on ahead and look for water at that place with the hope of finding it before the wagons arrived. I left the train on horseback about eleven o'clock p.m., in company with Olojio Danda, one of my herders, who had been in my service some time and had proved himself a very reliable man. He was a citizen of Presidio del Norte, and one of the reasons that induced me to employ him was because he was known as a great Indian fighter.

His reputation was acquired on the trail that passed between Presidio and Fort Davis, over which marauding bands of Comanches and other warlike tribes often passed when making raids into Texas, where the men of Presidio frequently intercepted them. Occasionally they fought them openly, but their favorite mode of attack was from ambush, and sometimes they proved themselves equally as expert as their red brethren by stealthily recovering all the horses the Indians had stolen on their raids. The services of such men were always in demand in that region because they were versed in Indian ways and their courage was equal to any occasion.

We arrived at the springs about one o'clock in the morning and made a thorough search for water, but none could be found anywhere. About that time we saw towards the north at the distance of a mile a dim light, and Olojio suggested that we should find out what it meant. I did not favor an investigation because I thought that it might be an Indian camp, but I made no objections to his proposition. I was riding a good horse and knew that I could make my escape if my suspicions were substantiated, and Olojio was riding an active little mule on which he kept ahead of me as we followed the windings of the drain through a heavy undergrowth of mesquite that extended in that direction.

We approached the fire cautiously, but our animals made considerable noise tramping on the loose rocks, that could be heard some distance. When within about fifty yards our curiosity was satisfied when a bunch of Indians sprang to their feet in the circle of light and instantly disappeared in the darkness. Olojio, who was a few yards ahead of me, gave the startling cry of "Indians!" as he quickly wheeled his mule, and the dreaded name was repeated when he dashed by me before I could turn my horse. There was no need for him to sound the alarm, because I had been shocked by the exciting apparition that stimulated his actions and I made no unnecessary delay. He kept in the lead a short distance, as we hurriedly retreated over the route that had led us into the danger, but when I got in front the mule was soon out of the race and I could hear Olojio's pleading voice in the distance pitifully appealing to me in Spanish, saying, "Boss! Boss! Don't leave me." It was a cry for help which I could not ignore, and it made me check the speed of my horse while I reproached myself for the thoughtlessness that led me to abandon him; but at that moment

Olojio's mule passed me without his rider and my belief was that the Indians had overtaken and killed him. The impression gave me a fresh start and added impetus to my speed, though I could scarcely keep up with the un-encumbered mule that, on account of his fright, ran as swift as a deer in the direction of the wagons after entering the road.

Our race did not relax its fleetness until we met the wagons, about two miles from the springs, where we came to a halt. Our sudden appearance created alarm and great excitement prevailed among my drivers and herders when I related what had happened. They too believed that Olojio had been killed by the Indians and we proceeded on our journey with the intention of finding his remains and giving them a decent burial, but we were greatly relieved after traveling about a mile when we saw the supposed dead man limping towards us in the distance. We were all glad to know, when we met, that he had escaped serious injury, and that he had not encountered the Indians. Olojio accounted for his lameness by explaining that his mule had stepped into a hole, and when the animal stumbled he was thrown over his head with such force as to cripple his leg. He also lost his gun when he fell, and it was recovered when we returned from Fort Stockton.

My reflections, when I seriously canvassed the incident, made me realize that I had done a very foolish thing by risking my life unnecessarily in a country that was full of dangers and under circumstances which made it a reckless enterprise. The fact that the Indians were as badly frightened as we were did not mitigate the folly, because if they had not been startled out of their sleep the episode might have had a different ending. I was taught a good lesson through my experiences in that connection, because I never afterwards hunted for trouble with Indians and was always glad when I did not see or hear of any on my travels.

During that period no precautions against marauding savages could be relied on, even in the vicinity of settled communities. To illustrate the fact, I had a lonely adventure a few years later, similar to the foregoing, within forty-five miles of San Antonio, that terminated very nearly in the same way and without injury to anyone.

I had been absent from my family about four months and naturally was anxious to get home. My train was camped at the High-hill, on the Fredericksburg and Fort Concho road, when I left it about one o'clock in the morning and started on horse-back for San Antonio by moonlight over a road that was familiar to me. I crossed the Guadalupe River, where Waring is now situated, and turned into a dim trail that was half a mile shorter than the wagon road to the point where I would re-enter it. The route was level and my longings to reach home as soon as possible prompted me to urge my horse forward in a slow gallop, but we had only proceeded about three hundred yards when my horse passed through a bunch of Indians lying beside the trail, who were evidently asleep. Some of them sprang to their feet as I rode among them, but before they could do any harm I realized the danger I was in, and at that instant my horse bounded beyond their reach as he felt the stroke of my whip, which I continued to apply until he was running at the top of his speed. How far he ran before checking his gait is not remembered, but I am sure that we traveled a considerable distance. I do not know how the Indians felt when I galloped among them, but they must have been as badly frightened as I was when I saw them. I was very much surprised at finding Indians that near San Antonio after passing through hundreds of miles of country in which they ranged without seeing any; but they were the real article, as was proved by the damage they did a few days later by killing two or three sheep-herders and stealing a number of horses in that section of country.

Very few of my acquaintances are aware of the fact that I was once engaged in the brewing business in Chihuahua, therefore I will relate my experiences in connection with the enterprise from its inception until I pocketed my losses and charged them up to my foolish confidence in human nature.

The man with whom I was associated introduced himself as John Kohler when I first met him in San Antonio, in 1873, immediately after his arrival in the city. He was then friendless, destitute of money, and shabbily clothed. He approached me and submitted for my inspection a certificate from a St. Louis brewer that highly recommended him as a first-class brewer, and endorsed him as an honorable man. His credentials appeared to be correct and I was satisfied that he understood his business, otherwise he could not have secured such commendations. After hearing him talk I became favorably impressed, and when he expressed a desire to start a small brewery somewhere in Texas, I offered to take him with me to Mexico and establish him in business in Chihuahua. The numerous advantages of the situation that I mentioned seemed to please him, and he accepted my proposition.

I provided for his immediate necessities, and with his assistance I purchased the outfit required for a small brewery, including everything required for the plant, which I agreed to haul. It was also understood that I was to furnish the capital to start the business, and that after my outlay was repaid the net profits should be divided equally between us.

Kohler accompanied my train which transported the outfit, in 1874, and the brewing establishment was successfully inaugurated in June. It was a small affair when compared with modern institutions of that kind, but it was distinguished as the first brewery that was ever established in Chihuahua. The enterprise was successfully operated, and Kohler demonstrated to the satisfaction of every one that he knew how to make good beer. His prices were reasonable and the public showed their appreciation by extending him a liberal patronage. He sold his beer in bottles only, for which he charged six dollars per dozen quarts, and pints sold at three dollars and a half a dozen. At these prices his supply of hops, bottles, corks, etc., was soon exhausted, but about that time I returned from San Antonio and replenished his stock.

I was astonished at his success, and the praise bestowed on his beer was merited, because it was excellent. With his knowledge of the business there was no reason why it should not be superior in quality, because it was made from the finest grade of hops that could be procured in the market. It was also cheaper than St. Louis beer that sold in Chihuahua at one and a half dollars a quart or twelve dollars a dozen bottles, or twice our prices, consequently we had no competition. The venture had surpassed our most sanguine expectations, and its future prospects encouraged me to entertain the thought of enlarging the establishment.

I again returned to San Antonio and did not get back to Chihuahua before December, with my usual quantity of freight, including additional supplies for the brewery. Much to my surprise and disappointment I learned that the brewery was closed, and my friends informed me that Kohler had anticipated my arrival ten days before by secretly departing from the city, but no one knew in which direction he had gone. He sold the property belonging to the plant for a small amount of money, but that received from the business represented a considerable sum, which, added to the expense I had incurred, constituted a heavy loss.

He knew that I would demand my share of the profits, in addition to the outlay of one thousand dollars I spent in starting the business, and he concluded that he would make a stake when he had a chance. He was one of the "get rich quick" sort, and the old story was illustrated over again in which I had the experience and he had the capital; but if he had pursued a different course and honestly conducted the business we would both have realized a fortune in a few years by continuing the enterprise. It was capable of being developed into large proportions because the location was excellent and the beer had won a reputation. Instead of doing so, Kohler chose to rob his benefactor, who had lifted him from poverty to competency, and he became a fugitive from justice. I traced him to Parral, but gave up the search under the belief that he had gone to Europe, and I have never heard of him since.

Chapter Eighteen:
Accused of Smuggling

I was in Chihuahua in 1874 after making an uneventful journey westward, and I quartered my teams as usual in the city at the meson de Massarre, where wagon trains and transient persons with animals usually stopped. The establishment was instituted for the convenience of travelers and freighters, and they are found in many cities throughout Mexico. Massarre was the owner's name and a meson means an inn or hostelry.

The buildings occupied a large square and they are worth describing. The stalls, with a cement trough each, sufficient for stabling fully six hundred animals, are built around the sides. The square inside has room for four trains of heavy wagons at one time, and in the center stood the granary, a peculiar stone structure, the shape of a bottle with a round tower that resembles the neck. It is seventy-five feet high and twenty feet in diameter, with steps that wind around the outside to a platform on top, up which the corn is carried and deposited in an opening. When the tower is full the opening is sealed up with adobe mortar that makes it airtight. Its capacity is about five thousand fanegas, about fifteen thousand bushels, and that quantity corn has been kept three years in perfect condition without weevils. The corn was taken out from an opening below that was secured by an iron gate and lock.

The meson was a private enterprise, and the charges were fixed for sheltering a train, but those for provender were governed by the market price. Sometimes a series of drouths caused a scarcity of corn and forage, consequently it was necessary to secure a large supply in seasons of plenty for such emergencies in order to facilitate traffic in the country by furnishing accommodations for those engaged in the business. Usually the price for a fanega of corn ranged from two to three dollars, but after a season of drouth it was more; or when the country was distracted by civil war, high prices prevailed, as in 1873, when I paid $12 a fanega for corn, and it was difficult to get at that price.

A few days after my arrival a large body of friendly Indians came into the city to celebrate a recent great victory they had gained over one of the hostile tribes toward the northwest, about fifty miles distant. The authorities had granted them the privilege of passing through the streets in a triumphal procession, for the purpose of displaying the trophies they had won in their foray into the enemies' country.

The wild Indians, represented by the Apaches, Comanches, Lipans, Navajos, and other fierce tribes, had desolated the State for a number of years, and had proved themselves a great scourge in the northern portion of Mexico, where they had materially injured the country. In order to suppress them, Governor Luis Tarrasas, of the State of Chihuahua, offered a reward of two hundred and fifty dollars for every scalp taken from the head of an unfriendly Indian. The agreement stipulated that the scalp should be identified by other trophies taken from the enemy, so that no impositions could be practiced. As the dress and ornaments, also the bows and arrows, of every tribe were different and could be easily recognized by those familiar with them, deceptions could not be practiced with impunity. These were turned over to the government officials, and, if the evidence was satisfactory, the reward was paid immediately.

The friendly Indians on the reservations, influenced by this reward, made a regular business of waging war on the wild tribes, and they would absent themselves from their villages for months, seeking opportunities secure scalps, by waylaying their victims in favorable localities; but frequently their object was effected by surprises which resulted in the extermination of entire settlements. The State did not concern itself with reference to their plan of warfare, and it approved their destruction by any method that might be adopted, because the hostilities were a constant menace. A natural enmity existed between the peaceable and warlike tribes and it was easy to excite the cupidity of the former by offering liberal rewards. By such means the State rid itself of a large number of uncontrollable savages and gave protection to its citizens.

The celebration I witnessed was not only approved by the city officials, but the programme was, evidently, arranged by them beforehand. The procession entered the city about ten o'clock in the morning, and a brass band in front discoursed appropriate music. The warriors followed on horseback, in their war-paint and decked out in all their finery, about fifteen of whom had long poles to which were secured the scalps of their victims killed in battle, together with the bows and other trophies necessary to prove their valor. The women and children of the tribe came next, on horses, also in single file, and their oddity added an attraction to the display. I was greatly impressed by the significance of the occasion, which had the appearance of a great festival, on account of the interest manifested by the citizens.

A few days after witnessing the parade I started with my train for Texas, having my wagons loaded heavily with freight, to which was added a large sum of money. Nothing of importance occurred until I arrived at place called Mula, situated about forty miles west of the Rio Grande, where a custom-house officer was stationed. The facts will show that it was a very unpleasant incident, and one that led to my arrest and the sequestration of my train, with its entire cargo, by an officer the government, under a suspicion that part of the freight was contraband. I was accused of smuggling, and under that charge I was tried before the Federal Court, but I was acquitted because the evidence was not sufficient to convict me.

Before stating the facts in the case, it will be necessary to relate the preliminary circumstances that associated me with it, and they were about as follows:

The Mexican Government, in order to get rid of the copper money that flooded the country, provided for the coinage of five-and ten-cent pieces, and the mint in Chihuahua was compelled to coin ten per cent of its total silver output in coins of those denominations. As the merchants in the city were opposed to retiring the copper money from circulation, because it was the money of the poorer classes, they agreed among themselves that they would not pay out the small silver coin received in their business transactions, consequently about twenty thousand dollars accumulated in their hands, and when the government learned that it was unpopular, and again made copper a legal tender, necessity compelled them to dispose of it in some way.

Small change was very scarce in San Antonio at that time, especially five-and ten-cent pieces, and such denominations readily commanded ten per cent premium. But the exorbitant export duties exacted by the government, amounting to a total of ten per cent, was prohibitory through legitimate channels. Therefore certain persons determined to avoid the imposition by smuggling this money across the Rio Grande, in order to take advantage of the excellent market that was offered them, and in that way the greater part of the holdings was transferred to the United States. A part of the sum, amounting to about eleven hundred dollars, was placed in a sack of beans, and shipped with similar freight on one of my wagons.

When I arrived at Mula, the officer stationed at that place inspected my freight without discovering the money, and everything was found to be correct. But before I was ready to move on, the Alcalde of the town interfered, and demanded a second inspection. Evidently he acted under certain information received from some source, because he did not hesitate when pointing out the sack, which, it was afterwards proved, contained the money, and he carried it away with him. A courier was dispatched to Presidio with the information, and with the entire train, was detained until a squadron of mounted custom-house guards arrived. The commander took me in charge and escorted my train to Del Norte. I gave bond for my appearance and was liberated until the following day, when I was placed on trial under an accusation of smuggling money out of the country.

Witnesses testified with reference to the facts, and as the evidence was conclusive, I was compelled to admit that the coin was found among my freight under suspicious circumstances; but I proved that the sack of beans in which it was placed was one of a large consignment sent to San Antonio, and I denied knowing the owners or the parties who placed it there. My defense was sufficient to show that I was innocent of conspiring to defraud the government, and that I had been imposed upon by others who were using my train for illicit purposes; consequently I was honorably acquitted and the money was confiscated by the government.

The laws of Mexico, with reference to smuggling, and the punishments imposed, were extremely severe, but they were not always vigorously executed. The penalty for transporting contraband goods required that the entire train and cargo should be confiscated. Those in charge of the train were assumed to be guilty and they were liable to a long term of penal servitude, consequently the risks attached to the business were very great.

The evidence in my case put me in a pretty tight place, and if my friends had not stood by me so faithfully and firmly I would not have been so fortunate in escaping the penalties. I had many good reasons for congratulating myself on the result, and I was concerned as much for the interests of my patrons as on my own account. They had entrusted to my care one hundred and eighty thousand dollars, in Mexican coin, on which the ten per cent duty had been paid, and it was all subject to confiscation under a strict construction of the law. My consignment of freight was also valued at a large sum of money, and my individual losses, if my train had been taken from me, would have ruined me financially.

The energy with which my defense was conducted, and the earnest efforts of my friends, who brought all their influence to bear in favor of my interests, was all that saved me from the penalties of the law. The court was persuaded to consider my case in a favorable light, and after my acquittal the government officials were liberal in their exactions, and courteous treatment was shown me, especially by Henrico Peña, who was in charge of the custom-house, from whom I received an unusually lenient inspection when passing me through his department. I became better acquainted with him afterwards, and I had many good reasons for esteeming him as one of my most intimate friends.

A few days after my release from custody I crossed the Rio Grande, passed the United States custom-house after a satisfactory inspection by its officials, and camped the same day twelve miles beyond the river. That night James Clark, who was then in charge of the American custom-house in Presidio del Norte, joined us with a party consisting of his wife, two young ladies, Hugh Kelly, and an escort of six men on horseback. They were traveling in an ambulance, and they had come out for a frolic. I made them welcome in my encampment, and after supper we decided to have a dance, for which purpose several wagon sheets were spread on the ground inside the corral that was made by the surrounding wagons. The Loza family, representing several persons, were traveling with me to their home, which is at 926 San Fernando Street, in San Antonio. Prof. Manuel Manso and his orchestra troop, comprising several members, also from Chihuahua, were with our party, and they furnished music for the occasion.

The music, from stringed instruments, was excellent, and as the wagon sheets on the level, hard ground furnished a splendid surface for the dancers, they enjoyed themselves to the utmost, until the caporal drove in the herd to be hitched, as day was dawning, and brought our pleasures to an end. Nothing similar to our frolic on that occasion was ever seen in that wild region, and, probably, its like will never be witnessed again, as the wilderness, perhaps, cannot be greatly improved. Everyone had entered into the spirit of the occasion and their pleasure found utterance in expressions of delight after it was brought to a close. The event might be termed a swell affair, because it was attended by the best people in the country, and though it lacked many accessories of civilization, the picturesque surroundings compensated for the deficiencies. After breakfasting with us, Mr. Clark and his party returned through the uninhabited country to their homes.

Mr. James Clark, who now resides in Denver, Colorado, was familiar with all the facts relating to my arrest in Mexico, and he amused himself later at my expense, when among my friends in San Antonio, by telling them about the supper he ate in my camp, and the beans that were served as the principal dish, in which five-and ten-cent pieces were found with every mouthful. The joke became current, and its meaning was understood, but I am inclined to think that its interpretation would place me in rather an unfavorable light in Mexico.

The pleasures we participated in and which have been so briefly described, were not confined to the occasion.

At Fort Stockton we were joined by Thomas Nelson, a worthy civil engineer, who now resides in San Antonio, and Pete Johnson, a well-known merchant at that time at the fort. They were jolly fellows, who could make themselves welcome anywhere, and such men always turn themselves loose when in camp. We always selected a camping place with a level space suitable for dancing, and every night the canvas was spread inside the corral, which was illuminated by the light of candles placed on the wagon wheels, and we danced to the sweet music discoursed by Manso's fine orchestra to the limit of endurance. The frolics were always full of fun, but Christmas and New Year's nights which we spent on that trip were both unusually lively, and those who are alive recall them as pleasant memories.

The journey was agreeable throughout, and nothing of a serious nature occurred to mar its pleasures, except my trouble with the Mexican custom-house officials, which was brought about by a traitor in my employ. This information was communicated by a reliable person, who was conversant with the facts, after I had pledged myself to secrecy on the subject. Until then I did not know who the informer was because he did not appear at the trial, and only the Alcalde with the sack of beans, with the money inside, appeared against me in court. I was told that the rascal discovered the money, and after marking the sack, he notified the Alcalde, who re-inspected my goods.

I had allowed him to return with me to Texas as a favor, and I would not dismiss him, but his treachery was suspected by the men in my train, and if I had not protected him it is doubtful if he would have reached his destination. I had promised not to betray his guilt, and I kept my pledge, although I felt inclined to punish him in some way, but I never did him any harm.

Chapter Nineteen:

Justifiable Homicide—Dr. Paschal—Buffalo Hunt

I was often accompanied on the long, tedious journey to Chihuahua by one or more friends, and their companionship was always appreciated. Business matters forced some of them to make the trip, and others made it with a desire to see the country, but, generally, their experiences did not tempt them to repeat the venture. Among them were Messrs. Gus Mauermann, San Antonio's former Chief of Police; Ernest Paschal, Fred Miller, Tom Nelson, Britt, Guinn, Allen, Henry Laager, and Judge Netterville Devine. These intimate friends of that period are still alive and any of them will sustain the truthfulness of my statements. The last named had often expressed a wish to travel over the route with me, and, in 1874, when he learned that I intended to return through the buffalo country, on the headwaters of the Concho, where these animals roamed in countless numbers, he arranged to go along.

I always traveled in an ambulance and otherwise provided for my comfort on such journeys, consequently Judge Devine had no hardships to encounter in his jaunt through a wild and rugged country. The prospects of sport, variety and adventure were the temptations that influenced him to go, and I determined to do all I could to have him realize his expectations. He joined us on Nueces Creek, west of San Antonio, on my usual route with a train of fourteen wagons loaded with freight for Mexico, and he was a pleasant addition to my company,

which consisted of Messrs. Jack Berry and Henry Vonflie, who are now well-to-do ranchmen and farmers near
Devine station on Briar Branch in Medina County.

Beyond Fort Clark an American, whose name was James,
stopped at my camp and made himself known to me. He
stabbed and killed a man when I was loading my wagons
in Luling, and it was approved by public opinion as a justifiable homicide. The assistance he received from people
in Luling enabled him to escape the clutches of the law,
and he was then traveling on foot towards Mexico, which
was a place of refuge for all such fugitives.

I was acquainted with the particulars connected with
the tragedy and my sympathies disposed me to help him
in his troubles. I made him a present of a good horse
and saddle, and Judge Devine gave him his Winchester
rifle, without considering his own necessities. He ought
to have felt grateful when he parted from us that night,
and I suppose he did, but we never heard from him afterwards, nor do I know what became of him.

We continued our journey westward and arrived at
Fort Davis in the morning and camped until two o'clock
in the afternoon. When we resumed our journey, to make
the sixty-mile drive to the next watering place, Judge
Devine decided that he would remain a while longer
with his friends residing at the post, with the expressed
intention of overtaking us before night, and I made no
objection to his doing so.

He did not leave the fort until the next day, or about
twenty-four hours after the train left there, and he rode
hard until two o'clock that night, when he arrived in
camp. In the meantime I had become anxious for his
safety on account of Indians, and my uneasiness kept
me awake. I heard him whistling as he approached, but
there was no tune to his music, and evidently he was in
a disturbed state of mind on account of not seeing the
wagons, or perhaps the silence of the wilderness made
him think of the dangers. It made me think of my boyish

experiences in dark and lonely places and the similar noises I made to keep up my courage. He was in camp before he realized the fact, and I scolded him severely for his imprudence that had caused me so much worry, at the same time telling him exactly what I thought on the subject, but he didn't seem to consider that it was a serious matter. Many things afterwards happened on the trip that I do not care to mention, because those involved might not like to see an account of their escapades in print, but the details would be entertaining.

We reached our destination within a reasonable time and found the people in Chihuahua very much interested in the preparations that were being made for a grand masquerade ball which was to be given by Governor Terrazas. Shortly after our arrival Judge Devine and myself received invitations, and, as a matter of course, suitable disguises were procured in which we appeared at the festival. All the prominent citizens of the city and many foreign visitors were present and participated in the pleasures without restraint. It was a brilliant entertainment throughout, including its lavish refreshments, and it was an occasion that the guests could always recall with pleasure.

Among those in attendance was Dr. Frank Paschal, a brother of ex-Mayor George Paschal, of San Antonio, who had earned an enviable reputation as a physician and surgeon in Chihuahua, where he was also highly esteemed by all classes for his talents and many excellent qualities that distinguish a man and win the confidence of his fellow creatures. They were natural to him, but he was indebted to his amiable wife for much of his popularity on account of her social attainments, that attracted the wealthy, and her charities, which, when added to his gratuitous practice, endeared them both to the poorer classes.

These statements will justify me in noticing a few incidents in his life as I recall them, because the facts are not generally known in his birthplace, where he has since become prominent. The information is of local interest, otherwise, on account of his having been professionally associated with Dr. Cupples, who was one of the ablest and most popular physicians and surgeons in San Antonio when Dr. Paschal commenced his practice. He was then about twenty-two years of age and had only recently returned from the university where he graduated in his profession. His subordinate position did not suit his ambitious temperament, consequently he looked abroad for a suitable location where he would encounter less opposition in his profession, and he selected Chihuahua as the most desirable. His early childhood was passed in Monterey with his parents, and he was not only familiar with Mexico and the customs of its people, but spoke the Spanish language fluently.

He received a friendly welcome from the people among whom he cast his lot, and for two years practiced his profession successfully before he again returned to San Antonio. The visit was made with a single purpose in view, and that was accomplished when he married Miss Lady Napier. Their bridal trip was made in the stage that was then running from San Antonio by way of Fort Concho and Horse-head Crossing to Fort Davis, where an ambulance with four mules and a driver awaited them, in charge of an escort, in which they were conveyed to Chihuahua.

A warm reception was extended to the newly married couple by the best people in the city, and in a short time the young wife was loved and admired by a large circle of acquaintances. The doctor soon became the leading physician, with an extensive and lucrative practice, but his services were not withheld from the poor, and he was greatly assisted in his charitable attentions by Mrs. Paschal, who devoted much of her time to such work. Many indigent people were relieved by his skill as a surgeon, and quantities of medicine were generously distributed to them free of cost.

When Dr. Paschal and his wife removed from Chihuahua to San Antonio, in 1881, his departure was greatly regretted by all classes, but such men are always a loss to any community. As an evidence of the appreciation in which he was held, he was often called to Chihuahua to perform difficult surgical operations or for consultation in serious cases of illness, until about five years ago, but since then he has been unable to absent himself from San Antonio on account of his large practice.

My stay in Chihuahua was not extended beyond the time necessary to load my wagons with freight destined for Texas, consisting of copper, hides, and a large amount of Mexican silver coin. We returned via Presidio del Norte to Horse-head Crossing on the Pecos River, where we diverged towards Fort Concho, in compliance with my promise to Judge Devine to take him to the buffalo country, which was many miles north of my usual route.

The plains and valleys that are traversed by the headwaters of the Concho River and its tributaries were then occupied by droves of buffalo whose numbers could not be computed with certainty. They seemed to be innumerable when we entered that region and passed through the herds which grazed quietly on all sides far into the distance, until they moved at certain hours toward the river to quench their thirst. Then they congregated from all points and formed masses which sometimes compelled the train to stop until they passed. On such occasions the drivers shot into them and many were uselessly killed or wounded, without any reason to justify their cruelty.

There was no trouble to kill buffalo under such circumstances, and of course the wanton destruction of animal life could offer no pleasure to a sportsman, consequently the gentlemen in my party were content to satiate their curiosity by admiring the wonderful sight. But soon afterwards Netterville Devine passed through an exciting experience when stalking buffalo, in which he had a narrow escape from Indians. He was walking ahead of the wagons when he saw a small herd of buffalo that tempted him to try a shot at them. He approached them cautiously and was creeping within range when luckily he looked behind and saw several Indians stealthily approaching him in the distance. He realized at once that the hunter was being hunted, and as he disliked the thought of figuring as game for Comanche sportsmen who coveted his scalp, he abandoned his game before they were disturbed, and made a hasty retreat. Fortunately he had a good start, and he improved the time by running at full speed on a bee-line until he reached the train.

The next day Mr. Devine, in company with Henry Vonflie and Jack Berry, gave variety to the murderous sport, after it became monotonous, by roping and necking together a pair of three-year-old buffalo, which, when released, joined the herd in that condition. We had an abundance of meat, and the men found more amusement in mastering the wild beasts than in slaying them ruthlessly for no purpose. They might have been driven into camp and butchered if the parties had been disposed to do so, in the same way that Mr. Vonflie did a two-year-old buffalo about two years afterwards in that region, where it was killed by the soldiers who were escorting my train from Fort Stockton to San Antonio.

The range of the American buffalo or bison in Texas did not extend very far south of the Concho River, in 1874, and they were only found in great numbers about fifty miles above that limit. They were not molested in that region to any great extent until afterwards, on account of the risk of encountering Comanche Indians, who occasionally hunted in that region in defiance of the United States troops which garrisoned Fort Concho. But their presence acted as a restraint, consequently the noble animals were partially protected in an area about thirty miles wide, where they were in the greatest numbers.

Buffalo were plentiful in that country until 1877, when hunters began to kill them for their hides, and thousands were destroyed by organized bodies of men for that object alone. The Texas & Pacific, the International, and the Southern Pacific railroads had then advanced far enough into the State to be accessible, and the demand for the hides induced unscrupulous persons, including many foreigners, to engage in the business. But the massacre was not confined to Texas, because it was greater in the Northwest, where hundreds of men enlisted in the barbarous destruction of "our national animal" when the Northern Pacific Railroad penetrated the plains where millions roamed at will.

Perhaps the percentage of merchantable skins that were placed on the market would represent only a fraction of the total number of the animals that were killed and which no one can estimate. Thousands were slaughtered in sport or for their hides, and perhaps more escaped to die from wounds. Sometimes the tongue and other choice pieces were cut out and the carcass fed the wolves and buzzards that followed in their trail.

Before the work of extermination was complete a new industry was suggested to those who dealt in buffalo hides and those who saw the millions of pounds of bones that lay bleaching on the plains. When it was ascertained that they had a commercial value, the dismembered skeletons were gathered in piles and hauled to the nearest railroads, which transported them to the East. The first person in Texas who appreciated the worth of such commodities was Mr. Louis Bergstrom, a brother of Oscar Bergstrom, Esq., formerly of San Antonio, but now a prominent lawyer in New York City, whose large practice extends into Mexico. Mr. Louis Bergstrom is now the general manager of the Alamo Dressed Beef Company of San Antonio, and he engaged largely in the business of collecting them, also in buying buffalo hides. He sent out dozens of wagons which delivered the bones in carload lots to the nearest railroad stations. Perhaps a larger sum was realized from the sale of bones by the parties who were engaged in collecting them than from the total number of more valuable hides and the quantities of dried meat, that were recognized as merchantable commodities.

The splendid race of animals is now represented by about two thousand individuals all told; and about half of that number are in the United States. The Federal Government has control of several herds and is making efforts to revive the race in suitable locations on the national reservations, where they will have permanent homes.

My opinion is that it was as necessary for the buffalo to be destroyed as it was that the Indians should be driven out of the country, because while they remained the Indians could not be controlled, and the range was needed for domestic cattle, also for homes of thousands of people who have since settled the country.

Chapter Twenty:

1875—Hauling A Meteorite to Philadelphia—
An Attempted Robbery

I was in Chihuahua again in the spring of 1875, and while there was told that several years before a large aerolite had fallen on the ranch of Mr. Henry Mueller, near San Lorenzo, about ten miles from the city, which was said to be one of the most massive known to the scientific world. I became very much interested in the subject and decided that if it was possible to secure the stone I would haul it to Texas and place it on exhibition at the World's Fair in Philadelphia.

Legally, the meteorite belonged to the owner of the land on which it fell, and as Mr. Mueller attached no value to it, personally, he agreed to let me have it. But in the meantime the Mexican authorities had asserted a claim, based on the assumption that as it came from space it was not subject to individual ownership, consequently the Republic had a right to dispose of it in any way it pleased. These pretentions were not disputed by the owners, although it is obvious that they could not have been sustained; but it was useless for me to oppose them, and I determined to secure it from the government on the most favorable terms.

The decision made it necessary for me to negotiate with the proper officials, and after I explained my intentions they graciously condescended to allow me to carry out my wishes under the following conditions, to which I subscribed: They permitted me to transport the meteoric stone out of the country free of export duty and to the Centennial Exposition buildings, at Philadelphia, at my own expense; but they required Mr. Mueller and myself to give a bond for a considerable amount, which stipulated that the stone should be safely returned to Chihuahua within a certain time without cost to the government.

The meteorite was composed of solid iron and weighed 5,400 pounds. It was shaped like a turtle, round on top and flat below. It measured about two feet through its thickest part and curved to the edges, where it measured three feet wide and four feet long across the bottom. Evidently when the mass of metal struck the earth it was soft enough to be flattened by the impact and retained the imprint of the solid rock where it fell among loose stone on the surface, which were imbedded in the lower part.

This visitant from another world was not very attractive in appearance, but I was fascinated by it and thought that others would be equally impressed when the curiosity was placed on exhibition. I was aware that it would be a difficult and costly undertaking, but I expected to consign it to one of the show places where sightseers would reimburse me for my trouble and outlay.

I hauled the mass of iron on a wagon assigned for that purpose, and it alone made a heavy load, which strained the team more than bulky freight would have done, because it was dead weight in the bed and the wagon had no swing. The other wagons were loaded with heavy freight in the bodies, including $200,000 in silver coin, and a bulky top weight of hides, which caused them to oscillate with a motion that relieved the teams. At Forts Davis, Stockton and Concho the aerolite attracted great attention among the soldiers, and when it arrived in San Antonio the wagon was unhitched and placed in the rear of the Veramendi House, which was then occupied by Mr. Weber, a brother of Jacob Weber, who resides on North Flores Street, where it was viewed by hundreds during the two weeks it was there.

The only incident worth noticing, that occurred on the trip, happened near the crossing of the San Saba River, where a company of rangers were stationed under the command of Captain Rufus Perry. About the time that I reached their camp several men went out hunting, and a short time afterwards they returned with the information that they had discovered a party of Indians. Captain Perry, with the greater part of his men, was absent on a scout, but it happened that Major Jones, who commanded all the State Rangers on the frontier and was then on a tour of inspection, had arrived in camp a short time before the news was reported. He hastily summoned his escort together, with several of Captain Perry's company, and quickly proceeded in search of the Indians. He soon overtook them, and a battle was fought in which three Comanche marauders were killed and several others wounded, but no casualties occurred among the Texans.

I got through with my train all right, but the meteoric stone caused a certain amount of trouble, and the expense was considerable, because the wagon carried nothing else. The others brought full loads of freight, for which I was liberally compensated, but the most valuable part consisted of the two hundred thousand dollars, in Mexican silver coin, that was entrusted to my care. The sum represented the first considerable amount of money that was ever forwarded from Chihuahua to Luling, and for that reason the fact is worthy of record.

Luling was then a new town that had sprung up in a few weeks at the terminus of the Galveston, Harrisburg & San Antonio Railroad, and the population was composed of all sorts of people, including many rough characters who were capable of committing any crime. In the midst of such surroundings I felt a natural uneasiness, on account of the large sum of money that remained on my wagons, during the two nights and a day that I was compelled to wait for a train on which to forward it to its destination. I guarded it continually until Mr. Dan Price, who is now Yoakum's efficient Mayor, witnessed my anxiety, and kindly offered me his services. I gladly accepted his valued assistance in watching the treasure, which was rendered until it was forwarded to the consignees, Messrs. Heick & Helfrisch, of Galveston.

I left the stone in Luling with instructions to send it to Philadelphia, but as my business called me back to Chihuahua immediately, I was unable to give it further attention. It was publicly exposed with the Mexican exhibit without my authority, and my claim was ignored, as if the contract was not in existence. When the Centennial Exhibition closed the meteorite was donated by Mexico to the British Museum. The opportunity had passed when I might have made it profitable, and I was glad to be relieved of the expense and trouble that would otherwise have devolved on me had I been required to comply with the exactions of my agreement.

The meteorite was my property under the contract until I was released from my bond, and I have never understood why it was taken from my possession and transferred to others without adequate compensation. Justice entitled me to a reimbursement of my actual outlay at least, and such generosity at my expense was inexcusable. As the matter now stands, individual acts, backed by the Mexican government, made me an involuntary contributor to science contrary to my expectations; and I will always believe that I have a claim resting against that stone, amounting to about five hundred and fifty dollars; but if proper credit was awarded for my services I might be willing to discharge the debt.

When I think about the great number of lawless men who frequented the frontier during the period that I was engaged in the business of staging and freighting, and the large sums of money I transported from Mexico every trip through to Texas, I wonder at the forbearance that restrained them from molesting me. They could have organized a sufficient force at any time, and under favorable circumstances they might have captured and plundered my train with impunity.

The only occasion that such an attempt occurred was in 1875, when I was returning from Chihuahua with a valuable lot of freight and one hundred and fifty thousand dollars in silver coin. We had crossed the Rio Grande, at Presidio del Norte, after passing through a customs-house inspection, and my train encamped that night eighteen miles east of the river in a dry and narrow cañon, across which the road passed, where it was not more than 300 yards in width. Under ordinary circumstances it was not a desirable camping place, but it was the best place I could find and I was not apprehensive of danger.

The usual precautions were observed for our protection by corralling the wagons, and the customary guard was selected to watch over the camp; the mules were grazing on a mountain-side towards the west end of the cañon under the watchful care of the caporal and his herders, and before the evening shadows closed around us the noises that had disturbed the silence of the wilderness were hushed and all was quiet except a tingling bell with the herd that proclaimed our presence.

The calm that surrounded us was not interrupted until some time after Henry Vonflie and his men, who were first on guard, had retired. I and Timps, a young American, and three Mexicans, had relieved him, but I cannot recall the hour that we went on post. We were seated outside of the corral near the two wagons that were loaded with money, when a shot was fired close to the train. Immediately afterwards we heard the tramp of men running over loose rock from the east. We knew then that an attack was being made on the train and instant preparations were made to meet them. I fired the first shot a few moments before my companions commenced firing, and our assailants answered with a volley which brought Mr.

Vonflie and his men to our assistance and doubled our force. We were armed with Winchester rifles and many shots were fired on both sides before our party of twelve men drove the enemy away.

The fight only lasted a few minutes, scarcely long enough for the wagon-master, who was with the caporal, and his men to drive the herd of mules into the corral before it was over. They were kept there and vigilance was observed until morning, because the excitement had banished sleep, and, besides, we expected that the attack would be renewed, but nothing unusual took place.

Early the following morning we visited the position that our foes had occupied in the skirmish, and also where their horses were tied, with the expectation of finding a few gory corpses, but our valor was poorly rewarded, because we could not find a drop of blood nor could we discover that our adversaries had suffered the slightest injury from our storm of lead. After making a diligent search we collected a couple of old hats, a gourd of water, and a few trifles of less value as trophies of our victory.

We afterwards learned that our assailants numbered altogether about forty cut-throats who knew that I was carrying a large amount of money and they had planned to rob my train. They had arranged to approach my camp through the cañon in two equal parties from the east and the west, with the design of making a simultaneous attack on foot when a signal gun was fired by a spy who was to have entered the corral secretly. But their plans were disarranged by the detachment which was to have advanced from the west, that was delayed by coming in contact with the herders and the mules that were grazing in that direction. Fearing detection, they used precautions which prevented them from making an assault on the west side when the signal shot was fired, consequently they did not participate in it and we did not see them at all.

A few months later several of the men who took part in the little skirmish were pointed out to me, but I could not prove anything against them, and as it was not safe to molest them during those rough times in that part of the country I thought it was best to leave them alone, and I also avoided making any allusion to the subject.

The possibility of a second attack being made by the robbers was discussed, and we were led to view our surroundings with considerable apprehension; but we continued our journey with resolute spirits, because there was no other alternative than to move forward. The large amount of money that I carried would have tempted the cupidity of thieves under any circumstances, and it was scarcely possible that the reckless scoundrels would abandon the booty they had hoped to secure without making another effort.

These and other similar impressions led us to anticipate an ambuscade, and that day, when about to start from where we stopped for dinner, about twelve miles west of Davis' ranch, a signal of alarm was given. My guard, who was stationed on a hill near by, reported that he saw about thirty men go into the high grass near a ravine at the place where we would have to cross, and it was his opinion that they had planned an ambush for our benefit.

We accepted the report in good faith, and naturally inferred that they were the same robbers who had attacked us the night before. Henry Vonflie and myself took ten men and cautiously ascended the hill, with the intention of making the necessary observations. The guard pointed out the place, about six hundred yards distant, where he had seen the men conceal themselves, and the truth of his statement was partially confirmed when we saw several men in the tall grass that was about waist-high.

We decided at once that our surmises were correct, and congratulated ourselves that we had anticipated the highwaymen's movements. There was no need of further investigation, and we commenced firing at those in the grass with a deadly purpose. We were all armed with long-range guns that were capable of doing execution at a greater distance, and we knew that our bullets reached them, but they made no response. We concluded that we were either beyond the range of their guns or else they were trying to conceal their position, until we had fired about fifty shots. We then saw a man signaling to us by waving his hat, from a hilltop off to one side, and I ordered my men to cease firing.

Evidently we had made a mistake, and as the man approached I advanced to meet him. When we met I recognized an old frontier settler I had known a long time, whose name was Landrum, who had lived on the frontier about a quarter of a century. In answer to my inquiries he explained that he was traveling with several men and had stopped to rest near the ravine a short time before, or about the time the guard saw them. When we began to shoot and the bullets struck among them he realized that his party was the target and that they were in great danger. To avoid being killed they threw themselves on the ground and crawled up the ravine some distance until they were out of range, and he ascended the hill where he could see the wagons, which he recognized. He then made his presence known by signaling to us, with the intention of correcting the erroneous opinion we entertained with regard to them.

Chapter Twenty-One:
Cardise Killed In El Paso—
Freighting Chihuahua to San Antonio

On my way to Chihuahua, in 1876, with the train loaded with freight received at Luling, it was necessary for me to diverge from my usual route at Fort Davis and travel the road leading to El Paso. The principal points of interest on that route were Barrel Springs, Eagle Springs, Van Horn's Wells, Fort Quitman, San Elizaria and Ysleta; but the town of San Elizaria was the only place of any importance, and it had only about four thousand inhabitants. About seventy-five years ago the little town, which is situated on an elevation in the valley, was in Mexico, on the west side of the Rio Grande, until the melting of snow on the mountain above caused a great overflow that covered the valley, which, at that point, was several miles in width. When the water subsided the river was confined to a new and permanent channel west of the town, and the inhabitants were made to realize that their possessions were in Texas.

It is claimed that the river cut off about ten thousand acres from Mexico, and that the loss of territory was the cause of considerable controversy between the two republics before it was finally settled according to international laws governing in such cases. Along the banks of what was called the old river the dead trunks of immense cottonwood trees could be seen, but the bed through which the water formerly flowed was dry. In fact, the

Rio Grande del Norte itself was sometimes destitute of water, and I have traveled up the river-bed on horseback for miles. In the summer only, when the snow melts in the mountains, there is a full flow of water, and occasionally destructive floods similar to that which caused the cut-off of San Elizaria inflicted considerable damage in the valleys along the river's course, but it is expected that when reservoirs are completed above, that such overflows will be extremely rare.

The importance of the great irrigation schemes that are proposed for the Rio Grande valley seems to be appreciated, and they will not only be of incalculable benefit to that region, but help to make El Paso the great commercial center of the middle Southwest.

When I first knew El Paso it was a straggling town of a few hundred inhabitants, and at the time that Charley Howard killed Louis Cardise it was a rough frontier place. The tragedy occurred when I stopped there on this trip, and I will state my recollections with reference to the causes that led to the encounter. They differ somewhat from other versions of the story that have been published, but I believe my recollections of the original trouble are correct.

Forty miles northeast from El Paso there is a lake that is strongly impregnated with salt which the sun evaporates continually. It was known throughout the northern part of Mexico and it supplied all that region with salt. Numerous carts were constantly engaged in hauling the salt into Mexico, where it found a ready market at $12 a fanega of 240 pounds, and at that price it was remunerative.

The salt at the lake had been free to the people from time immemorial, and it could be had for the labor of gathering, until Mr. Cardise, who was a government mail contractor, began to collect a revenue of $2.50 on each cartload that was taken away from the lake, which was paid reluctantly. The lake was on vacant land, which was a part of the public domain belonging to Texas, and Cardise never acquired any title in the property, consequently his charges were illegal and he had no authority to make them; but the people submitted to the imposition rather than be deprived of the necessity.

Subsequently, when these facts became known to Mr. George P. Zimpleman, of Austin, Texas, he was influenced to locate the land on which the lake was situated, and he placed it in charge of Mr. Howard, his son-in-law, whose home was in El Paso. Mr. Cardise was enjoined from levying further exactions for salt, and the collections were made by Mr. Howard. The ill feelings produced by these transactions grew into bitter enmity, and as both men were popular, they exercised their influence to the prejudice of each other until the feeling developed into an open feud. Both men were fearless, and it was expected that the quarrel would end in bloodshed, when Howard forced the issue by looking up Cardise and killing him before he could offer any resistance.

The death of Cardise exasperated his Mexican friends on both sides of the river, and as many of them were devoted to his interests when alive, they organized a party with the intention of wreaking their vengeance on his slayer. The attack was made upon Howard and his friends in a small house containing three rooms, in which they took refuge, where they stood their assailants off for three days, but finally they were all killed.

Before I started for Chihuahua, the Galveston, Harrisburg & San Antonio Railway Company was rushing its track towards San Antonio, which was designated in its charter as the terminal point, and the belief was generally entertained that the road would not be extended beyond that city for many years. Naturally I was of the same opinion, because I was thoroughly acquainted with the country northward and to the western borders of the State, and I could not believe in the possibility of a locomotive marking its course through that uninhabited region with its smoke, or that its whistle would startle its silent wastes. Even if it was practicable to build a railroad to El Paso, many persons thought, and I among them, that the Indians would destroy the track as fast as it was built and cause it to be abandoned.

Years afterwards, when I saw the wonderful work that had been accomplished under the direction of skillful engineers, I recalled my mistaken ideas on the subject. Though it broke up my business I could appreciate the benefits that were conferred on the country when the road was completed. It has introduced civilization, and a large area of the desolate wilderness with which I was so long familiar has become one of the most prosperous regions in Texas. But at the time my story opens it was a wild and inhospitable region that promised to remain a desert for ages.

I found the wholesale merchants in Chihuahua rejoicing at the prospect of having a railroad terminus at San Antonio, within nine hundred miles of them, and they were considering the best means of reaping the greatest advantages that could be secured in the transportation of goods. They thought it was possible to avoid the enormous expense on large shipments of merchandise that necessity required them to order at one time, by arranging for quick transportation of goods in smaller quantities. As a single consignment sometimes weighed about 80,000 pounds and was valued at $100,000, this capital, with an additional outlay of $50,000 for freighting and custom-house duties, had become a serious burden, because the goods had to be stored in warehouses six or eight months until the supply was exhausted.

Several of the most prominent merchants interviewed me on the subject and inquired if it was possible to make an arrangement so that they could get their consignments through in smaller lots at regular intervals by introducing a system that would insure rapid transportation and thereby avoid the great outlay and expense that wholesale dealers were obliged to bear in order to supply their customers.

I gave the subject careful consideration before coming to a decision, and then I proposed to them that if a certain number of merchants in the city would obligate themselves, for a period of ten years, to import 72,000 pounds of merchandise every month, exclusive of heavy machinery, and export all their remittances and freight through me, I would start thirty-six small wagons with five mules to each. I explained that I intended to divide the wagons equally into three trains, and that each wagon would be capable of hauling two thousand pounds of freight; that after the line was established the trains would run on schedule time, and make the trip to Chihuahua in thirty days, by leaving San Antonio on the first and fifteenth of every month, and return in the same time after leaving Chihuahua on the seventh and twenty-fourth of each month.

I agreed to provide specially constructed wagons for the protection of merchandise from the weather and from pilferers, and arrange for their safety on the route by placing each train, with its twelve drivers and three herders, in charge of a competent wagon-master and arm all of the sixteen men with improved weapons, so that they would be strong enough to protect themselves against Indians and outlaws.

I stipulated that I should receive eight dollars per hundred, or $80 per thousand pounds for hauling freight from San Antonio to Chihuahua, and that the rate on copper and other back freight from Chihuahua was to be five dollars per hundred, or $50 per thousand pounds; also that the charge for transporting Mexican money and silver bullion should be two and a half per cent, or twenty-five dollars on every thousand dollars.

My proposition was accepted with the understanding that the contract should provide for the discontinuance of the line in the event that a railroad was completed to

Chihuahua at any time within ten years. This stipulation did not concern me in the least, because the remote possibility of such a road being built was beyond my conception, and I was very much elated over the prospect of building up a safe and lucrative business. After perfecting the agreement I realized that the undertaking was too great for me to handle alone, and I decided to associate Mr. Edward Froboese with me as a partner in the enterprise. He was then in San Antonio, where it was necessary for me to complete my arrangements, and I proceeded immediately to load my wagons with freight destined for Texas.

Before I was ready to start, Mr. Russell Norton, of the firm of Norton & Deutz, of San Antonio, who was awaiting an opportunity to return to Texas, requested permission to travel with me, and I readily granted him the privilege. Business affairs had called him to Chihuahua some time before in the interest of his house, which transacted a large business in cities and mining districts of the State through local agencies.

Mr. Thomas Cordero, a man of prominence in that country, with his family and servants, also accompanied the train in three ambulances, with a wagon that carried their luggage. His individual wealth was estimated at a large amount, and he, with his brother, Augustine Cordero, was once the owner of the largest irrigated farm in the State of Chihuahua, which they sold in 1872 for $250,000. Mr. Cordero expected to be absent from Mexico several years, and had planned a tour through the United States and Europe, with the expectation of returning by the way of Vera Cruz and the City of Mexico. They were refined and educated people, with agreeable manners, and his was the nicest family that I ever traveled with.

The third day after leaving Chihuahua, when we were making the ninety-mile drive between the two watering places, at Julimes and Chupadero, Mr. Norton met with an adventure that might have terminated seriously but for a fortunate coincidence. About twenty-two miles east of Julimes I ordered the driver of the ambulance in which Mr. Norton and myself were riding to go ahead of the train to a place about three miles beyond, where I expected to camp for supper.

We stopped near the bank of a dry branch, that was covered on both sides with a growth of brush, and a few minutes later Mr. Norton walked down into the dry channel about one hundred and fifty yards from the ambulance, where he was suddenly confronted by eight or ten Comanche Indians where no one would have expected to find them. I could not see them until they circled around him, and then I perceived that he was in an awkward if not a dangerous situation. I knew that he did not have his rifle or other weapon with him, and I, with the driver, hastened to his assistance, but we stopped in an advantageous position within forty yards of them. This was not what they expected, and they undertook to get us inside the ring that surrounded Norton, by advancing in our direction, but we made threatening demonstrations which kept them back until they desisted after several attempts.

They did not injure Mr. Norton in the slightest manner, but I have no doubt that they would have killed him if we had not been present. Their actions indicated that they were in a bad humor, and when they showed Mr. Norton how they scalped white men in Texas it was plainly intended as an expression of their hatred for the race. I expected that serious trouble would grow out of it, but we were prepared to meet it and watched for the first threatening movement. I thought the time had come for action when one of them mounted his horse and rode through the place where we expected to camp, because his actions showed that his intention was to provoke a fight; but luckily for all parties concerned, the herd of mules, driven by the caporal and his men on horseback, and followed by the train of wagons, appeared a short distance beyond as they came over the hill.

The Indians seemed to be disconcerted when they saw my outfit, because they believed that we were traveling alone, and it is probable that they calculated on getting our scalps. They realized the disadvantages that confronted them at a glance, and after mounting their horses with as little delay as possible they rode off, yelling in regular Comanche style. We were glad to see the last of them, and Mr. Norton, who seemed to understand that he had escaped a serious danger, was more careful in his movements thereafter and never wandered about unarmed.

The weather was pleasant until we arrived at Fort Stockton, and then it commenced to rain. From there on to Fort Clark we traveled through almost an incessant downpour of rain, which made our journey very uncomfortable and delayed us beyond the time I had calculated on for making the trip, consequently a change in my plans became necessary on account of a large sum of money I was transporting on two of my wagons, amounting to $180,000, which I had obligated myself to deliver in Galveston before the steamer sailed for Europe that brought the goods which were to be conveyed under bond on my next trip to Chihuahua.

To meet my engagements I was compelled to leave the train at Fort Clark in charge of the wagon-master, and make forced drives with the two wagons containing the money, which had fourteen mules hitched to each of them. The commandant of the post furnished me with an escort of fifteen men and a wagon, in charge of a sergeant. I hastened forward to Luling, and thence by train with the money to Galveston, where I delivered it to Messrs. Heick & Helfrisch two days before the steamer's departure.

Mr. Norton had become impatient to get home, and he also left the train at Fort Clark, where he took a seat in the stage; but Mr. Cordero and his family remained with the wagons, which were heavily loaded with copper and hides, until they arrived in San Antonio. He had made arrangements with me to take charge of his servants, teams, and vehicles, with the understanding that I was to convey them to Chihuahua with my train, and I complied with my agreement the next trip.

I made no unnecessary delay, but immediately returned to San Antonio and interviewed Mr. Froboese, with reference to my contract for the transportation of goods between San Antonio and Chihuahua, and laid before him the whole scheme, with the evidence of my agreement with the merchants. I offered him an equal partnership with myself in the enterprise, which he accepted with the understanding that it was to be equipped at our joint expense. We then had an interview with Col. T. C. Frost, the banker, who was then the agent for the Mitchell Wagon Company, and I requested him to ascertain the price and how soon the factory could deliver thirty-six wagons to be made as follows: Wagons to be built of the best materials and with a guaranteed capacity to carry 2,000 pounds over rough roads; the box to be four feet wide, six feet high, and twelve feet long, with a door on hinges in the rear end, that could be locked; the roof covering the bed to be made stationary, with sloping sides made of light boards and covered with heavy ducking; the driver's seat to be in front, outside of the box, like those on a Concord stage-coach, and placed where the brake could be controlled by the driver's foot.

All the thirty-six wagons were to be exactly alike, and numbered so that when loaded the contents of each could be specified on the bills of lading. The door in the rear was to be closed and locked after the goods were packed for the journey, and the roof was to secure them against thieves, but principally to protect them from the weather when in transit.

In due time Colonel Frost received a satisfactory reply from the wagon factory with reference to the order, and about the same time a communication came to me from Messrs. Kedelson & Degetau, of Chihuahua, stating that an engineer corps had surveyed and established a line for a railroad from El Paso to Chihuahua, and that the company was then negotiating for land belonging to Governor Terrazas and Henry Mueller. The company had also deposited a bonus of $200,000 as a guarantee that the road would be completed to Chihuahua inside of three years.

Fortunately the information reached me opportunely, otherwise we would have placed our order for the wagons and possibly other expenses might have been incurred. I was thankful that unnecessary outlays had been averted, but my disappointment was irritating, because I had planned and expected to perfect one of the largest freighting enterprises in the West. In ten years I could have made the business profitable in many ways, and at the same time our trains would have saved the merchants of Chihuahua an incalculable amount of expenses. But the "Rapid Transportation Company" was only a vision that ended like a dream before its name became known to the public. Froboese and I continued to run our regular freighting business separately, as before, until we entered into a partnership in other enterprises that continued for years.

Chapter Twenty-Two:

Revolution in Chihuahua—General Ord—
Final Trip to Chihuahua—Chloroform

I was accompanied on my last trip to Chihuahua, in 1876, by Mrs. Santleben and our two children, Sophie, now Mrs. Ed. McAllister, and Carlotta, who died in early childhood. Dr. Rufus Watkins, of Corsicana, traveled with us from San Antonio, and Miss Emily Stienly joined our party at Fort Stockton, both of whom went through to Chihuahua. Miss Stienly, who is now Mrs. Garby, of San Antonio, traveled with my wife from Castroville to that point two years before, and had been visiting her sister, Mrs. Mary Arnold, the mother of Martin Arnold, Esq., of San Antonio.

Nothing occurred on our western journey that is worth noting except an adventure with a large rattlesnake that was discovered in a tarpaulin that was used for the children to play on when in camp. The night before, when in use, the snake crawled between the folds, and when taken up it was placed on the rear of Mrs. Santleben's ambulance. It remained there until we stopped for breakfast the next morning, when it was taken out to be spread as usual for the young folks to romp on. As the folds were opened the snake dropped out, and considerable excitement followed until it was dispatched.

Before starting on this journey I received information that a revolution was brewing in the State of Chihuahua, and I was advised to travel the El Paso route, which is over three hundred miles further than that by way of Presidio del Norte, because I would avoid a wilderness of one hundred and forty miles, in which there was not a single habitation, that was dangerous in troublesome times; but the country along the other route was more thickly populated, and I could hope for protection or advice. I made a fortunate decision, because before I arrived at El Paso the revolutionary party, with Angel Treas at its head, had risen against the government, and he pronounced himself governor of the State of Chihuahua.

Orders awaited me at El Paso from Messrs. Kedelson & Degetau directing me not to cross the Rio Grande until I received further instructions. I was compelled to obey, because the freight, consisting of valuable goods, with which the fourteen wagons in my train were loaded, belonged to them. I moved my train to the table mountain southeast of El Paso, near Fort Bliss, and camped them there; but I engaged apartments for myself and family at the old El Paso Hotel, that was then kept by Mrs. Roman, where Miss Stienly and Dr. Watkins also secured rooms.

We remained in El Paso forty-five days under a heavy expense. In the meantime the war was going on between the regular troops and the revolutionists, until the latter were badly defeated in a battle that was fought near the city of Chihuahua, in which the gallant General Paralta, of the Mexican army, was killed. The rebels were driven to their strongholds in the southern part of the State and eastward to the Rio Grande, where Treas held possession of Presidio del Norte and the country in that direction.

Messrs. Kedelson and Degetau informed me of the state of affairs, and instructed me to cross the river and hasten forward with my train as quickly as possible before the revolutionists could rally. I lost no time in obeying their orders, and after passing through the American and Mexican custom-houses, made a quick trip to Chihuahua without being molested, and arrived with everything in good condition, including Mr. Cordero's property, which I delivered to his agents.

Among the friends who welcomed me was Mr. Moye, a brother-in-law of Governor Tarrasas, who was absent.

He kindly placed the governor's house and servants at my disposal, and I occupied it with my family during the seventeen days that I remained in the city. The time was spent pleasantly, and the attentions we received were appreciated.

The delay was occasioned by the anxiety of the merchants to get their money out of the country on account of the unsettled condition of affairs, and the fear of losing it should the revolution gain strength. The insurgents had captured Henry Mueller, the millionaire and father-in-law of Emil Kedelson, before the battle took place in which Paralto was killed. He was taken to the mountains near Santa Lorenzo, and a ransom of twenty-five thousand dollars was demanded from his family, which was paid, and he returned home before my departure.

My stay in Chihuahua was attended by an enormous outlay on account of the scarcity of forage and provisions caused by the disturbances in the country. The hay that was fed to each mule cost about fifty cents per day, and corn was sold at twelve dollars a fanega. The supply was limited even at those prices, and their feed was much less than it should have been preparatory for hauling their heavy loads homewards.

I was compelled to return by way of El Paso, because Angel Treas still held possession of Presidio del Norte; and I started back with the largest amount of money and copper that was ever brought from Chihuahua. I carried three hundred and fifty thousand dollars in Mexican silver, for which I received two and a half per cent, or $8,750; and forty thousand pounds of copper, the freight on which was five cents a pound, or two thousand dollars. These sums added to the charges on 75,000 pounds of up freight made a total of $17,500 that I received for my round trip.

The great sum of money placed in my care made it necessary for me to protect my customers' interests as

much as possible, and for that purpose I engaged the services of Captain Maximo Aranda, who had made himself
conspicuous in his opposition to the revolution. I paid
him one thousand dollars to escort my train to El Paso
with his thirty men, and he performed his duty faithfully. Captain Aranda, who then owned a large stock ranch
seventy-five miles southeast of El Paso, in Mexico, at a
place called Conta Recio, was well and favorably known
in El Paso, Texas, where he once served as a guard under
Mr. Mills when he was United States customs-house officer at that place.

After crossing the Rio Grande at El Paso we traveled
down the north bank of the river a distance of ninety
miles, to Fort Quitman, where we took the road for Fort
Davis. About twelve o'clock that night, when twenty miles
beyond the fort, a party of six men came up with us, who
told me that they had in their possession twenty-four
thousand dollars in silver coin, that had been sent to me
from Chihuahua, but they had no writing to show from
the person who sent the money. The captain, who was in
charge of the party when they started, had received instructions from the owner, and knew to whom the money was consigned, had been captured by the revolutionists. He, with two of his men, visited a ranch on the way
with the intention of buying something to eat, but got
into trouble, and when the others realized the danger
they made their escape with the money. With no other knowledge than that the coin was to be delivered to
me in Texas, they hastened to overtake me. They might
have proven unfaithful to their trust, because I learned
afterwards that the owner never could find out what became of the men, and thought that, probably, they were
killed or captured by the rebels, until he learned through
me that they had honestly performed their duty. I took
the silver in charge, without giving the men a receipt,
and conveyed it to San Antonio, where I kept it in my
house for months, awaiting information from Heick &

Helfrisch, of Galveston, to whom I communicated all the facts.

When I arrived at Fort Davis I ascertained that Angel Treas and a majority of his followers had been driven out of the State of Chihuahua, and that he, with some of his men, passed the fort a few days before on their way to San Antonio. I was cautioned by my friends, Captains Quinby and Stibers, who were stationed with their companies at Fort Davis, to be very careful, by avoiding unnecessary risks, as it was widely known that I was carrying a large sum of money on my train, and it was not improbable that the outlawed revolutionists would attempt to capture it at some point on my route. They advised me to ask for an escort, and when I did so, a telegram to that effect was immediately sent to General Ord, the commandant of the Department at San Antonio, who approved my request by ordering that an escort of twenty-five men under an officer should protect me to Fort Stockton.

The detachment, with two wagons, accompanied me to that point, and another guard was furnished from there to Fort Concho, where similar orders had been received, providing the same number of soldiers to go with me to Fort McKavitt, and from there it was arranged that the escort with their outfit should go through to San Antonio.

The good behavior of all these detachments deserves commendation, and I could not help feeling more than grateful for the interest they manifested in guarding my train. The generous protection of the government, through its officers, insured the safety of my charge and relieved me of the anxiety I would otherwise have felt. But I had no opportunity to show my appreciation, in a substantial way, except to the last detachment, who guarded me to San Antonio. When they were preparing to return to their post I presented them with two boxes of good cigars and a cask of Budweiser bottled beer, including a dozen glasses, which they highly appreciated. I visited General Ord, at his headquarters, soon after my arrival, and expressed my thanks for the kind assistance he had rendered me. I had reason to value the favor shown me because mine was the first overland train on that route for which an escort was ever furnished.

I talked quite a while with the general, and at his request gave him all the information I could with reference to the revolution in Chihuahua that was headed by Angel Treas, who had visited the general a few weeks before my arrival. I never saw Treas myself, but was told that he was a fine-looking and well-behaved man.

I remained in San Antonio eight days, during which time the well-known banker, Mr. Lockwood, arranged with me to convey to Galveston an additional fifty thousand dollars, in Mexican silver, which he had boxed for shipment to New York, where it commanded a higher premium than the seven per cent he had paid. I accepted the responsibility and placed the sum with the three hundred and fifty thousand dollars I brought from Chihuahua and loaded the amount on four wagons, each of which was drawn by ten of the best mules picked from my herd.

I started from San Antonio at nine o'clock p.m., with thirteen men, including myself, five of whom were drivers, with an extra man as guard on each wagon, and two others rode with me on horseback. We were all armed with Winchester carbines and six-shooters, and felt that if there was any significance attached to the unlucky number "thirteen" we were well prepared to meet contingencies. Mr. Lockwood was present, and looked a little uneasy when the wagons pulled out of the yard, on Dallas Street, where I was then living; but after seeing the preparations I had made for the safety of my train, and the number of armed men that guarded it, he was satisfied and remarked "That looks all right."

We traveled from nine o'clock that night until daylight before stopping to rest the teams and eat breakfast. We waited until ten o'clock before hitching up, and arrived at Kingsbury, east of the Guadalupe River, about three o'clock that evening. I chartered a box-car from Captain Cook, the railroad agent at that point, and the money was unloaded into it before dark. I had arranged to take five men with me in the car, and after securing my six passes we started for Galveston, but did not arrive there until two o'clock the following evening. The $350,000 that I brought from Mexico was consigned to Messrs. Heick and Helfrisch and was delivered immediately, likewise the fifty thousand dollars belonging to Mr. Lockwood, to the bank to which it was consigned.

I told Messrs. Heick and Helfrisch all about the twenty-four thousand dollars that had been delivered to me under such peculiar circumstances and informed them that I had left it in my house in San Antonio where I was holding it for identification. I also notified them that I had sold a half interest in my train to Henry Vonflie, who would accompany the wagons thereafter, because I had other business to attend to, and it was probable that I had made my last trip to Chihuahua.

Three months later Messrs. Heick and Helfrisch informed me that a firm in Chihuahua had requested them to solicit information from me regarding twenty-four thousand dollars they had forwarded to me after I left Chihuahua, as they were unable to trace any of the parties to whom it was entrusted, and it was probable that if they did not deliver it, they were killed by the revolutionists. The uncertainty with reference to it and my failure to report its receipt, made them fear it was lost, because all the other merchants who forwarded money through me received correct returns from their consignees, and they hoped that I could throw some light on the subject. Messrs. Heick and Helfrisch immediately relieved their anxiety by communicating the facts as I had related them, to which they replied giving the necessary instructions for its disposition, and I forwarded the money by express from Kingsbury to their agents in Galveston, who paid the full amount of my charges. Although I had other transactions with Messrs. Heick and Helfrisch afterwards, this is the last time they will be mentioned. Mr. Helfrisch is dead, but as Mr. Heick is now a prosperous merchant in Abilene, Texas, he will testify to the truth of my statements.

After the twenty-four thousand dollars was taken to my house, a lot of bonded goods in my care was placed in the same room and the key was given to Mr. Ogden, the father of Charles Ogden, Esq., then United States revenue agent in San Antonio, who knew all about the money. But I took no chances on that account, and saw that it was properly guarded until the responsibility ceased.

I was certainly pleased at the prospect of being relieved of the money that was turned over to me in the wilderness under such mysterious circumstances after months of careful watchfulness. Fortunately Mr. T. Monier was making preparations to start for Kingsbury with his train the following day, and after making arrangements with him to haul it to that point I sent the money to his house on Zavala Street early in the morning by Henry Wagenfuhr, a trusty drayman. In the meantime I learned that certain persons in San Antonio had found out in some way that the money was moved, and were planning to rob Monier's house, but fortunately for them they did not put in an appearance, because arrangements had been made to give them a warm reception. Charges were made against the guilty parties before the grand jury, of which Henry Elmendorf was foreman, but the matter was finally dropped.

This last trip to Chihuahua was the longest and most expensive in my experience. It was commenced on the 10th of July, 1876, after loading my wagons in Luling, and it did not end until I returned from Galveston, seven months thereafter. In the meantime I had unloaded the copper on my wagons in San Antonio, on the 11th of January, 1877, and the money at old Kingsbury, nine days later.

The gross income that I received on the trip was over seventeen thousand dollars, and my total expenses amounted to over fourteen thousand dollars, consequently I only netted about three thousand dollars as a compensation for all my hardships and disappointments. But for the enforced delays I would have received profitable returns from it, and also from a second trip I might have made in that length of time.

Dr. Watkins remained in Chihuahua, but our party was increased by the following persons, who returned with us to San Antonio: Mr. Markt, a retired merchant of Chihuahua, his wife and five children, who now reside in Medina County; a son of Mr. George McManus, and Henry Fischer, a nephew of Henry Mueller. These, with my own family and Miss Stienly, enlarged our company to fifteen persons, and our associations were pleasant throughout the journey.

The only unpleasant incident of the trip occurred in connection with one of my men soon after leaving Chihuahua. Francisco Ruiz was a confidential driver to whom I entrusted the care of a brick of gold valued at two thousand dollars. A short time after receiving it he became afflicted with nervous prostration, which affected his mind, and when I attempted to recover possession of the gold brick I could get no satisfaction from him in regard to its hiding place, but I continued to look for it until it was found. The poor man had completely lost his mind, and for seven days he ate but little and never slept. He never lay down, and a constant watch was kept over his movements, but nothing could be done to relieve him until the eighth day, when I tried an experiment which restored him to a normal condition.

He was sitting near a camp fire, with several of his companions, about eight o'clock at night. His head was resting in his hands and he was crying. I determined to quiet him, and if possible, put him to sleep. I saturated a towel with chloroform and placed it slowly under his face, where I allowed it to remain until he went to sleep. Captain Aranda and Henry Vonflie, of Briar Branch, laid him down and put something under his head that served as a pillow. He slept about two hours, and when the effects began to wear off I administered more chloroform. About three o'clock in the morning we persuaded him to get into a wagon where he would be more comfortable. He then asked for more of the sweet-smelling medicine and I gave him some on a handkerchief, but not enough to hurt him. He fell asleep before I left him and an hour later the train started. When we camped at nine o'clock Ruiz was well rested and he talked very sensibly. He commenced searching immediately for the gold brick that I had trusted to his care, but I told him it was useless, as I had it in my possession and showed him the place where I found it. No indication of his disorder was perceptible, and after we crossed the river, at El Paso, he was again able to drive his team.

He continued his services as a driver with the train until a year later, when on his way to Chihuahua. He then had a similar attack, which came on him in a camp three miles east of the Nueces River, on the El Paso road. He died almost instantly, and was buried the following morning at that place. His grave can yet be seen, and it is a satisfaction to know that I can identify it and testify to his worth.

He left a wife and three children, who then lived in San Antonio on the Rock Quarry Road, in a small house south of Captain Smith's residence. I took care that his family should not suffer, by giving a standing order to my brother-in-law, Henry Wagner, for supplies at his store, and supported them for two years. At the expiration of that time I arranged with Telamantes to convey them with his train to Santa Rosalia, near Chihuahua, and when I last heard from them they were all alive and in comfortable circumstances.

Chapter Twenty-Three:

San Antonio Transfer Company—First Telephones—
Ill Health—New Rules At Eagle Pass—Betrayal

Before the Galveston, Harrisburg and San Antonio Railroad was completed to San Antonio I anticipated that important event by founding one of the first two transfer lines that were ever established in the city. Messrs. Berg & Bro. started the other at the same time when the road was opened for business, in 1877, and our individual wagons delivered the first commercial freight that was ever hauled into San Antonio over a railroad.

I could not give the business my personal attention because I was frequently absent with my train, and for that reason I entered into a partnership with Messrs. Wolfing and La Batt, who were then conducting a commission business on Market Street. We organized under the firm name of "The San Antonio Transfer Company," in 1877, and it was entirely under their control, except that I had a voice in the general management.

About that time telephones were being used as novelties, and we introduced the first instruments that were ever put in operation in San Antonio. The line was a private enterprise and the wire was stretched from our office nearly in a direct line to the freight office of the Galveston, Harrisburg & San Antonio Railroad depot by passing it over buildings and attaching it to trees or other objects. One phone was in our office and the other was attached to the desk of our shipping clerk in the depot, Mr. Ed. Dieselhorst, who now lives in San Antonio. They were not as perfect as those now in use, but they answered our purpose equally as well and they certainly gave satisfaction. The wonderful invention was then a curiosity, and as it excited a great deal of interest, many persons visited the office to test it personally. Its marvelous powers were commented on, but no one predicted that it would grow in favor until it became a necessity in the business and social world.

We secured a liberal patronage and the firm prospered, but soon afterwards Mr. La Batt sold his interests to Mr. Wolfing and withdrew from the firm. A new partnership was then formed under the name of Wolfing & Santleben and we opened our office in the old Odd Fellows' Building, on the corner of Houston and St. Mary Streets, where the San Antonio Transfer Company was run in connection with the commission business. After the transfer business was started I devoted the greater part of my time and attention to my freighting interests, but I became dissatisfied with the management of the new company and determined to dissolve partnership with Mr. Wolfing.

Mr. Ed. Froboese owned and was then running a large wagon-train, and as I had before offered to associate him with me in the "Rapid Transportation" business to Chihuahua, I proposed that he and I should establish a Mexican commission business in connection with our freighting service. I also suggested that if he would purchase Mr. Wolfing's interest in the transfer line we could combine all three enterprises under one management. He willingly entered into my plans, and when Mr. Wolfing was made acquainted with them, he reluctantly sold out his interest in the transfer company to Mr. Froboese, who entered into partnership with me in 1879 under the firm name of Froboese & Santleben. We conducted our business in the same office two years against continual opposition, but we met our competitors successfully by uniting our energies and concentrating all the resources at our command after the sale of our trains when freighting ceased to be profitable. We had been competing with

Messrs. Berg & Bro. all the time in a friendly way until John Monier, C. Villemain and Martin Muench entered into open opposition against our transfer line and then we all had to hustle for patronage. Fortunately our company was able to hold its own and in a short time our three competitors were willing to sell out to Froboese & Santleben at a reasonable price and quit the business; but their wagons were old and useless to us after we bought them, and our only returns were the worth of the irons.

Later on Mr. La Batt started an independent transfer line with four floats of Wilson & Childs make, but soon afterwards he proposed to consign his outfit to the management of the San Antonio Transfer Company and it was not long before we made the same arrangements with Messrs. Louis and Henry Berg, whereby we controlled their eight floats. Under our agreement Messrs. La Batt and Berg & Bro. were to receive a certain percentage of the net earnings of their twelve floats during the continuance of the contract. In this way we removed all competition and the San Antonio Transfer line was conducted to the satisfaction of all the parties concerned until we closed out our business, and at the same time we continued our Mexican commission enterprise as an independent concern in which Froboese & Santleben alone were interested. During eight months of the time Mr. Froboese was in Europe and the business was entirely under my control.

In 1882 felt the necessity of visiting Mexico for the benefit of my health, which had been seriously impaired after I gave up freighting five years before. I determined to visit the San Lucas Springs and made suitable preparations for the trip by providing an outfit with everything necessary for the comfort of my family, including my sister, who was also in bad health, and others who accompanied me on the expedition with expectations of pleasure and excitement.

The party consisted of Mrs. Santleben and my sister, Mrs. Mary Rheiner; a niece, Anna Weyel; my two nephews, Henry Wagner and Willie Rheiner; James Durham, now postmaster, business man and owner of the water-works at Sabinal; Ernest Hausman, now of San Antonio, and four servants. We started about the 10th of May and traveled leisurely in our four vehicles over the Eagle Pass route which, on account of my feeble condition, was made by easy stages.

We stopped at the Dolch Hotel in Eagle Pass and were welcomed by my old friend who had frequently entertained me on former occasions. Ten years had passed since I had visited the place or crossed the Rio Grande at that point, and many new rules and regulations had been introduced in the custom-houses, especially at Piedras Negras, with reference to travelers entering Mexico. These were known to me, but I thought I could avoid the exactions, vexations, and delays in my case by seeking a personal interview with the officials. Although scarcely able to make the exertion I crossed the river the day after my arrival, and visited the office of the Mexican custom-house, where I hoped to meet some of my old acquaintances, but those who received me were assistants and strangers. They were very civil and I was politely requested to state the purpose of my visit. I informed them that I wished to enter Mexico with my party and outfit without unnecessary delay, and that it was my intention to visit and bathe in the waters of San Lucas Springs with the hope of benefiting my health. They explained that it would be necessary for me to make an inventory of all my belongings, such as vehicles, animals, arms, and our three months' supply of provisions; and that an import duty of thirty per cent on their value would be levied, which when paid would be deposited to my credit with an understanding that the amount received on each of such entries as specified on the inventory, should be refunded when I again passed through the custom-house on my return. I thanked them for their courtesy and requested an interview with the officer in charge of the custom-house, who occupied an adjoining room, which was granted.

I walked in and after introducing myself, stated that I was an old frontiersman who once ran a stage line between San Antonio and Monterey when the custom-house at Piedras Negras was in charge of Nicolas Gresanto and his assistant, Pedro Morales, who were then and afterwards intimate friends of mine. I also told him that I had since freighted to Chihuahua and crossed the Rio Grande many times at El Paso and Presidio del Norte. When I saw that he appeared to be interested I talked about many prominent persons in Mexico, some of whom were my friends, who were well known to him, until I was agreeably interrupted by the appearance of Juan Muscos, the chief clerk of the custom-house, who to my knowledge had held the office for eighteen years, whom I recognized in a moment after he entered the room. He knew me instantly and immediately rushed forward to greet me. With his arms around me he told his chief that I was a very dear friend of his whom he had known since 1862. He then inquired of me what had brought me back to Mexico, but before I could answer, the officer had told him the object of my visit, and that as I wanted to arrange for my passage through the custom-house with as little delay as possible, he instructed his clerk to issue me a pass that would permit me to cross the river with my party and outfit at once.

The next day I crossed over, and after I drove up to the custom-house the ladies were invited to the residence of the officer in charge, where they were entertained by his family while an inventory was being made of our belongings, which were thoroughly examined and valued; but not a cent was exacted as a deposit on the valuation, and my verbal obligation was the only stipulation for the return of the animals and vehicles. Finally a pass was given me which stated that I was an old frontiersman and that as I was visiting Mexico for my health I and my party should be permitted to go wherever we pleased without being interfered with in our travels.

We left Piedras Negras about four o'clock in the afternoon and in about an hour and a half we arrived at Vieta, where we were welcomed by Jose Maria Perez, the principal owner of the town, who was a highly esteemed old gentleman. He was an old friend, who, in 1871, brought his infant son all the way to San Antonio because he wanted me to stand as his god-father. He was an uncle of Pedro and Nicanor Valdez, of Sabinas Station, who were then prominent in Mexico, and were also intimate friends of mine. I remained with him four days, and when I left he sent his son, a mounted custom-house officer, to escort us and extend his protection, because the country was unsafe on account of Indians.

Our next stop was at Santa Rosa, on the third day, where we were hospitably entertained by the Muenzenberger family for four days, and they were unremitting in their attentions, and I have every reason to feel grateful to them because they have always been my good friends. Mr. Muenzenberger died several years ago in El Paso, but his widow and sister-in-law now reside on Avenue B, in San Antonio. When we left we were accompanied by Anton Burgelman, with two men, who gave us additional protection until the morning after we passed Puerto Ovio, where two families were killed by Indians two days before. The next night we stopped at Luis Serna's ranch, within five miles of the spring, and the next morning we reached our destination.

San Lucas Springs is situated north of the Serna ranch in a rough cañon, due west from Eagle Pass and about one hundred and eighty miles from the Rio Grande. To distinguish it from hot springs in other localities, it is known as the cold spring, although the water is temperate, and it flows from a large and deep basin in the mouth of a cave, where it forms a brook which passes through the cañon. The curative properties of the water are well known, and many invalids visit the spring on account of the medicinal qualities it possesses, independent of the sulphur with which it is strongly impregnated.

I had little faith in the efficiency of the water and at first refused to bathe in it, but was overcome by the insistence of my wife and sister, and was surprised at the beneficial results I derived from it. It far surpassed my expectations, and I continued to improve after my first bath, which was repeated twice a day for six weeks, or until my health was entirely restored.

I had borrowed two cows from Mr. Serna and also bought a lot of hens to furnish my camp with milk and eggs, and they gave us an abundance during our stay. We passed our time pleasantly in camp and introduced many diversions. The day that Guiteau was executed we thought it was our duty to notice his foul crime, and when Durham formed us in line those with weapons fired a salute to express our approval of his fate. On account of Indians and to prevent a sudden attack a strict guard was maintained by sentinels who were stationed every night around the camp.

Mr. Serna had information of our intended departure from the springs, and the day we arrived at his ranch he had a sumptuous dinner prepared for our benefit. We expressed our appreciation of his hospitality by doing full justice to his entertainment, and we retain pleasant recollections of the many acts of kindness manifested in our behalf.

After I returned to San Antonio, much improved in health, Mr. Froboese and I decided to dispose of our business interests and invest in a cattle ranch. We sold our entire interest in the San Antonio Transfer Company and the Mexican commission business to Messrs. Berg and La Batt and soon afterwards our ranch was established on the Rio Frio in Uvalde County under the firm name of August Santleben & Company.

Although we had cut loose from all business entanglements in San Antonio we continued to feel an interest in the transfer company, and it was with sincere regret that we learned of its troubles. It seemed that they commenced in a disagreement with B. F. Yoakum, who I believe was at that time the general manager of the International & Great Northern Railway Company, and it led to the establishment of an opposition transfer line by Yoakum, who instituted it as a private enterprise. He bought six four-horse floats and turned them over to Mr. Orr, who had been a contractor on the International & Great Northern Railroad and owned a lot of horses, mules and wagons which were then idle. In a short time the San Antonio Transfer Company found that it could not compete with the methods that the new company introduced into their business, and Messrs. Berg and La Batt were compelled to sell out to them. The Orr Transfer Company then controlled the entire transfer business in the city, and it was run to suit the managers without reference to the wishes of their patrons. The principal cause of discontent was their refusal to pay the freight at the depots according to the custom that was established by Messrs. Berg and myself when the G. H. & S. A. depot was first opened.

I kept posted with reference to what was going on in San Antonio, and after Froboese and I realized that we had not only made a mistake when we went into the cattle business but were actually losing money on our investment, we determined to engage in other employment independent of the ranch. We soon found out that the merchants in the city were dissatisfied with the way the transfer business was conducted, and when some of them requested us to re-establish ourselves, I visited all the wholesale houses and made contracts with them to haul their freight at a stipulated price for two years. We ordered twelve floats from Wilson & Childs, and Froboese went to St. Louis to buy the necessary number of large Missouri mules that were required. Inside of two months our opposition line was in operation and Mr. Orr was immediately thrown out of business. Messrs. F. Groos & Company were the bankers for the Orr Transfer Company and they bought the entire property and sold it to us for eleven thousand dollars. We gave our notes for the amount, which was paid in less than two years out of our earnings.

When Froboese & Santleben took possession of the property, an inventory showed that they owned seventy-two floats and old wagons and one hundred and ten head of horses and mules. These numbers included their recent purchases and all the floats and animals that were formerly owned by every one of the defunct companies. From them the San Antonio Transfer Company selected forty of the most serviceable floats and seventy-five of the best animals with which to carry on its business. The remaining trucks were either stored away or sold as junk, and the surplus horses were placed on the market and disposed of as quickly as possible. It then ran forty odd floats with over one hundred animals.

Our company monopolized the transfer business of the city during the two years that it operated under the contracts with the merchants; but when the time expired competitors with from two to four wagons opposed us on all sides, and during the next four years we had the struggle of our lives. Among them was Mr. Louis Scheihagen, an old retired merchant, who started four floats, but after running them a while he sold them and his business to F. A. Piper, a prominent and successful merchant in Uvalde, Texas, who purchased largely from the leading commercial houses in San Antonio. His influence and standing secured him a certain patronage and made him a formidable competitor, and we saw the necessity of removing the opposition. We found that Mr. Piper favored a partnership, and an agreement was negotiated whereby he became associated with us in our business.

Under the arrangement that we perfected in 1892, Mr.
Piper purchased a half interest in the San Antonio Transfer Company at a fair cash valuation, and put in his four
floats and animals at cost as part payment. The San Antonio Transfer Company then expired, after an existence
of about fifteen years, when the new organization took
the name of the Merchants Transfer Company. But the
firm of Froboese & Santleben and also that of A. Santleben & Company, in which A. B. Frank and Max Krakauer
were interested, survived, because neither was connected with the new company.

The general management of the business was entrusted to Julius Piper, a brother of F. A. Piper, under the supervision of the stockholders; but it was not conducted to the satisfaction of all the parties concerned, and
a disagreement arose that made me wish that I was out
of the firm. Froboese and I discussed the business in the
presence of an employee of the house who had been befriended by me and in whom we both had confidence.
We decided that we would get out of the company and
re-establish the San Antonio Transfer line, but as Froboese was indebted to Mr. F. A. Piper for a considerable
amount of money and was not in a position to sell to
advantage, it was agreed that the subject should be left
open after it was settled that one of us should sell to
the other. The party who was present was thoroughly
acquainted with our affairs and we had every reason to
trust him because he was under many obligations to us;
but we afterwards learned that he was scheming to sev-
er our connection with the firm, and subsequently he
used his information to effect his purpose.

I was sick in bed at the time the Judas visited me and
submitted a plausible proposition in which he represented that Froboese wanted either to purchase my interest in the company or sell his own to me. He urged
that as I was unable to attend to the business I should
make Froboese my successor, and as I was then still

more inclined to sell and knew that he wanted to buy, I entertained no suspicions of a shady transaction until I ascertained afterwards that the proposition was made without Froboese's knowledge. The terms submitted for my consideration appeared to be free from entanglements, and I was so well satisfied that I agreed to dispose of my stock to Froboese at once. The next day a clerk was sent to my house with the necessary documents, which I signed when propped up in bed, thereby terminating my connection with the firm without any money being paid, and I was forced to institute suit for the amount.

That was the way I got out of the transfer business in San Antonio, after having spent many of the most active years of my life in its management. Froboese severed his connection with the company in a tragic manner a few months later when he realized that he was inextricably involved in debt. I then ascertained that he was financially mined when he purchased my shares in the transfer company, and that he had hypothecated them for their full value to protect his credit after encumbering all of his property for every cent it could carry.

I knew that Froboese owned considerable property, but I did not suspect that any of it was encumbered, nor do I believe that he intended to ill use me when he bought my shares on the strength of his credit, and I am confident that pressure was brought to bear by his creditors through the Judas who betrayed us both under the guise of friendship. It was a well-laid scheme to swindle us, and the hand that manipulated the triggers knew when to spring them when there was no means of escape.

This information disposes of the transfer business so far as I was concerned, but I have not noticed my connection with other private enterprises or political experiences during that period otherwise than in a bare reference. I will now call attention to them, and will first give an account of the street-sprinkling business, that has not been noted, in which I engaged long before I was identified with any local business in San Antonio.

The enterprise was instituted during the administration of Mayor French, under contracts with the city and merchants, to sprinkle the plazas and certain streets in San Antonio, also the main avenues leading to the depots after the railroads were completed to the city, under Mayors Callaghan's, Paschal's and Elmendorf's administrations. I purchased the first sprinkling outfits, of both the Miller and Studebaker patents, that were used in San Antonio, through Messrs. Staacke Bros., and introduced them for that purpose. These contracts were extended through a period of sixteen years, and then it were permanently interrupted by the San Antonio Water-works, Company, which secured an injunction to prevent the use of water from its hydrants. The city controlled the business afterwards, at its own expense, under an arrangement with the company, and doubtless it will continue to manage it to an indefinite period.

I had been connected more or less with politics for years, but I was never a candidate for an office until nominated and elected City Alderman of the Fourth Ward in 1890. The best evidence I can give of my services is the approval awarded me by my constituents, who were granted all their demands, and it is pleasant to remember that my associates, with Mayor Callaghan at their head, always seconded my efforts in their behalf. The only city ordinance that I can recall which originated at my suggestion, was the naming of Main Avenue, that for 150 years was known as Acequia Street. I was an alderman eighteen months, and when I resigned in August, 1891, to accept the office of Registrar of Votes for Bexar County, to which I was appointed under Governor Hogg's administration. I was succeeded by Mr. Thomas E. Dougherty, who served as alderman for the unexpired term.

The office to which I was appointed had been recently created, and after I was installed in September, 1891, my signature approved the first registration certificate that was ever issued in Bexar County. I held the office six years, in which time I served three terms for the county and three terms for the city, and when I resigned, in August, 1897, Captain Philip Shardein was appointed to succeed me.

I then entered into partnership with Joe Meyer and engaged in the produce business, on Houston Street, but I soon discovered that the business was unprofitable, and as it did not suit me I closed it out as soon as possible. In this connection I will notice the fact that soon after I disposed of my transfer business, in 1893, the partnership of Froboese & Santleben was dissolved, and a year later the firm of Santleben & Company discontinued the ranch business; consequently when I disposed of the produce business I was out of employment, and my natural inclinations led me again to engage in politics. I became a candidate for the office of Tax Assessor for Bexar County, in opposition to three other aspirants, and was defeated.

I supported Marshall Hicks, Esq., for Mayor of the city in the next political campaign, in 1899, and after he was elected I was offered, and accepted, the position of Superintendent of Streets and Sanitation. I held the office four years under Mayor Hicks' administration and that of his successor, Dr. Fred Terrell, who was appointed Mayor to fill the unexpired period of Senator Hicks' second term. The records of the Superintendent's office during my incumbency will bear inspection, and I know that my duties were honestly and properly executed; but the best evidence is noted in the credit the city received on account of its cleanliness throughout that period.

This was the last of the political offices I have had the honor to fill either by election or appointment, which occupied eleven and a half years of my life. Although I do not regret the time devoted to such employment I am convinced that if I had given the same attention to my personal affairs that was received by the public, my compensation would have been more remunerative and I might have spent the time more pleasantly. I do not believe that I lost any friends during my political career, although I opposed several with whom I was intimate, but never with bitter feelings.

The interest I felt in municipal affairs engaged me in politics more than personal aspirations, and I have manifested the same sentiment through aid extended to many public and private enterprises that have been started in San Antonio, under the belief that they would advance the city's prosperity; and among them I will notice the Opera House and the Lone Star Brewery. I believe that I was influenced by a laudable ambition and that the money was well spent, because it has encouraged me to do all I could towards helping to make San Antonio the greatest city in Texas.

I will now bring this subject to a close by saying that since the date on which my last political appointment expired I have engaged in many other business undertakings, but none of them could be considered as permanent enterprises, although it may be stated that I have continually held from two to three government contracts, each for a limited period, up to the present time.

Chapter Twenty-Four:

Claim Against The Government—126,000 Miles—
My Family

Before concluding those experiences in which I have
reviewed my humble services and other subjects of a
personal character, I will notice the settlement that re-
imbursed me for a part of my losses on the frontier. I
always believed that in the course of time I would be
paid for the mules that were stolen from me, because
the Federal Congress had made provision for such compensation and a Court of Claims had been organized in
Washington, D. C., for the purpose of considering the
evidence referring to Indian depredations on the exposed settlements of the United States. Numbers of such
claims had been filed, including my own, some of which
were for losses sustained in 1865, and the total amount
of those docketed represented many millions of dollars.

Some time after the Court of Claims convened in Washington, the judges ascertained that no headway was possible on account of the nature of the claims, which required close investigation through evidence that could
not be secured except at an enormous expense, consequently it became necessary to transfer the sittings of
the court to San Antonio and other central points near
the frontier. Provision was accordingly made by amend-
ing the law to allow the court to be moved from place
to place, so that the judges could make an exhaustive
examination into the merits of each case without incom-
moding the witnesses.

The first Texas city in which the court convened was San Antonio, in 1902, and there Judges Spooner and Palmer presided alternately until 1905, when the sessions were brought to a close. So far as I was able to decide, every claim that was presented before the court was impartially investigated and the evidence carefully considered with a view to do the claimants justice and at the same time protect the government against fraudulent or exorbitant charges.

The court held to the opinion that all the depredations that had been perpetrated on the southwestern frontier were committed by Mexican outlaws, from points west of the Rio Grande, and not by Indians, as represented, until positive evidence was offered that proved the contrary. My testimony was conclusive with reference to horses I saw in the possession of Indians in Mexico, bearing the brands of ex-Congressman Noonan, and other well-known ranchmen in Medina County. The fact was so well substantiated that it influenced the court to dismiss the assumption, and thereafter the justice of the claims was considered entirely on their merits.

Much of my time was occupied as a witness during the sittings of the court, because of my knowledge of events that transpired during the period in which all the depredations were committed. I only testified with reference to the facts and responsibility of the claimants from a disinterested point of view, and it was a pleasure to know that nearly every case in which my evidence favored the justness of the claim it was approved and paid. The proceedings of the court have been published, and the decisions will show that many claims were set aside as fraudulent, also that the court reduced the amount of damages specified in the original affidavit of every legitimate claim before a judgment was rendered.

My claim against the government for the value of mules that were stolen by Indians in 1871, was filed in Washington, D. C., in 1872, by my lawyers, Messrs. Eckford and Robertson, of San Antonio, whom I employed for a contingent fee. Afterwards I was represented, first by Judge Pray, next by Colonel Upson, of San Antonio, and then by Messrs. Wilson and McManus, of Washington City. When Mr. McManus died, in 1888, Mr. Wilson continued to represent me until Messrs. Werner and Schramm, of San Antonio, became my lawyers, in 1891, and Mr. Wilson was retained by them to attend to my claim in Washington. The case was in their hands twelve years and I became impatient at the delay which seemed as if it would be prolonged indefinitely. I had given them ample time before I employed Mr. Clark, an attorney in Washington, in 1904, to attend to the business for me. Six months afterwards when my case was called for trial, Mr. Clark secured a judgment in my favor; which amount was paid to me in full after deducting the attorney's fee that the law allowed for such services, and Mr. Clark made a satisfactory settlement with Mr. Wilson out of the amount he received.

The case was pending thirty-two years, and I have no doubt that the gentlemen who represented me at various times did all they could to bring it to trial, but they were hampered by contingencies and official delays which Mr. Clark was in a position to overcome. I was not under obligations to retain an attorney when I believed that my interests could be served to better advantage by another, and as the compensation was contingent, after bringing it to a settlement, I was not responsible to any of them for a fee except to Mr. Clark, who was a lawyer of high standing, and I made a satisfactory settlement with him. This explicit explanation is submitted for the purpose of counteracting any unfavorable criticisms which reflect upon my actions in the premises, that, I understand, have been put in circulation.

The tedious delays that the government imposed upon me, and others, were extended through an ordinary lifetime, and then its responsibilities were scaled below actual values, that prevailed when the losses occurred, before its constitutional obligations were discharged. But the amount I received was appreciated, though it was much less than I expected. The fact that my claim for losses of animals on the frontier was recognized by the Federal Court as having been perpetrated by Indians confirms my statements on the subject. It was only an incident in the past, that has been sketched in these reminiscences, but it recalls the active life with which I was associated, and leads me to sum up my travels as noted in my experiences with a view to accentuate my services.

I will only notice the distances covered by me between 1865 and 1880, and in these fifteen years I claim that I traveled a greater number of miles as a mail contractor and when staging and freighting than any man then living. This assertion is not made as a boast, but because the facts will confirm my exertions during those years.

I will first review my employment from January 1, 1866, until June 30, 1867, as a mail contractor when I drove a weekly stage from San Antonio to Eagle Pass, a distance of about one hundred and sixty-five miles, without missing a trip. I made seventy-eight round trips over the route, going and returning, each estimated at three hundred and thirty miles, or a total of twenty-five thousand, seven hundred and forty miles.

The stage that I always accompanied from San Antonio, Texas, to Monterey, Mexico, started on its first trip the first day of August, 1867, and the line was discontinued July 30, 1869. The distance between the two cities is five hundred and twenty-five miles, and I made forty-eight round trips of one thousand and fifty miles in each, or a total of fifty thousand, four hundred miles.

After abandoning my stage line, I engaged immediately in the freighting business, and from 1869 until 1880 ran a train of wagons from seaports and railroad stations in Texas, to the city of Chihuahua and other prominent places in Mexico, also to frontier posts in Texas. A reasonable estimate of my travels, during those eleven years, would amount to fifty thousand miles, and I believe the total would far exceed that distance if accurately estimated.

These three overland enterprises alone will sum up over one hundred and twenty-six thousand miles, or about five times around the earth, and if my journeyings during the other active years of my life were added, the totals would foot up much more. They were made through a wild and uninhabited country, over routes that were continually beset by savage Indians, who were inveterate enemies of the white race, and by equally lawless men who frequented the frontiers of Texas and Mexico. Though I risked my life continually on these travels and jeopardized all the property I possessed, besides much that was entrusted to me by others, I generally reaped a reward that compensated me for all the hardships and dangers I encountered. Although I sustained many losses in various ways on my own account, which aggregated a large amount, I can truthfully say that not one of my customers who entrusted money and merchandise to my care, or the Federal Government under my mail contracts, ever lost a cent through my negligence.

The value of freight that I transported to and from Chihuahua and other parts of Mexico, on my own wagons and under contract on other trains, amounted to millions of dollars. I will also state that I hauled more money from Mexico during that period, on stages and wagons, than any other person, the greater part of which was consigned to parties in Europe. No security was ever exacted to insure the safe delivery of money, and it was only necessary to give my personal receipt for large sums that were entrusted to me, or for freight, the greater part of which consisted of valuable merchandise.

The outlay on each trip that I made with my wagon-train was always heavy, and several times my profits were all consumed on account of unavoidable delays. I usually had from eighteen to twenty men in my employ, including several extras for service in cases of necessity, and tried to secure experienced and reliable persons, who were paid good wages in addition to their board. My wagon-master received $75 per month; my caporal $30; my drivers from $18 to $20; and my herders from $15 to $18. I also gave my stage drivers $60 per month and board when I ran the stage to Monterey. I will also notice that the firm of Froboese & Santleben, of San Antonio, paid the following liberal salaries to their employees: Their book-keepers received from $100 to $125 per month; their shipping clerks, at each of the depots, received $100 per month; and their float drivers, $1.50 per day. They were all competent men and earned wages that will compare favorably with the salaries allowed for such work since the advent of union labor organizations, which are trying to regulate such matters; and I want to correct an erroneous impression by saying that I am not opposed to labor unions in general, because I recognize that they have become necessary, but I have denounced those who advocate extreme measures or appeal to their strength, otherwise than through arbitration, to enforce their demands. In my opinion wages should be graded according to efficiency, and in every order members ought to be rated with reference to their qualifications and receive pay corresponding to their abilities. I always observed this rule in my business, and I never lost anything by paying worthy men good wages, because it was always cheapest in the end.

I often found destitute American citizens in Mexico, where they had no friends, and it was always a pleasure to aid those who solicited my assistance. I brought many of them back to Texas on my stage from Monterey, when the fare alone was $75, and paid their expenses all the way. Afterwards, when freighting from Chihuahua, I often did as much for Americans who were stranded in that region. I also brought many poor Mexican families to San Antonio, who were furnished provisions free of cost from the train. These never failed to express their gratitude, and there is a well-known and respectable Mexican woman, now living on the Castroville Road, near the crossing of Leon Creek, who came to Texas under such circumstances in company with thirty-five other emigrants. This woman now earns a support from a small store which she owns and manages, and she shows her thankfulness in various ways for the help I gave her about thirty-five years ago under the belief that she never can do enough for me or my family. Many similar incidents might be noticed in this summary of facts, but they would only prolong the story of my life unnecessarily, and I only call attention to these because it is a pleasure to recall them.

The subject has been confined to my personal experiences and those with whom I was associated, and I have only noticed incidentally a few members of my father's and my own families, but it was because I could not find a place in which to introduce the records referring to them. The information does not extend beyond the birth of my parents, because I remember nothing of their ancestry, and my references only include their descendants of the third generation.

My father, Christian Santleben, was born in Hanover, Germany, on the 27th day of July, 1809, and my mother, Sophie Haas, was born in the same city on the 25th day of October, 1810. They were married in said city on the 13th day of January, 1837, and it was their place of residence until they emigrated to America, in 1845. Three children were born to them in Hanover and two in Texas, whose names, with the dates of their birth and christening, are as follows: Christian, born January 20, 1838, and christened January 25, 1838; Wilhelmina, born May 22, 1842, and christened June 5, 1842; August, born February 28, 1845, and christened March 11, 1845; Mary, born July 8, 1850, and christened July 25, 1850; Ferdinand, born, 1852. My mother died November 30, 1886, and my father died March 11, 1889, at their home near Castroville.

My brother, Christian Santleben, married Wilhelmina Ammann, of San Antonio, in Castroville, on the 27th day of July, 1867, and the names of their children are as follows: Charley, Willie, Lena, Mary and Christian. He died in December, 1893.

My sister, Wilhelmina Santleben, married Henry Wagner, of San Antonio, on the 13th of July, 1863, and the names of their children are as follows: Mary, Henry, Gusta, Willie, Lena, Sophie, August, and Lizzie. Wilhelmina died July 28, 1883, in San Antonio.

I, August Santleben, married Mary Anna Obert, of Boerne, Kendall County, Texas, on the 30th day of December, 1870, and the names of our children are as follows: Sophie, Charlotta, Henry, August, Graves, Alfred and Ella.

My sister, Mary Santleben, married Peter Rheiner, of Uvalde County, in San Antonio, on the 1st of January, 1872, and the names of their children are as follows: Peter, August, Ferdinand, and Mannie. Mr. Rheiner died in 1878, and his widow married Charles Barnard, of Rochester, New York, in 1884, and Mary died in 1888.

My brother Ferdinand married Louisa Grosenbacher, in 1878, in San Antonio, and the names of their children are as follows: Emma, Mary, Dolly Bell, Eddie, Oscar, Johnny, and Alfred.

The offspring of the second generation number thirty-five souls, of whom twenty-six are now living, and several of them are married, who have a total of thirty-two children, six of them being my grandchildren by my daughter, Mrs. Sophie McAllister; consequently the living descendants of my parents at the present time number fifty-eight persons.

In this brief reference to the Santleben family I have stated all the facts that it is necessary to notice, and as my existence on earth is drawing to a close, it is suitable that I should introduce a latter posterity of my father's descendants before concluding this sketch of my life.

Mr. George Obert and his wife, Mary (the parents of my wife), came to this country in 1853, and settled in New Braunfels; the names of their children were Eva, Adam, Lizzie, Margaret, Valentine, and Mary (my wife).

The succeeding chapters are reminiscent of early times in west Texas and Mexico, and refer to historical and social conditions that no longer exist. Those who read them will, perhaps, appreciate the efforts that have done so much for civilization in the past and encourage the present generation to greater exertion towards improving the opportunities that the future offers for extending the territory tributary to San Antonio far beyond its present limits.

Chapter Twenty-Five:

Settlement of Castroville—First Colonists

The settlement of the northern and western regions of Texas was retarded many years by hostile Indians who opposed the advance of the white race into their hunting grounds. The enticing wilderness, extending from the Colorado River to the Rio Grande and covering an indefinite area northward which lured the American colonists by its attractions, was controlled by the Comanche tribe, whose habitations were on the headwaters of the Brazos. They were a brave, cruel and vindictive race numbering many thousands of warriors whose horsemanship was marvelous; and they roved at will over the immense territory which they were always ready to defend against trespassers, or gratify their thieving propensities by robbing those of their possessions who succeeded in gaining a foot-hold in that country.

When Anglo-American pioneers and colonists began to ignore all barriers and ventured to occupy the prohibited region in greater numbers they were checked by brutal murders and revolting outrages. The Comanches' fierce and bloodthirsty nature delighted in such crimes and they served to intimidate their determined enemies while satisfying an implacable vengeance. Experience had taught the native occupants of the soil in all parts of America the hopelessness of coping with their white adversaries in open warfare, and they undertook to oppose them through the horrors inflicted by the tomahawk and scalping knife. But such tragedies only restrained the timid, through the dread they inspired while they invoked the fearless to merciless retaliation, and a struggle commenced for mastery which led to a carnival of crime that threatened to destroy the hopes of those occupying the outposts of civilization.

For many years marauding bands of Indians swept down from their northern strongholds and spread destruction in the territory surrounding San Antonio, when that city was the only place of refuge in the western country. The population of the town in 1843 numbered less than two thousand, and their rude habitations were confined for safety to a small area in the vicinity of the public square. Wild Indians constantly hovered in the suburbs and frequently entered the town to depredate on the people, and occasionally they committed murder.

Such statements seem to be incredible, but several old residents of San Antonio are now living who have seen citizens killed by wild Comanches in the vicinity of the Post office. The fact will be more clearly emphasized by quoting from Henry Castro's diary, where he says that when his first colonists arrived in San Antonio in February, 1843, "no settlements existed west of San Pedro Creek to the Rio Grande." His enterprise attracted but little attention because no one in the town then thought that it was possible to establish a settlement such as he proposed. Nor was this opinion changed when they were joined by other immigrants during that and the following year. But a sensation was created when Henry Castro, in company with Louis Huth, appeared, on the 19th of July, 1844, and announced that it was his purpose to carry out his undertaking. He stopped at Antonio Lockmar's, on Soledad Street, "then the best house in the city," and while there, on August 26th, he says that "five or six Comanches came within two hundred yards of the house... and succeeded in capturing eleven mules that were grazing in the enclosure...Such acts of audacity on the part of Indians intimidated my colonists and tended to injure my enterprise."

Castro had not then seen the land that was specified in his grant, but a few days afterwards he went west with an escort of five men furnished him by the famous ranger captain, Jack Hays, which increased his party to twelve well-armed men, and spent several days in riding over a part of it. When the short-sighted citizens of San Antonio saw that he was determined to carry out his project they became alarmed at the idea of a town being established between them and the Rio Grande which would cut off the trade that came to them in dribbles from Mexico. With a view to hinder his plans they attempted to discourage his colonists and were aided by interested property owners who wanted their labor. But he overcame their selfish schemes and a few days later established the town of Castroville, where he settled his people, far beyond the limits of the most remote habitation. In the face of difficulties, with the aid of armed bodies of Texas Rangers who kept the Indians in check and guarded the outskirts of the settlements, he installed the first progressive enterprise that promised to develop the western country. These fearless citizen soldiers of Texas, to whom they were so much indebted, were always ready to pursue the raiders without considering the odds against them, and frequently inflicted retributive justice for their misdeeds when driving them back to their distant haunts. Posterity can not too greatly extol the memory of those gallant men in the service of the Republic, who constantly exposed their lives through their efforts to protect the frontier, and they deserve a monument in San Antonio that will commemorate their performances during that period.

The town of Castroville was founded on the Medina River, twenty-five miles west of San Antonio, on the 12th day of September, 1844, by colonists brought out from the Rhenish provinces by Henry Castro. On the same day Messrs. Louis Huth and G. S. Bourgois were elected Justices of the Peace and Louis Haas Constable by the authority of David Morgan, Chief Justice of Bexar County. In the morning of the same day the ceremony of laying the corner-stone of the church of Saint Louis was performed by the Rev. Bishop Odin, with the assistance of his grand vicar, the Rev. Abbe Oge, in the presence of all the little colony. The events of the day were celebrated that night with "discharges of musketry, bonfires and the usual libations."

The following day Bishop Odin departed for San Antonio and Mr. Castro accompanied him part of the way. Before they separated the Bishop gave him the following certificate:

> I, the undersigned, bishop of Claudiopolis, affirm to whom it may concern, that upon the invitation of Mr. H. Castro, who has received from the government of Texas a large grant of land in the county of Bexar, I visited, accompanied by Abbe Oge, of my diocese, his settlement, situated on the Medina River, twenty-five miles west of San Antonio de Bexar, to lay the corner-stone of the first Catholic church to be constructed in the first settlement of the said Castro, and that we placed the same under the invocation of Saint Louis. We have seen a good number of colonists at work building their houses with a view of forming a solid and permanent settlement.
>
> In faith of which I signed and affixed my seal to these presents.
>
> ODIN, B*ishop of Claudiopolis.*
>
> CASTROVILLE, Sept. 12, 1844.
>
> Seen for legalization of the signature of Odin, bishop of Claudiopolis.
>
> F. GUILBEAU,
> *French Consular Agent at San Antonio de Bexar.*

"This document, signed by Bishop Odin and dated Castroville, September 12, 1844, is no doubt the first time that the name Castroville was ever signed or printed, as it came into existence at that time" according to A. J. Sowell, *The Early Settlers and Indian Fighters of Southwest Texas*, p. 136.

The colonists proceeded immediately to provide shelters for themselves and families, which kept them constantly employed, and it seems that they did not have leisure to draw up and sign the following document until the twelfth day, though it was dated the day of their arrival:

Process verbal of the possession taken of the lands situated on the concession made to Mr. H. Castro by the Texas government, on the 15th day of February, 1842, situated in the county of Bexar, and other lands belonging to him.

We, the undersigned colonists engaged in France by Mr. H. Castro to participate in the advantages of the grant above mentioned within the limits assigned by the government of Texas, the terms of which are more particularly set forth in a contract passed between us and the said H. Castro, do declare:

That the said Castro having assembled us at San Antonio de Bexar as our leader, conducted us on that which had been assigned and given us by him, in consequence of which we left San Antonio on the 1st of September to go to the Medina River, twenty-five miles west, which place we reached on the 2nd instant. We declare that, independent of our contract and without any obligation on his part, Mr. H. Castro has made us the following advantages heretofore expressed, in order to facilitate to us our speedy settlement.

Here are the advantages above mentioned:

First. To each of us forty acres of land of his property on the Medina.

Second. The necessary transportation and our rations secured until our homes shall be constructed.

Third. Horses and oxen until our next crop.

Fourth. Bacon and corn to those who may want it until the next crop is gathered.

Fifth. The use of his milch cows.

We declare that Mr. John James, deputy surveyor of this district, came and surveyed the lots assigned to us. We declare since twelve days that we have reached our destination our labors, being well conducted, promise to give a comfortable shelter for ourselves and families within seven or eight weeks. We are satisfied, by the experience that we have acquired, that the climate of Bexar County is among the most salubrious, the water exceedingly good, timber sufficient, and the land appears to unite the qualities needed for great fertility. Such is the protection under which we have established ourselves and which forms the base of our hopes. We have unanimously resolved to name the town of which we are the founders Castroville.

Done at Castroville, on the Medina, in the county of Bexar, September the 12th, 1844.

Signed, Jean Batiste Lecompt, Joseph Haguelin, N. Rosee, Theodore Gentil, Auguste Fretelliere, J. S. Bourgeois, Zavier Young, Louis Huth, George Cupples, Charles Gonibund, J. Fairue, N. Forgeaux, P. Boilot, C. Chapois, J. Maeles, Leopold Menetrier, Michel Simon, Theophile Mercier, Anthony Goly, Louis Graff, G. L. Haas, Joseph Bader, Bertold Bartz, Charles de Montel, Sax Gaspard, J. Ulrich Zurcher, George Spani.

Certified to at Castroville, September the 12th in the year 1844.

G L. HAAS, *Constable.*

Louis Huth and J. S. Bourgeois, Justices of the Peace.

Republic of Texas, county of Bexar. I, the undersigned, do hereby certify that Louis Huth and J. Simon Bourgeois are justices of the peace and G. L. Haas constable of Castroville in this county.

Given under my hand and official seal at San Antonio de
Bexar, this the 5th day of October, A. D., 1844.

DAVID MORGAN,
Chief Justice of Bexar County.

Seen for the legalization of David Morgan's signature,
the consular agent for France ad interim.

FAUTREL AINE.

Recorded by T. H. O'S. Addicks on the 7th day of October,
A. D., 1844, in the records of Bexar County.

Several shiploads of colonists had arrived before the
settlement was made at Castroville, but evidently the
signatures in the foregoing list represent the heads of
families of all that were present on that occasion. Some
were then on the way, and they continued to arrive until
1847. A complete list of the colonists that were brought
out by Castro was transmitted to the Secretary of State
immediately after the arrival of each vessel, and they
are supposed to be on file in that office in Austin. The
following family names are all of those who settled in
Castroville between the years 1844 and 1850 that I can
recall: Rien, Tunder, Eldiero, Bowl, Sharp, Magilien,
Kichley, Criesly, Varnet, Ichhorn, Riechheartzer, Halde,
Hans, Grimwald, Meny, Bentely, Huechler, Frauger, Ful-
mer, Drougheorst, Inchin; Schmitt, whose two sons, Emil
and Louis, are living; Johanes Loesbeog; Burger, whose
sons, Louis, Robert and Joe, survive; Trawalter, whose
sons reside in San Antonio; Vollmer, father of John and
Jacob; Conrad, father of Peter and Joe; Biedeger, father
of Joe and Jack; Huehner, father of August and Mrs. Louis Huth, Sr., of San Antonio; Vonflie, father of Henry
Vonflie, of Briar Branch; Steinley, who has a son living
in Dunlay; John Buser, who has a son living in San Antonio, and family; Halde and family; John Kreisle and family; Walter, who has six sons residing in San Antonio;

Alberdie and family; Drodcour and family; Eldise and family; Mangold, whose three sons, George, Jacob and August, reside in Medina County; Tschierhart, whose six sons, Emil, Joe, Louis, Nic, Henry and Sebastian, reside in Medina County; Schwendeman and family; Dreier and family; Andrew Keller and family; Jacob Pippert, father of Jacob, John, Fritz, Dave, Emil, Mrs. Tuerpe, and Mrs. Zoller; Zimmerman and family; Hoak and family; Berry, father of Jack, Joe and August.

After the town site of Castroville was surveyed into lots and the people were settled in their new homes the business of its citizens was directed to varied industries. The church, a school house, a saw and grist mill, a brewery and stores, etc., were built, and in a few years evidences of prosperity were perceptible in the community. The following list will show who were the first business and professional men who located in the village when it was a frontier settlement:

The first Roman Catholic church and the first Lutheran church west of San Antonio were built in Castroville.

The first Catholic minister was the Rev. Father Dubuis and the first Protestant minister of the Lutheran denomination was the Rev. Mr. Offinger.

The first survey of land west of the Medina River was made by Mr. John James, of San Antonio.

The first school teacher was August Kamp, who was afterwards County Clerk of Medina County for fifteen years. He was the father of Aug. Kamp, Jr., the present County Clerk of said county.

The first store and brewery was established by Louis Huth, who was one of the two first Justices of the precinct, and he was first County Clerk after Medina County was organized.

The first corn mill and cotton gin was owned and operated by Louis Haas, the first Constable of the precinct.

The first bakery and dance hall was owned and conducted by Hichling.

The first meat market and boarding house was opened by Mr. Crust, the father-in-law of C. Villemain, who is San Antonio's present City Tax Collector.

The first hotel was opened by Mr. Dardie.

The first physician was Dr. Hoffman.

The first lawyers were Judge Noonan and Colonel Upson.

The first sheriff of Medina County was Thomas B. McCall.

Although the name of Castro was thus honored by the people with whom he was personally associated, and though the State of Texas has perpetuated his memory in an act of the legislature which gave his name to one of the northern tier of counties in recognition of the benefits he conferred on the Republic in the most trying period of its existence, no effort has been made to eulogize his services to the extent that they deserve.

We know what Stephen F. Austin and his colonists and others did towards braving the dangers and hardships of the wilderness, and afterwards when they secured their freedom and established the Republic of Texas. Their fortitude and bravery deserve all honor and praise, and the statesmanship which laid the foundation for a great commonwealth will receive consideration in all ages; but those who came afterward and gave strength to the community, as producers or otherwise, especially those who placed themselves in the van of civilization near the more exposed western border where they opened the way for others, should not be forgotten.

The most prominent of the latter class was Henry Castro, and we are constrained to believe that the territory west of the Guadalupe River is more indebted to his personal perseverance, energy, and liberal expenditure of wealth, than to any other individual that appears in history. In a short period after settling his colony west of the Medina River he did more towards promoting the material prosperity and safety of the country by giving value to property in that region than had been done in the previous one hundred and twenty-eight years of its occupancy.

Castro brought to Texas a total of five thousand two hundred desirable colonists, or, according to another statement, four hundred and eighty-five families and forty-five single men, on twenty-seven ships, in five years, and settled them beyond the western limits of the most remote white settlements, on land granted him by the Republic of Texas in 1842, in that portion now comprising part of Medina, Uvalde, Frio, Atascosa, Bexar, McMullen, LaSalle and Zavalla counties. These people were transported across the ocean and conveyed to their destination at his own expense, and he not only complied with his contract in every particular with regard to the donation of land, but he added forty acres and a town lot to the allowance of each family, and assisted them out of his means in every possible way until they were able to provide for themselves. He injected his own spirit into them, and encouraged them and others to occupy the desirable wilderness beyond until the western frontier was extended to the Nueces River.

This man was born in France in July, 1786, of wealthy Hebrew parents, and he could claim a descent from one of the oldest Portuguese families. He was a soldier under Napoleon until his overthrow, when he emigrated to the United States, and in 1827 he became an American citizen. He returned to France, in 1838, and engaged in the banking business as a partner of Mr. Lafitte. Later he undertook to colonize the large grant of land in Texas that was awarded him at his own solicitation, after exerting himself in General Henderson's behalf to negotiate a loan of $7,000,000 in France for the young Republic which interested him in its fortunes; and his services in that connection secured him the honorable appointment of Consul-General of the Republic of Texas for the Kingdom of France.

The concession and distinction were conferred on account of his natural abilities and wealth, which commanded great influence in commercial circles and which were extended to the government. He was not an ordinary man, otherwise he could not have persuaded so many persons to abandon their homes and associations in the old world and take up their abode in a wilderness among savages with a confidence that was based entirely on his promises and representations.

In a letter written to the President of the Republic of Texas, at Washington-on-the-Brazos, on January 14, 1844, he refers to serious obstacles he had encountered and overcome, and also to the large sum of money, amounting to $40,000, which he had expended up to that date. Castroville was not then established and evidently he distributed a much larger sum in carrying out his enterprise, which, when added to his generous distributions to all who needed assistance, exhausted his means and encumbered him with debts that impoverished him in his old age. He died at Monterey, in Mexico, when on his way to visit the graves of his relatives in France, and not one of his immediate family is alive.

Texas has worthily perpetuated the memory of many of her citizens who have conferred honor and benefits on the commonwealth. A similar sentiment has prompted communities in Texas to erect memorials to prominent individuals as an evidence of gratitude, and the spirit that suggested them should be encouraged, because hundreds have and will live who deserve such monuments.

When the descendants of the first settlers within the limits of Castro's colony learn to appreciate Henry Castro's character and begin to realize the importance of his efforts, they will petition the State to show him reverence by removing his remains from their obscure resting-place in a foreign land and entomb them in the State cemetery at Austin. Then perhaps a marble statue will be erected in San Antonio, the metropolis of Texas, which has been so greatly benefited by his energies and wealth. When such a movement is inaugurated I will gladly show my respect for his memory by contributing to the fund, because of my gratitude for many favors that he conferred on my father, who, though not one of his colonists, was intimately associated with him.

Chapter Twenty-Six:

History of Medina County—
Settlements and Settlers

Castro's land grant covered an area of several thousand square miles between the Medina and Nueces Rivers, which bounded it on the east and west. The country within these limits lies among the foot hills of the Rocky Mountains, in Medina and Uvalde counties, and spreads out on the plains below. Several spurs that jut out from the range of mountains further north represent its roughest portion, but their rugged sides are beautifully clothed with evergreens, and between the elevations are wide valleys of rolling or level lands covered with succulent grasses and groves of forest trees in endless variety. Sparkling streams and rippling brooks of crystal water meandered through them and added to the charms of that region until they escaped into the open country southward. The highlands, lying in plain view a few miles north of the Southern Pacific Railroad, mark the outlets of the cañons in which there are now many villages and numerous prosperous homes of farmers and ranchmen.

Further southward the land is rolling with occasional level prairies that formerly were carpeted with perennial flowers mingled with luxuriant verdure, but now the greater part is covered with mesquite brush and occasional mots of live-oak or other timber. The country was then well watered by a number of tributaries with seemingly an inexhaustible flow of water which emptied into the river on its borders, and all of them were lined with belts of pecan or other large forest trees. The land generally is fertile, and the numerous attractions that the country presented led many pioneers to settle there when the Indians were dangerous. In recent years thousands of home-seekers have bought up and divided the land that was owned in large bodies by ranchmen and speculators, who have demonstrated on their smaller holdings that the soil is unsurpassed for agricultural purposes. These facts in connection with the present prosperity of the country, will be enlarged upon later. A number of flourishing towns with substantial business houses, beautiful residences, churches and educational institutions, where the usual occupations are represented and all modern conveniences have been introduced, are found in that region.

In addition to this vast territory Castro controlled a tract of land containing sixteen leagues, which was bounded by the Medina River on the west, and fronted his grant on the east above and below Castroville. This body of land was secured from John McMullen, of San Antonio, through private negotiations, to prevent its occupation by others who might have come in conflict with his enterprise, and it was a part of his scheme to colonize it also after establishing the settlements under his contract.

Many glowing descriptions have been written about Texas when the country was in a primitive condition, and that part west of the Medina River has received its share of praise. A more attractive region did not rest under the dome of heaven, and as I remember it when in a natural state, it is my opinion that the representations so frequently made are not exaggerations. Myriads of wild horses roamed the prairies at will, deer were everywhere and other game was abundant; the clear, running streams were full of fish, and quantities of honey in caves and hollow trees waited those who cared to take it.

A natural supposition suggests that with such an abundance of nature's provisions at the disposal of Castro's colonists a scarcity of food was impossible; but strange to say they sometimes lacked a sufficiency the first few years. The fact that the new settlers had been raised in towns and thickly settled districts and knew nothing about hunting wild animals will explain the situation. Besides, very few brought guns with them, and only a small quantity of ammunition, none of which was suitable for killing large game or defense against Indians. With the exception of a few who were in prosperous circumstances they were destitute of money, consequently their only dependence for ammunition was on the Rangers, who occasionally gave them small supplies until their condition improved. The Rangers also relieved their necessities by killing and delivering large game, and they also relied for food on the Lipan and Delaware Indians, with whom they traded until the former became hostile, but of course many helped themselves as they gained experience.

Even if the emigrants had been well equipped they could not have been compared with the American pioneers accustomed to frontier life and who were expert shots with the excellent rifles they always carried; therefore the colonists were at every disadvantage and almost helpless, individually and as a body, in their exposed situation. Castro had taken preliminary steps to protect his people by representing the situation to the government, with the result that Captain Jack Hays, who was stationed at San Antonio, was ordered to protect them with his company of Rangers. The efficient service they rendered kept the Comanches from destroying the settlement in its infancy, although they continued their depredations at intervals.

My recollections of the country extend back to a period when it was very sparsely inhabited by small communities wide distances apart. In order to convey a comprehensive idea of the subject I will first locate each settlement west of San Antonio, with the date and names of those who made them, and then I will give similar data with reference to those north and northwest.

The first settlement, four miles west of the city on the San Antonio and El Paso road, was made in 1850, by William Waldenpalt, where Herd Johnson's grass farm is now situated. He started the first dairy farm there, from which the first milk was sold in the city. It was on Leon prairie, which extended from the Alazan Creek, near San Antonio, to within one mile of Leon Creek, or about five miles in width from east to west, and it was between ten and fifteen miles long. Then it was bare of trees and covered with native grasses that grew about two feet in height, but in later times a growth of mesquite brush made its appearance.

Five miles beyond the dairy farm was a settlement that Placito Olevirra and Cetro made, in 1844, on Leon Creek, shortly after Castroville was established. The latter was the foreman of the Nat Lewis horse and cattle ranch, which was projected soon afterwards on Leon prairie.

The Lewis ranch became well known, and the "No" brand of Don Louis al Pelon, which was a popular title that distinguished the owner, was familiar to everyone in west Texas. During the years in which it flourished many poor families of settlers within fifteen miles of San Antonio earned a support by milking the Lewis cows with his consent, some of them as many as twenty-five head. They sold butter and cheese in the San Antonio market and fattened their hogs on the sour milk. Until 1860 the Lewis ranch owned a greater number of horses and cattle than any other in western Texas, and they were mostly raised on Leon prairie. He and his excellent wife, who resided in San Antonio, were always ready to extend their hospitality to strangers, and their liberality in helping the poor was known to me, because we lived as neighbors in said city for many years, and they were my best friends. Their two sons, Messrs. Nat and Dan Lewis, are now prominent citizens in San Antonio.

Five miles west of Leon Creek is Arroyo Medio, which was first settled in 1850, by Noah Bowles, who was an old friend of my father and they were neighbors when they lived on Castro's ranch.

Four miles further is Potranco Creek, which was first settled, in 1850, near where it empties in the Medina River, by Billy Lytle, a brother of Sam Lytle and an uncle of John Lytle, a well-known ranchman who owned large herds of horses and cattle that were recognized by the L brand.

Two miles beyond is San Lucas Springs, that was settled in 1850 by the Adams family, represented by the following seven brothers: John, Bill, Dave, James, Pete, Mart, and Henry. They also owned large herds of horses and cattle in the JA brand.

Four miles further west is Saus Creek, that was first settled in 1854 by Samuel Etter, Sr., who engaged in farming as a business, and also raised cattle on a small scale.

On the same creek, and adjoining Mr. Etter's, was my father's farm, which he settled in 1855, where he resided until the date of his death.

Four miles beyond is the town of Castroville, on the west bank of the Medina River, that was settled in 1844.

Ten miles west of Castroville on the San Antonio and El Paso road is Hondo Creek, where a settlement was made, in 1855, by the Harper, Burnet, Benian, and McLamore families.

Four miles above, on the same creek, is the town of Quihi, where the first settlement was made, in 1846, by Louis Bailey, Jack Reef, Sardoff, John Rieden, the father of Frank Rieden of San Antonio; Baptist Schmidt, Amb. Reitzer, B. Bonekamp, G. Garsting, H. Wilpert, H. Gerdes, Jans Sievers, B. Brucks, Bickman, F. Bauer, Brinkhoff, Opus, Denters, John Toucher, H. Schneider, Rensing, Gasper, Eisenhauer, Louis Korn, Rudolph Charobiny, and Dr. Acke, whose descendants reside in San Antonio.

Three miles west of Quihi is the town of Vanderburg, that was first settled, in 1847, by Zavier Vanz, Mumme, White, G. Bridge, Stegler, and Decker, whose entire family, with the exception of two sons, Joseph and Carlo, died from eating wild lettuce, and Carlo was raised to manhood by my father in his family.

Four miles southwest of Vanderburg, on Worthy Creek, is the town of New Fountain, where a settlement was first made in 1845, by the Leinaweber, Grossenbacher, and Goehring families, all of whom have representatives now residing in San Antonio.

Ten miles west of Hondo Creek, on the San Antonio and El Paso road, is the old town of D'Hanis, that was first settled in 1847 by Nic Ney, John Ney, the father of Joe Ney, the present sheriff of Medina County; Donald French, Finger, Hagemueller, Barto, Joe, Nic and Sebastian Wipff, Mike, Wolff, Mathias Koch, father of Mathias Peter, John, Jacob, and Steve Koch; Braden, Carr, John Rieddenmann, Peter Britz, John Schreiber, John Raiber, Antone Ludwig, John Ruedinger, Joseph Wollehker, Anton Strausser, Frank Bihl, John Nehr, Joseph Reudinger, J. B. Deckard, Dr. Marrell, John and Chris. Schumacher, Ben Grosenbacher, Riesmann, Kaufmann, Joseph Echtile, John B. Zeher, August Zeher, Leonard Esser, Peter Koch, O. W. Koch, Joe Rieber, Joe Wippf, John and Austin Gardieser, Herbert Weynand, John and Austin Lutz, Leopold Zuercher, Joe Zuercher, Jack Souter, Tob Souter, Richard Riley, Paul Brotz, Joe Richarz, and Martin Nester.

Two miles further west on said road is Saco Creek, that was first settled in 1850 by Mr. Reuter, the father-in-law of the well-known stockman, Fritz Rhode, and in the same neighborhood Tobe Reiley, John Reinhart, and Captain Richarz established themselves.

Fort Lincoln was established in 1850 on Saco Creek, two miles from the old town of D'Hanis. It was named for General Lincoln of the American Revolution. Major Longstreet of the United States Army, who was afterwards a famous general in the war of secession, was its last commander.

A settlement was made in 1850 on Ranchera Creek three miles east of Sabinal station by John Davenport, John Bowles, and two brothers, John and Ross Kenedy.

The next settlement was on Sabinal Creek, that was made in 1850 by Warren Allen's and George Hammer's families.

Four miles beyond is Blanco Creek, where, in 1858, the Wish family settled.

Eight miles beyond is the Rio Frio, where, in 1854, the Sanders family settled.

Eight miles beyond is the town of Uvalde, that was first settled in 1850 by Mr. Bowles, the father of Duck and Peter Bowles, John Weimiller, Pullion, Greiner, and Nance.

Four miles below Uvalde was Fort Inge, on Leon Creek, that was established by the United States government in 1850 for the protection of the frontier, where a company of dragoons was stationed.

The next and furthest settlement towards the west until after the Civil War was at Fort Clark, that was established by the United States government in 1856, on the north side of Las Moras Creek, fifty miles from Uvalde.

On the east side of Las Moras Creek, opposite Fort Clark, is the town of Brackett, which was settled in 1852, by James Connell, Mrs. Rose, Henry Rudolph, and the Brackett family.

Fort Ewell was also established by the United States government in 1850, on the Nueces River, about ninety miles below Uvalde, now in La Salle County.

A settlement known as San Francisco was made in 1850 on San Francisco Creek, west of the Medina River, six miles in a southwest direction from Castroville, below the San Antonio and El Paso road, by Mr. Haas, the father of Valentine, Philip, Fritz, and George Haas, and their sister, who afterwards married Mr. Benderley; Mr.

Vonflie, the father of Henry Vonflie of Briar Branch; also by Roatsman, Blase Meyer, Cristiles, Bater, and Haller. This settlement was repeatedly raided by Indians and many settlers were killed.

A settlement was made in 1850 where Devine station is now situated, which is eighteen miles below Castroville, on the International & Great Northern Railroad. It was named in honor of Judge Devine, the father of Netterville, Albert, and Joe Devine of San Antonio. Of the following settlers Big-foot Wallace was the first, then came Tom Galbreth, Thomas A. James, Lou Moore, Gip and Bee Tilley, J. W. Winter, West Davidson, James Long, George and James Crawford, Reese Moore, W. M. Bromlett, George McCombs, John Craig, Tobias Long, Holly Laxon, and Rev. Newton. Big-foot Wallace claimed that he built the first log cabin on the west bank of the Medina River, ten miles south of Castroville, four years before it was established.

Five miles below Castroville a settlement was made on the west side of the Medina River in 1848 by the father of Emil and Louis Smith, in company with Berges, Trawalter, John Lisburg, Miller, Brown, and Cole.

In 1845 a settlement was made by my father on land known as Castro's corner, that was also known as Castro's ranch, in a bend on the east side of the Medina River, six miles above Castroville, and his was the most remote white man's habitation in that direction; but he was not one of Castro's colonists, though he lived there eight years and then removed to land he bought on Sans Creek.

Four miles above Castroville were the farm and sawmill of Charles de Montel, the father of Ed. de Montel of Hondo City, where he settled in 1846. The Laman, Hagerly, and Zinsmeier families settled in the same neighborhood.

The Harby settlement, which was situated eight miles above Castroville on the Medina River, was made between 1847 and 1850 by the Harby, Spattle, and Koenig families, and afterwards the Wusbach, Tuerpe, Sedar, Berley, Felter, Dr. Bohm, Monier, and Villemain families settled in the same neighborhood.

About all of the settlements west of San Antonio have been noticed that were in existence before 1860; but there were others in the Fisher and Miller grant, northeast and north of said city, that were made by German immigrants sent out by an incorporated society in Germany in charge of Prince Salms-Braunfels, to whose efforts the colony is principally indebted for its success.

On Good Friday in 1845 Prince Salms-Braunfels crossed the Guadalupe River with an escort of a few men and selected the present site on which the beautiful city that bears his name has since been built, where he located his first colonists. The names in the following list represent a few of those he introduced between that date and 1850: F. Heidemeyer, F. Salmuller, W. Kracke, Chris. Hans, A. Sauerborn, Carl von Domersmark, George Klappenbach, Gus. Hoffman (the first Mayor of New Braunfels and a colonel in the Confederate Army), Dr. Theo. Koester, Nic Zink, Carl Thomas, H. Wilcke, Geo. Ulrich, F. Holekamp, L. Vogel, Theo. Sterzing, Ad. Benner, Peter Home, G. Remley, Thomas Schwab, Albert Dreiss, father of Adolph and Edward Dreiss; Nic Zircher, Silvester Simon, E. Kaderli, E. Scherz, P. Margerle, E. Winkler, Gab. Sacherer, and E. O. Meusebach, father of Ernest, Otto, and Max Meusebach; George and Philip Obert.

Sisterdale was settled by a colony of German immigrants, in 1847, and it was known as the Latin settlement, because they were all familiar with the Latin language. It was composed of the following members: Edward Degner (afterwards a member of the United States Congress), Professor Kapp, Dr. Hertzberg, Nicolas Zinks, Mr. Baer, Julius Dressel, Dr. Runge, A. Simmering, Hugo Klocke, A. Neuber, O. Neuber, Kuhler, Ernst. Flack, Philip Braubach, Fritz Degner, Joe Moses, Mr. Donaup, and Mr. Langbein, father of August, Carl, and Gustave Langbein.

Fredericksburg was laid out in May, 1846, by John O. Meusebach, and settled by B. Blum, William, August, and Daniel Arhilger; also by Lawrence Schmidt, Fritz and Henry Lohde, Heinrich and John Behrens, Mrs. Carl Schwarz, Heinrich Strackbein, Mrs. John Turst, Mrs. Steubing, Martin Heinemann, Mrs. Anton Novian, Anton and John Klein, Mrs. Leyendecker, Mrs. Young, Carl Megrih, Ernst. Besler, Mrs. Peter Boun, and L. and H. Wahrmund, father and uncle of Otto Wahrmund.

Boerne was laid out for a town in 1851, by Mr. Deussen, who was the first hardware merchant in San Antonio, and Judge James, the father of Vinton, Sidney, Scott, and J. H. James, who is now Judge of the Fourth Court of Civil Appeals of Texas. But before that date, in 1847, the following persons had settled in that vicinty: Adam Vogt, Leopold Schuz, Dr. Ferdinand Herff, Fritz Sauer, and Kreuer. In 1849 they were joined by Jacob, Thomas, and Peterson Sasuma, and Judge G. W. Kendall; and afterwards came Fritz and Henry Wendler, August Staffer, Matthews Banman, Captain Adolph and Fritz Zoeller, Julius Faber, John Schartz, Joseph Bergman, Charles Dienger, Jacob Deussen, Guenther Froebel, Franz Werner, Bernhard Hagerman, Judge Brown, and Mr. Spitz.

Bandera was settled in 1850, and among the first were P. D. Sauer, R. H. and DeWitt Burney, Milstead, Odum, and Macon Gillis. A saw-mill owned by Charles de Montel was located on the present site of the town before 1854, which turned the fine cypress timber in that vicinity into lumber and shingles. In 1853 Amasa Clark settled there, and a few years later came August Pengenot, V. and Auten Audewald, John and Adam Adamietz, Charles Montague, T. L. Miller, Mrs. D. Oborski, G. W. Lewis, Mrs. Mahala Jones, J. P. Rodrigues, Mr. Klappenbach, Mr. Dahlmann, and Captain Reese's family.

Comfort was laid out in 1851 by Ernest Altgelt, who conducted the first store and also a saw-mill near by. Mr. Altgelt was the father of H. H. Altgelt of New Braunfels, and George C., August, and Ernest Altgelt, of San Antonio. Mr. Altgelt was a very prominent attorney and highly esteemed by all who knew him, and died in 1878. The following is a list of the first settlers of Comfort: Ernest Altgelt; Theo. Wiedenfeld; W. C. Boerner; Wm. Heuermann; Fritz Goldbeck; Theodore Goldbeck; Mr. Ingenhuett, father of Peter, Thomas, and Martin Ingenhuett; H. Allerkamp; Louis Boerner; Schelbhase and family; Fritz Holekamp; Mr. Hartenbrock; Mr. Hinneber; C. W. Telgmann; Mr. Harms; Mr. Stecher; Mr. Timpke; Hy. Werder; H. Liesman; Mr. Karger; O. Roggenbucke; Ed. Steves, father of Albert, Ernest, and Edward Steves; Otto Brinkmann; Geo. Holekamp; Charles Herbst; W. Fellbaum, father of Charlie and Ernest Fellbaum; Schladore; H. Stieler; Dr. Melis; Mr. Brunks; A. Bruns; H. Boerner; John Horner; L. Breitenbach; Mr. Schimmelpfening; Herman Wille; Justus Seginnis; Mr. Johns; Paul Hanisch; E. Serger; Mr. Herder; O. Rosenthal; C. and E. Vetterlein; Mr. Schwethem; H. Schulz; H. Witbold; Mr. Schmidt; E. Schilling; F. Perner; C. Flach; Mr. Joseph; Jacob Kuechler; Louis Berger; Fritz Sauer; Dr. Pfeiffer; V. Pfeiffer; A. Faltin; Paul and Otto Bellow; L. Strohecker; H. .Seidenstricker; Emil Oberwalter; Chris. Boerner; and M. Lindner.

A party of Mormons drifted into the country from Missouri in 1854, and stopped first on Verde Creek, but soon after they moved to Bandera, where they remained a short time before settling at a place still known as "Mormon Camp," a few miles below Bandera.

The following families settled on the Salado, before 1850: Ackermann, Gembler, Ries, and Eisenhauer; Thos. Applewhite, Ross Houston, Craighead, Claiborne Rector, "Uncle Billy" Evans, and J. H. Polly, on the Cibolo; and Harrison Pressnall, John, Jesse, and Stephen Applewhite, on the east side of the Medina.

The Indians were very bad and made raids on the unprotected settlements about Bandera at regular intervals until 1855, when Governor Pease made an effort to check them by authorizing the citizens on the frontier to organize themselves into minute companies under a provision which stipulated that they should receive pay for actual services performed. The same year a company of infantry was stationed by the Federal government on Verde Creek, but the absurdity of foot soldiers undertaking to cope with the wild nomads of the plains soon became apparent, and they were relieved the following year by a company of dragoons, under the command of Captain Palmer, who erected the necessary buildings, and Camp Verde became a permanent station.

The Indians were not deterred by the preparations to resist them, but continued their murderous and thieving raids as before, until the more timid settlers abandoned the frontier through fear of death and the horrors of captivity. These conditions continued, in violation of the Constitution, which required the United States to protect its citizens, until the State of Texas undertook to shield them in 1861 by placing a regiment beyond the limits of the settlements, which kept back the marauding savages and insured the safety of that region during the following four years.

Chapter Twenty-Seven:

Indian Depredations On The Frontier

Castro's colonists were not molested by Indians during the first two years after Castroville was established. Immediately after that event Castro entered into a treaty with the Comanches, which placed them on friendly terms, but in 1846 outside white men killed several of that tribe and the settlers were made to suffer through a series of years for that act of indiscretion. The Lipan Indians who occupied Castro's grant were very friendly with his people until one of the tribe was killed by a discharged Ranger in a drunken frolic, for which reason they became bitter foes of the white race. They removed in a body to Mexico, where they occupied a mountainous country in Coahuila without the consent of that government, and thereafter they continually depredated on the frontier settlements of Texas.

The New Braunfels and Darmstadt colonies were more fortunate, because the treaty that was made in their behalf by Meusebach, Spies, and Von Koll, with the Comanches, in 1847, on the Verein Shegal, or Union Hill, in said town, was not violated. But for the concession of land lying between the Llano and San Saba rivers the colonists would have been exterminated, and on that account Baron von Meusebach was called the savior of Fredericksburg.

The Texas Rangers proved themselves faithful guardians and kept the Indians under restraint for two years, but when Captain Jack Hays raised a regiment of Rangers, in 1846, to serve with the United States army in the invasion of Mexico, many of the most prominent Indian fighters of the frontier enlisted under him. The entire western portion of the State was practically unprotected, and during his absence the scattered settlements in every direction around San Antonio were exposed to the ravages of wild Indians, who availed themselves of the opportunity to vent their vengeance without restraint. They did not confine their attacks to the exposed border region only, but actually invested San Antonio with a display of boldness, and even entered the town, where they killed several inhabitants on the Plaza.

Under such circumstances the inoffensive people in exposed situations were compelled to resort to every available means for self-protection, and it was only their ceaseless watchfulness and precautions that saved them from destruction. During that period, and prior to 1850, many persons were brutally murdered, though it has only been possible to get the names of a few of those that were killed; but the people were poor and they had few animals, consequently the plunder the marauders secured was light.

After the settlements extended further west the pioneers were not only exposed to depredations from the Comanches, but they were constantly harassed by the Lipans and other implacable foes from Mexico. These enemies were, perhaps, partly composed of remnants of tribes who were exiles from their ancient homes and sacred associations, after centuries of warfare with Anglo-Americans in the east, and an intense hatred governed their actions towards the white race. When an occasion offered to avenge their past wrongs after finding a refuge in a foreign land, they made incursions across the Rio Grande to the settlements in Texas with a secrecy and celerity that defied opposition. There they stealthily committed a series of revolting crimes before escaping

with the plunder of their victims, and often with captured children and many stolen horses, to their strongholds in the mountainous regions of Mexico, where they
were safe from pursuit.

About fifteen small settlements only, representing a
few families in each, had been able to establish themselves west of the Medina River in the first eight years
after Castroville was located, several of which were
made by Americans in the last three years of that period, who managed to maintain themselves by fighting
frequent battles. The Federal government was dilatory
about guarding the frontier after Texas was admitted
into the Union, and five years passed before the State received the inadequate protection afforded by the establishments at Forts Inge, Ewell, Clark, McKavitt, Concho,
Lincoln, and Camp Verde, which attracted many people
to the country. Experience proved that the small companies at those points could neither suppress the Indians
nor prevent their raids, consequently the settlers in exposed situations were obliged to depend on themselves,
with the aid of a few companies of gallant Rangers in
the service of the State, and the dangers constantly increased.

These enemies usually entered the country on foot,
about the full of the moon, and prowled through the settlements in search of horses on which to mount themselves, and then they collected others in large herds, with
the intention of driving them out of the country. When
the frontiersmen discovered their presence, which, very
often, was not done until some bloody crime had been
perpetrated, runners were sent out to collect all the
available fighting men at a designated place, where they
embodied themselves under a chosen leader and pursued the marauders with untiring energy. When overtaken, no mercy was shown by either side, and many
bloody battles were fought, in which the white men were
generally victorious. In that way retributive justice was

inflicted, but frequently the raiders escaped across the Rio Grande, or northward, with large numbers of stolen horses.

The troops at the United States forts were commanded by efficient officers, and they performed the duties assigned them with diligence, but their services generally were inefficient because the Dragoons were mounted on large, heavy, Missouri-raised horses that were too clumsy for the duties required of them. When in pursuit of the small, hardy, and active native animals that the Indians rode, which had great vitality and were accustomed to hardships of every kind, the soldiers were usually outdistanced and the raiders escaped. Nevertheless, their presence inspired confidence and helped to settle up the country, and on many occasions they performed efficient service, or their deficiencies were supplied by companies of Texas Rangers, which from time to time were raised by the State of Texas for the purpose of effectually guarding the frontier.

Through a period of ten years prior to the commencement of the Civil War the whole western border region of Texas was a scene of rapine and bloodshed perpetrated by Indians and outlaws from Mexico, which that government was unable to prevent, and which the United States, whose duty it was to exert its powers for that purpose, took no steps to suppress. The most daring and dastardly acts of outlawry were committed until a large area of country was laid waste on the lower Rio Grande, in which, according to the official report of Major Heintzelman, of the United States army, "there was not an American or any property of an American that was left to be destroyed"; and many Mexicans, citizens of Texas, were likewise robbed of their possessions. "Their horses and cattle were driven into Mexico and there sold—a cow with a calf by her side for one dollar."

These and other acts of defiance and robbery were committed by a lawless element who have been identified, whose operations were confined to that region and along the border about El Paso. Between these two sections of country the Indians depredated more frequently than elsewhere, and the record of murders they committed in those years will show that they penetrated to the interior within thirty miles of San Antonio on the north, south, and west, where Federal troops were stationed and State Rangers always were in the field to oppose them.

The Indians made but few predatory incursions during the war of secession, and the frontier was remarkably free from their attacks, although it was not always exempt from raids and at several points severe engagements took place. This immunity was secured by a regiment of cavalry, that was raised by the secession government of Texas, in 1861, for the protection of the frontier. The companies were stationed at intervals along the outskirts of the settlements from the Rio Grande to Red River, and scouts constantly rode between the stations to watch for Indian trails going into or returning from the settlements. This regiment, after serving the State one year, was turned over to the Confederate government, and it was retained in that service until 1864.

The constant movement of troops along the border and the vigilance that was observed in all quarters kept them quiet. When the Civil War closed, these restraints were removed, and shortly afterwards marauding bands of outlaws and hostile savages resumed their depredations. They not only harassed the border settlements, but frequently penetrated the interior to within fifty miles of San Antonio.

The conditions prevailing at that time throughout that large territory are expressed in a letter, written by Governor Throckmorton, on September 29, 1866, to the Secretary of War of the United States, in which he says: "The frontier is suffering great devastation. Murders, rapine, and the most revolting outrages are of daily occurrence.

Unless the government will send sufficient and immediate protection, the State will be compelled to undertake it, without a dollar in the State Treasury to defray the necessary expenditures."

When the Federal government failed to send troops to the border in compliance with the request made by the Governor of Texas, the State Legislature passed an act authorizing him to call one thousand men into service to protect the frontier settlements for a period of twelve months. Three battalions of Texas Rangers were raised accordingly, under a provision which required every volunteer to furnish his own arms, horses and necessary equipments, and this little Texas army performed efficient service in the field, under amended acts of the Legislature, until the enemies of civilization on the frontier of Texas were suppressed.

The following extract from the exhaustive report of Adjutant-General W. H. King, referring to the latter period, says:

> The disturbed condition of the country, the lack of a stable and permanent State government, the widely scattered and helpless condition of the border settlements, the absence of mail facilities or other means of easy communication, and the small number of newspapers then in the State, all united to make it nearly impossible, in many instances, to get specific information in regard to Indian raids and depredations, even though it was positively known that the border was being scourged by such raids. In this way and from these causes scores of murders and outrages in the dark and bloody past have found no place in the written pages of Texas history, though leaving ruined homes, aching hearts, tearful eyes, and frightful memories as evidences of their dread reality. The history of Texas for almost forty years shows an almost continuous state of warfare between her people and the blood-thirsty devils of the...Indian race along her western and southern borders. Many counties that had organized and were becoming populous before the

Civil War, were depopulated by these Indian forays, and the whole line of frontier settlements was kept for years in a state of mind alternating between fear and fury by these incessant predatory attacks.

The Comanches, Sioux, and Kiowas in their raids would follow down the Red River, cross into the northwestern counties and ravage the sparsely settled section of the northwestern part of the State. They even carried their depredations into the more thickly settled parts. The Kickapoos and Lipans, from the secure camping ground in Mexico, made periodical raids into Texas, crossing the Rio Grande above Eagle Pass generally. These hostile bands frequently traversed the entire southwestern section of the State, murdering the white settlers and pillaging wherever they went.

A corroboration of these statements is partially verified in the following evidence, and if it was possible to procure a complete list of the killed, the destruction of human life west of the Guadalupe River during the years enumerated would be increased enormously.

1843. In the battle in Bandera Pass, seven miles above Bandera, 5 of Capt. Hays' Rangers were killed.

1844. An Irishman, one of the Hays Rangers, was killed in the Nueces cañon, name unknown.

1844. Z. Rhien was the first of Castro's colonists that was killed, 48 miles southwest of San Antonio.

1845. Wesley Deer, one of Capt. Waxfield's Rangers, in Sabinal cañon; Heck, a Ranger, one mile west of "Sunset" railroad crossing over Sabinal on El Paso road; an unknown Ranger, one of Capt. Walker's company, near Sandy branch, in Medina County; Noah Mangum, a Ranger, on the east side of the Leona, ten miles below Uvalde.

1846. F. H. Gulled, Vincent and Joe Jonnes, and Joe Bessale, the first of the Castroville settlement on the Medina River, seven miles above Castroville.

1847. Mr. Meyer, by Kickapoo and Lipan Indians near Quihi.

1849. Two men with Dr. Lyon's wagons at Deadman's Pass.

1850-1860. The following persons from Boerne and Comfort were killed by Indians in these ten years: Stahl, Grober, Mikel, Henrich, H. Kensing and wife, H. Runge, Dunlop, Peter Metzger and daughter, Taylor, Joy, and Gusta Schumann.

1851. Seven men, near Fort Ewell, on the Nueces River, when a U. S. government train was captured; one of them was August Sartor, aged 18 years, a brother of Alex Sartor, a prominent jeweler of San Antonio; Lieut. Hollibird, a United States dragoon, below Laredo; Ad. Gillespie, of Ford's Rangers, between Fort Merrel and the Rio Grande; Baker Barton, in a battle fought by Lt. Burleson 25 miles from Laredo.

1852. A Mexican mail-rider and several persons between Corpus Christi and Laredo.

1854. Lowe, a Frenchman, who lived with E. D. Westfall, near Fort Inge; Forrester and two children on the Helotes, 18 miles west of San Antonio.

1855. Willis Jones, of Capt. Callahan's Rangers, a brother of Capt. Frank Jones, at Piedras Negras; Gesser, a French peddler, and ten Mexicans, 15 miles west of Gonzales; Jesse Lawhorn, on Curry Creek, in Kendall County; Amanda Davis, a child of Richard Davis, near the river, 8 miles north of Bandera.

1856. Louis Thompson, near Frio cañon; White, on the Hondo, where Joe Richards' ranch is now; Hans Ney, an uncle of Sheriff Joe Ney, in Medina County; four persons on J. H. Hill's place in Frio canon; Dr. Thompson, by robbers, five miles west of San Antonio.

1857. Mr. Murry, assessor of Bandera County, in Sabinal cañon; Mr. and Mrs. Johnson Gilliland killed, and two children captured, in Refugio County; Bilhartz, an uncle of Mr. Bilhartz of San Antonio, at Lacoste Station; Valentine Haller, near Castroville; Berry Buchalow, on the Saco; John Martin, a soldier, at Kickapoo Springs near Fort McKavitt; Dan Murff, 8 miles north of Kerrville on Guadalupe River; Newt. Price, 8 miles north of Kerrville on Guadalupe River; 11 Mexicans, on Ranchero Creek, 2 miles east of Sabinal station.

1858. John Hoffman, of Castroville, 8 miles north of Sabinal station; Sebastian Wolfe, of D'Hanis, 8 miles north of Sabinal station; Lewis, at D'Hanis; Gotthardt on the Guadalupe River; his 3 sons now reside in San Antonio; Nat Magnum, ten miles below Uvalde, on Leona Creek; Capt. John Davenport, on El Paso road near Sabinal station; Jones Bowles, on El Paso road near Sabinal station; Jack Bowles, at Guide Hill, 7 miles below where Sabinal station is now; Nick Baker, in Uvalde County; Brinkhoff, killed, and his two sons captured near Quihi; Jule Bouchois, at the head of Hondo Creek, related to the Zinzmeyer family in San Antonio; Herman Rotzman, on San Francisco Creek 6 miles east of Castroville; Vonflie, father of Henry Vonflie of Briar Branch, Medina County; Louis Magee, near Boerne, a son of Rev. John Magee; John W. Davis, at Barrel Springs, beyond Fort Davis; Mr. and Mrs. Amlung, their 3 children and 7 men at Deadman's Pass; Young Hardin, 4 miles south of Bandera.

1859. Rowland Nicholas, about 5 miles above Kerrville; Saartoff, in Medina County; Jack Mechler, uncle of Mechler brothers in San Antonio; Jack Walters; John Bowles, between the Rio Frio and Sabinal cañon, near Pilot Knoll; Reuben Smith, near Hondo Creek; Harms Gaddis, father-in-law of Judge Haas, of Castroville, near Quihi; W. Houston, at 18th crossing of Devil's River, near Beaver Lake; a captive white boy, mistaken for an Indian in the Nueces cañon; Henry Fraiser, a boy, near Sesquadara Creek in Medina County.

1860. Long, on Hondo Creek, and his sister was scalped, but she recovered and afterwards married Mr. Smith, known as "Sago" Smith; Peter Ketchum was killed with Long on Hondo Creek; five members of the Braggart family in Comanche County; Ed. Watkins, near Knox's ranch on the Frio, 8 miles east of Uvalde; Richards, near Knox's ranch on the Frio, 8 miles east of Uvalde; Hans Youngman, an uncle of Mr. Youngman, a merchant of San Antonio, near Lacoste station, on Mustang Prairie; Martin Grace, on the Medina River near where Idlewild is now; White, in Hondo cañon; a Mexican boy between Elm Creek and the Medina River; an unknown Frenchman, in the Hondo canon; Samuel Lane, a few miles above Comfort on the Guadalupe River; Leonard Eastwood, near the Leona, in Frio County; B. F. Wilkins, on the Rio Frio about 8 miles from Uvalde; George Robinson, on the Rio Frio about 8 miles from Uvalde; Theodore, the shepherd, one of the first settlers near Sabinal station.

1861. James Winters and Harrington, both of Pleasanton, on Hondo Creek; William Herndon, on Hondo Creek; two negroes belonging to Mr. M. French, on Hondo Creek; John Schreiber, near D'Hanis; Anderson and O'Bryan; Decker, near D'Hanis; Henry Adams and Henry Robinson, in the Nueces cañon, near Chalk Bluff; Henry Robinson's sixteen-year-old son, in the Nueces cañon, near Chalk Bluff; Henry Richarz, an uncle of Captain Richarz, near Pleasanton; Harrington, near Pleasanton; "Mustang" Moor, on Laredo road, near Moor's station; a detachment of ten Confederate soldiers of Company D, of the 2nd Texas Cavalry, Capt. James Walker's company, under Lieutenant Robt. Mays, consisting of John Walker, Thomas Carroll, Sam Shelby, John Parker, Calvin Jones, John Brown and four others, were all killed; the following three members of Capt. James Walker's company of 2nd Texas Cavalry were killed between Fort Stanton and Fort Craig, viz.: William Pemberton, Joseph Moss, and Joseph Amanicker.

1862. Young Hart, lived on Patterson's ranch, killed on Hondo Creek between El Paso and Laredo road; David Adams, brother of Henry Adams, 40 miles east of Rio Grande; Stockhouse, a brother-in-law of Capt. Richarz, 5 miles from D'Hanis; Vincent Trahea, in Atascosa County; W. Hudson, at 18th crossing on Devil's River.

1863. Mr. Williams, on Llano River; Tom Black and Jones, 3 miles from Beaver Lake on El Paso road; Sawyer, on Dry Frio; Zach Deckert, near D'Hanis; Zavier Gollett, in Medina County; three Confederate soldiers, members of Capt. Bradley's Co., southwest of Uvalde; Adolph Schauffhausen, in Uvalde County; Eastwood, about thirty miles southwest of Uvalde.

1864. Mr. Hall, on Richland Creek, in San Saba County; a ten-year-old son of Mrs. Youngblood, on Grape Creek in Blanco County; "Gunsmith" Gebhard, of Castroville, on Salado Creek, twenty-five miles east of the Rio Grande on El Paso road; Rudolph Koenig, of Castroville, on Salado Creek, twenty-five miles east of the Rio Grande, on El Paso road. Texas scouts fought a large body of Kickapoo Indians on Dove Creek near its juncture with the Concho River, in the vicinity of Fort Concho, when on their way from their reservation on the Kaw River, in Kansas, to Mexico. The Indians were at first defeated, but rallied and routed the rangers with heavy loss. Among the killed were Don Cox, Tom Parker, Capt. Sam Barnes, Albert Everett, Noah Gibbs, John Stein, James Mabrey, Joseph Byers, Wm. Epps, Capt. Gullentine and his son, besides others.

1865. Ed. Terry, and 2 of his children, two and a half miles south of Center Point; Samuel Bennion, brother-in-law of Jack Davenport, in Burnett County, on Sabinal Creek; Bud English, 10 miles west of Frio River, in Frio County; Dean Oden, 10 miles west of Frio River, in Frio County; Frank Williams, 10 miles west of Frio River, in Frio County, and about six others; John Bockney, his wife and children, 8 miles east of Fort Clark in El Paso road; Chris. Wachter's mother-in-law, near Kerrville; Henry Cox lost a daughter 4 years old on west prong of the Nueces, a 13-year-old son on the El Paso road, and a married daughter, her husband and 3 children near Brackett.

186—. Rause, during the Civil War on Tuhuacana Creek in Frio County; Hood, a boy, on Redus ranch in Hondo cañon.

1866. Valentine Gunley, 6 miles west of Castroville below El Paso road; Thomas Clark, in Medina County, above Bandera; Bob Leakey, in Uvalde County; George White, in Uvalde County; George Wheeler, in Hondo cañon; George Miller, in Hondo cañon; Thulle, near Castroville; Mrs. Bowlin and child in Sabinal canon; David Cryer, about 10 miles north of Bandera; B. C. Buckalew, near Lexon Creek, in Sabinal cañon; Thos. B. Click, above Bandera on Medina River; Samuel Love, 2 miles above Kerrville; Sam Long, on Blanco Creek; B. Slaack, above Bandera, on Medina River.

1867. John Sanders, on the Eagle Pass road; Mrs. William Alexander, 18 miles above Kerrville, in San Saba Co.; Jack Miller, near Saco Creek; Joseph Moor, his wife and mother, where Medina city is now; Mr. Jones, where Medina city is now; W. B. Derry, and 2 children, on Guadalupe River 10 miles below Kerrville, and his 8-year-old daughter carried off, but was recaptured later in the Frio cañon, by Chris. Kelly, John Paterson and Ed. Meyer, a brother of Albert

Meyer, of San Antonio; Schlossen and Baptist, on G. W. Kendall's ranch in Kendall Co.; George Mayer; Henry Robinson, in Frio cañon, on El Paso road; John Rowland, an uncle of Frank Rieden of San Antonio; John Davis, brother of Davis, an express driver in San Antonio; John Dawson, at Barrel springs on El Paso road; nine Mexicans 15 miles from Eagle Pass, on Eagle Pass road.

1868. James Dowdy's four children, Fanny 20, Alice 18, Rilla 15, and James 12, on Johnson's creek in Kerr County; three persons in the Bickle family 5 miles east of Boerne; Roumon Gross and his son George, near Lacoste station in Medina Co.; Pablo Hernandez and 3 men, near Chichon on the Laredo road; Spanneburg, 5 miles east of Boerne; Hardin, a youth 15 years old, 4 miles southwest of Bandera.

1870. Mrs. Wanz, the mother of Zavier Wanz, on Verde Creek; a Mexican on Charley Vivian's ranch; two Mexicans on Ed English's ranch near Carrizo springs; Walter Reese, on Verde Creek; Bird, of Capt. Rufus Perry's rangers, near Shovel mountain in Hays County; Mr. English lost a son and his two companions in a fight with Indians on the Rio Frio, between Eagle Pass and Laredo road; Bedeger of Capt. Richarz's rangers, near Carrizo springs; Walter Richarz, a son of Capt. Richarz, six miles west of Sabinal Creek on El Paso road; Joe Rief, of Capt. Richarz's rangers, 6 miles west of Sabinal Creek on El Paso road; Mrs. Wallace, on Verde Creek.

1871. Mr. Stringfield and his wife, and his son, captured on the Rio Frio below Laredo road; a white boy in the employ of J. T. Patterson, in Hondo cañon.

1872. Frank Clark, among the Salt Creek mountains in Brown County; a negro who joined a party from John Kenedy's ranch, near Sabinal station; two Mexicans, at a sheep-pen in Live Oak County; one Mexican, in the Crough sheep-pen near Frio town; three Mexicans, near Frio town; one unknown white man near Frio town; one unknown white man in the Bennett settlement near Leon Creek; Ludwig Spath, on Sandy Creek in Gillespie County; Anastacio Gonzales and 8 Mexican teamsters at Howard's well; Freeman Clark, on Salado Creek; Frank Camp, at Round Rock, now in Ward's pasture, in Frio County; Mr. Redbug, on Elm Creek, in Frio County; Massey, on Elm Creek, in Frio County.

1873. Two Mexicans employed by Ross Kenedy and Frank Rooney, on the Rio Pecos; Capt. Williams and 2 of his men, in Babyhead gap, in Kimble County; Thomas Black, near Beaver Lake.

1874. Glass and Batley, two rangers, in the Lost Valley fight in Jack Co.; a boy on Black Creek, by Indian raiders, who carried off 100 horses; Bailey, in Uvalde County.

1875. Frank Jones, in Mason County; Isaac Galbraith, and three other persons, near Devine; George White, the father of ex-Sheriff White of Edwards County, near Devine; Jack Phillips, on his way to Sabinal cañon.

1876. W. B. Perry and 2 children, 10 miles below Kerrville on the Guadalupe River; a white man, & miles west of Johnson city; Mrs. Sawyer, in Frio County; a 16-year-old boy, one mile west of Johnson city; a Mexican herder, about 3 miles west of Johnson city; W. R. Terry and 2 of his children, on Verde Creek, near its juncture with the Guadalupe. The Indians made their last raid into Sabinal canon and killed 16 persons in the wide circle they made back to the Rio Grande.

1877. Joe Wilton, below D'Hanis.

1879. Five U. S. soldiers, by Victoria's band, west of Fort Davis; Baker, west of Fort Davis; John Coulson's wife and two children in Nueces cañon.

1882. Mrs. McLaurin, Allen Lease, near Knox's ranch, in Frio canon, 8 miles east of Uvalde, in the last raid made by the Lipan Indians, in the Frio cañon, when they were pursued by Lieut. Bullis into Mexico and whipped at Horseshoe Bend.

NOTE. This list gives a total of three hundred and ninety-two persons that are known to have been killed by Indians between the years 1843 and 1882.

This partial list of people that were killed by hostile Indians on the western frontier in thirty-nine years must suffice. No official record of such murders was kept, consequently the list is imperfect, and a great many names might be added of which I have no knowledge. It is certain that many persons were slaughtered by marauding bands of Indians, whose bodies have never been found. Numerous skeletons of other unfortunates have been found in remote places, which could not be identified, and the cause of their death is unknown. The greatest destruction of life occurred on the Texas frontier through a period extending from 1850 to 1877, and those who traveled the exposed route leading from San Antonio to El Paso suffered more than elsewhere. The following incident in my own experience will help to illustrate this statement and serve as a fitting close to the subject:

The incident happened in a wild, desolate country, west of Devil's River, in 1876, and I was accompanied by Captain Stocker of St. Louis, the manager and one of the principal stockholders of the Knox Mining Company of Parral, in which I was also interested. Captain Stocker went hunting and entered a ravine, where he discovered the bones of six or eight men that were lying exposed on top of the ground, and he directed my attention to them. Evidently they had been killed by Indians, because the skulls showed the marks of the scalping knife. The place was a short distance away from the road, and possibly they had retired to the shelter of the ravine during a cold spell of weather, where the Indians found and murdered them. The indications showed that the tragedy occurred years before, probably in 1849, when on their way to California. We could not find the slightest clue to their identity and their remains were left undisturbed.

285

Chapter Twenty-Eight:
Reminiscences of Old San Antonio

My personal recollections of San Antonio extend back to 1854, and they are vividly retained, although at that time I was only nine years old. Believing that the information will prove to be interesting, I will submit my youthful impressions of the city as briefly as possible, and after giving a general description of its area and appearance in connection with its prominent features, I will close with a sketch of the city's development in each decade until the present time.

My first view of San Antonio de Bexar was from the highlands towards the west, and the first object in that direction that I distinctly remember was the Catholic Cemetery, which included all of Milam Square and the land now occupied by Santa Rosa Hospital, that was enclosed by a stone wall about eight feet high. I was greatly impressed by its appearance, because it was the first graveyard I had ever seen, and when I was told that it was the burial place for all the people who died in the city the evidence was conclusive that we were approaching its limits.

From that point, the wagon on which I rode, with its team of oxen driven by my father, moved slowly forward to the crossing on San Pedro Creek, thence onwards through the center of the town and down Market Street to the ford where Navarro Street bridge now spans the San Antonio River. Nat Lewis' gristmill, which was run by water power, was situated just above the ford, on the north side of the beautiful stream, and the general camping place for wagons was in that vicinity. There the oxen were unyoked and turned loose to graze on the open lands east of the river, with hopples on to prevent them from wandering to a distance.

I was afforded many opportunities for sight-seeing while encamped there, and I took advantage of them to view the city, which was then confined to a small area around the public squares, where all the business houses were located, and to a couple of blocks in each direction from that point, that represented the residence portion of the town. All the land north of Houston Street, and that, equally distant, south of the Plazas between the San Antonio River and San Pedro Creek, which could be irrigated from the ditches, was in cultivation. The town was supplied with products of the soil derived from that source and a few small settlements in the surrounding country.

The population of the city at that date probably did not exceed four thousand inhabitants of all races, and of that number a large majority were of Mexican descent, many of whom were in destitute circumstances. It was a poorly built town of unattractive one-story adobe structures, with walls extending two or three feet above flat cement roofs, that resembled the houses commonly seen in Mexico; this style of architecture was observed in the business houses around Main Plaza and in the two stores that stood near the center in front of the present Court House, also in the Governor's Palace, on Military Plaza, the Veramendi house on Soledad Street, and others of less consequence on Main and Dwyer Avenue. A few buildings were constructed of stone, but the most stately edifice was San Fernando Church, and the only one of two stories in height that I remember was the James residence on Commerce Street, where General Worth died in 1849, and in which General R. E. Lee was a frequent guest. A majority of the dwellings were rude huts with walls built of poles set upright in the ground and plastered with mud.

The rear portion of the present Cathedral, the old Palace, the Veramendi house, and a few others of less importance are all that remain. The Alamo, of course, stands as solidly now as it did then in its solitude overlooking the city, where I visited it often and spent many hours playing among its ruins. The only residence east of the river, unless I am mistaken, was owned by Colonel S. A. Maverick, on the corner occupied by the Gibbs building, west of the Federal building. The Post Office was then kept in a small house on Dwyer Avenue, which is still standing.

Several buildings of that period, on Main and Military plazas, that have disappeared, are noted in history. One was the Council House on the corner of Market Street, where the fierce Indian fight occurred with a party of Comanche chiefs, in which all of them were killed; and another was the first schoolhouse, on Military Plaza, in the rear of the Cathedral. There were others that were notorious gambling places, where many bloody encounters took place, which gave San Antonio a bad reputation before it began to improve.

I have endeavored to recall the names of all the early settlers of prominence and worth, of Anglo-American origin and of European birth, who resided in San Antonio prior to 1857, and the list is inserted at the close of this chapter. They made themselves conspicuous in the upbuilding of the city through the exercise of civilizing influences, in opposition to a rougher element whose efforts to terrorize and disgrace the community as robbers and murderers retarded its growth.

The names of merchants and their places of business, who were established in San Antonio between 1844 and 1857, are given in the following list:

Cook & Lockwood; on corner opposite Kampmann building, in 1844, now occupied by Frank Bros. Bryan Callaghan, Sr.; on Main Plaza, in front of Court House, in 1844.

George Caldwell; on West Commerce Street, in 1853.

Daniel Devine; adjoining Cook & Lockwood's store, in 1844.

Dr. Dignowity; on Soledad Street.

Marcello French; on West Commerce Street.

Louis Groesbeck; on Main Plaza, in front of Court House, in 1844.

Griff Jones; on north side of Main Plaza, in 1844, where Saul Wolfson's store is now.

Jones & Ulrich; north side of Main Plaza, in 1844, where Saul Wolfson's store is now.

King & Carolan; north side of Main Plaza, in 1844; where Saul Wolfson's store is now.

Frank Paschal; north side of Main Plaza, in 1844, where Saul Wolfson's store is now.

Dr. A. Nette; the first drug store in San Antonio.

Post & Hedges; on north side of Main Plaza, where Saul Wolfson's store is now.

Rose & McCarty; on West Commerce Street, where A. B. Frank's store is now.

Wilson I. Riddle; on corner of Commerce and St. Mary streets, in 1844.

Sweet's furniture store, in 1850.

Sweet & Lacoste; where Critzer's Jewelry Store is now, in 1850.

William Vance; on West Commerce Street, in 1844, succeeded by Vance Bros.

Wallace & Evans; on West Commerce Street, where A. B. Frank's store is now.

The following resident lawyers practiced before the Bexar County bar between 1844 and 1855: Mack Anderson, T. T. Anderson, Jack Cock, James H. Denison, Thomas J. Devine, Judge Duncan, T. S. Harrison, Hart, Alford & Willie, James Henson, Hewitt & Newton, Russell Howard, Volney Howard, George H. Noonan, J. A. Paschal, Simpson, T. T. Teel, Columbus Upson, Vanderlip, Jacob Waelder.

These names will probably suggest others, but, doubtless, a complete list of the persons who were engaged in business during that period could be made from the court records by anyone who might feel disposed to undertake the task. Many persons named in the two lists became prominent and their character is stamped on the work they performed.

The town did not improve materially on the plazas in the twelve years following my first visit, but its habitations were extended considerably during that interval on account of large accessions to the population. The estimated number of inhabitants in 1857 was about seven thousand; and in 1860 they are stated to have been between ten and twelve thousand; but it is probable that numerous transient residents were included in the last estimate, who were awaiting a development of events threatened by the signs of the times. Texas was preparing to secede from the Union, and other important movements were in contemplation which made San Antonio the rendezvous of many adventurers.

The act of secession was anticipated by a demand for the surrender of the Federal troops in Texas, and the capitulation to the State authorities was accomplished in San Antonio. Texas then became a State in the Southern Confederacy and the great Civil War followed, with its four years of horrors that spread a blight over the country. That era of misfortune to the Southern States was succeeded by the evils of the reconstruction period, which were prolonged through twice as many years.

The conditions that prevailed, immediately after the war ended, hampered business energy generally throughout the South and hindered an active interest in commercial enterprises; but in no place was there manifestation of less activity than in San Antonio, where it seems that the welfare of the city had ceased to be a matter for consideration.

The people of the town could not have been placed in a worse situation, or one that could more thoroughly expose the inefficiency of the city government. My knowledge is derived from personal observation, because I made the city my home about the time that the disgraceful state of affairs was at its worst. A lawless element, composed of bandits, thieves, and murderers, infested the town, where they defied the authorities and terrorized the community with no fear of punishment, and with the same impunity that led tribes of marauding savages to ravage the outlying settlements within a few miles of the city. The crimes and murders that were perpetrated by white degenerates under the shadow of the law were less excusable, more cowardly and equally as brutal as those committed by savage enemies in their mode of warfare.

Before the interests of society could hope to advance it was necessary that the evils which held San Antonio in their grasp should be overcome, otherwise the city could not improve, nor was it possible to develop the natural resources of the country until they were removed. In other words, the conditions demanded that the city should be purged of turbulent and corrupt men in order to remove the contagion of bad example; and also that the country should be protected against savages, so that peaceable, orderly citizens might enjoy tranquility in the pursuit of their vocations when striving for the general good of the commonwealth. These problems were hard to solve, but they were worked out successfully in the course of time.

The conditions in west Texas could not have been more unsatisfactory than they were in 1866, when I assumed my duties as a mail contractor under the Federal government, over the routes from San Antonio, via Eagle Pass, to Fort Clark, and another from San Antonio to Laredo. Indian raids from the north and west were frequent occurrences, and the entire frontier was unprotected by a military force, consequently the dangers that lurked in every direction compelled those who traveled the roads, and the people in every settlement, to take care of themselves. Naturally, under such circumstances, all rural pursuits languished, immigration almost ceased, and communication with Mexico was hampered until intercourse between San Antonio and that country was continued with difficulty on account of the dangers that menaced those who passed over the route.

A state of affairs such as I have outlined could not continue in opposition to the enterprising spirit that began to assert itself in defiance of existing discouragements. Business men grasped the situation and began to work in earnest for the city's welfare and the country's safety, and though the obstacles seemed insurmountable they labored harmoniously until every obstruction in the way of progress was removed. Active steps were taken to improve the city, and in the next few years several public enterprises were inaugurated, many new, substantial buildings were erected, and the city was better governed than it had ever been before.

Among the most prominent measures and institutions worthy of notice, that were adopted or established in 1866, was the organization of the first national bank of San Antonio; a charter for the first street railroad was secured; the city was first lighted with gas; and an ice factory was erected. In 1867 the first city ordinance against carrying concealed weapons was passed by the council, and the first raid was made by the police on gamblers. In 1868 the first fair of the Agricultural and Industrial Association was opened; the first stage-line between San Antonio, Texas, and Monterey, was established; the first steam fire engine arrived; the first Jockey Club was organized; and the corner-stone of the first cathedral in west Texas was laid with imposing ceremonies. In 1869 San Antonio was first designated as a money order office. In 1870 the city was re-incorporated; improvements of the Plazas was begun; foot bridges were built across the river on Commerce and St. Mary Streets; sidewalks were laid; agitation of city water-works commenced; the city donated to the Federal Government forty acres of land near the present site of Fort Sam Houston, which was officially begun in 1865; and a more extensive wagon trade, in which "Prairie Schooners" were introduced, was opened with distant points in Mexico than had ever existed before.

A brighter future confronted San Antonio then, and the city's appearance had been greatly improved in a manner that comported with its commercial importance. But in the next decade it made far greater strides and both the business and residence portions were greatly extended in every direction and the river was spanned on Houston Street by the first iron bridge. An excellent public school system and a number of public enterprises were inaugurated, in addition to which many churches, stores and other buildings were erected. In 1875 Fort Sam Houston was permanently established and the city voted a subsidy of $300,000 to secure the Galveston, Harrisburg and San Antonio Railroad, which was completed in 1877. The water-works system was finished in 1878, and in the same year the Belknap system of street car lines was operated to San Pedro springs.

The danger from Indian raids had been lessened after military posts were established far out on the frontier, and telegraph lines connected them with military headquarters in San Antonio. In consequence of those measures the western and northern settlements became comparatively safe and the industries increased in proportion. Immigration poured into the country and a considerable area of land in the territory tributary to San Antonio was put in cultivation. Large herds of horses, cattle, and immense flocks of sheep grazed in safety on the western plains, and San Antonio became a prominent market for live stock and wool.

Throughout this period my identification with the freighting business from Texas seaports and railroad terminuses, through San Antonio westward to El Paso, placed me in a position where I could see the progressive steps that were made when bringing about the country's development, and I realized that a trans-continental railroad had become a necessity. When I saw that the Galveston, Harrisburg & San Antonio Railroad would be extended to El Paso and form a junction with the Southern Pacific Railway, I knew that my freighting business would be ruined. These impressions led me to anticipate that event by disposing of my outfit to advantage, and thereafter I became personally associated with affairs in San Antonio, and took an active interest in promoting the city's improvements and general prosperity.

During the next ten years San Antonio developed rapidly, and many large buildings, some of which were of considerable importance, were erected. A telephone system was established in 1881. The Sunset Railroad made connection with the Southern Pacific, and through trains were run from San Francisco to New Orleans in 1883. The International and Great Northern was completed through San Antonio to Laredo in 1885, where it connected with the Mexican Central, which established a through route to the City of Mexico. Trains were running over the San Antonio and Aransas Pass Railroad to Kerrville, in 1887. The street car system was extended; plazas and streets were improved, important bridges were built, the Army Post and Federal Building were finished; the business and residence portions of the city ere greatly enlarged; and many new enterprises were inaugurated.

The last decade of the nineteenth century was the most active period in the history of San Antonio, and the impetus the city received through the commercial energy and civic pride of its citizens made it the metropolis of Texas, with a total of 53,321 inhabitants, according to the last census. During that period business centers were changed; property values largely increased; the residence limits expanded in every direction, and new additions were made where property was purchased with avidity. The city was lighted by electricity; the street car service was greatly extended and electric cars were introduced which gave efficient service and did much to equalize the value of property; a more complete system of water-works was perfected which supplied the city with delicious water from artesian wells; an expensive sewerage system was introduced; many miles of asphalt and macadamized streets were constructed; the city was adorned by numerous costly business houses, public buildings, including a county court house, a city hall, churches and institutions of learning, in which several millions of dollars were invested; and it was also beautified by a number of public parks in choice localities, which are among the city's greatest attractions. It also became an educational center, because its public schools, colleges and seminaries ranged among the best in the United States and were patronized by students from abroad. Every denomination of the Christian religion, also every fraternal and benevolent order was represented and liberally sustained.

These improvements and benefits, that are recognized as a necessity in every civilized society, are associated with a healthful climate, a variety of agreeable natural features which are universally admired, and the locality is appreciated as an ideal place of residence. Identified with these attractions are the fascinations of a romantic history, which extends to a remote period, that casts a spell over the city, on account of its connection with many heroic performances in the story of its evolution, and distinguishes it as the most interesting city in America.

The prospects that unfolded before San Antonio in every direction at the beginning of the twentieth century, presented a future that was exceedingly promising. The reputation it had acquired as a health resort drew invalids from every civilized country, and its renown attracted visitors from all parts of the world, who naturally contributed to the city's prosperity. The city was also indebted to the Federal Government for its preference shown by selecting it for its military headquarters in the southwest, with a present property valuation of about $5,000,000, and the people appreciate the incalculable advantages derived from that source through the government's large disbursements, amounting to about $3,000,000 annually, and its military features.

The inducements that have made San Antonio a city of homes, and lured others from the outside world to seek its hospitality, are accepted as facts and they are fully substantiated, consequently there is no necessity for exaggeration. They largely increased the resident population, and gave encouragement to rural industries which brought large bodies of emigrants who settled contiguous territory partly on account of the flattering inducements and other opportunities that nature offered them.

The advantages possessed by San Antonio at that period made the city one of the most important commercial and military centers in the country, but they have been much improved in the past eight years. The evidence is perceptible in the character and value of the buildings in the business and residence portions of the city, which will bear a favorable comparison with similar structures in other localities, and in values of real estate that have increased enormously. An estimate based on the resident population at this time of one hundred thousand souls, and taxable wealth amounting to $65,000,000, will convey a crude idea of the changes that have taken place. But the metropolis of Texas owes its importance to its geographical situation and transportation facilities, more than to local attractions, through the opportunities for trade that have been opened since the country tributary to San Antonio was developed, and close connection with the Republic of Mexico was secured, but the last has conferred more benefits than any other contributory cause.

In 1854 Mr. Sartor, father of Alexander Sartor, Sr., was the owner of a small brewery on West Commerce Street, near the bridge, that was called the Lone Star Brewery, and a large star hung in front of it to represent the name, but I do not remember the length of time that it remained in existence. It is possible that this ancient enterprise suggested a name for the present wealthy corporation known as the Lone Star Brewery in San Antonio, but I am not informed on the subject.

The present association under that name was organized in 1880 by San Antonio capitalists, among whom was Herman Kampmann, J. E. Muegge and F. Kalteyer, who furnished most of the money. Mr. Otto Koehler was placed in charge of it as general manager. The greater part of the stock of the company is now owned by the Anheuser-Busch Brewing Association.

Mr. Otto Koehler is now president, and Mr. Otto Wahrmund is vice-president of the famous City Brewery, that is well known throughout the State of Texas, and these gentlemen, together with Messrs. John J. Stevens, the present postmaster of San Antonio, and Oscar Bergstrom, of New York city, are its principal stockholders.

The friendly and commercial relations that have been established through the energy and perseverance of business men in San Antonio, and more recently by the exertions of International Associations, have exercised an influence in both countries under the encouragement of a liberal government, instituted by President Diaz, to whose talents Mexico is so much indebted. They have accomplished a great deal of good, and the advantages are seen in the increase of trade between San Antonio and that country which shows that the plans were properly based and it is possible to benefit all the interests involved by executing them successfully.

The subject might be extended indefinitely, but this brief sketch of San Antonio must suffice, and I will close the account with a list of prominent American, German and French families who resided within its limits between the years 1845 and 1857:

Adams, father of Captain Bill, Captain John, Jim, Pete, Henry, Dave and Martin Adams.

Alexander, father of Dave and Rob Alexander, also of Mrs. Stribling.

Alsbury, E. P., and family.

Artzt, C. P., father of Charles and Theodore Artzt.

Baetz, Joseph, father of Henry and Robert Baetz.

Baylor, Mrs. S. M., widow of Dr. John Baylor, U. S. A., father of General J. R., Colonel G. W., Henry, Charles, Walker, Sophie, Mary and Fanny.

Beck, James H., father of James, Edward, Mary, John, Lucien, Hugel, William and Walter Beck.

Becker, Reinhold, father of Max Becker.

Beckmann, father of Charles and Joe Beckmann.

Bee, General H. P., father of Carlos, Ham P., and Tarver Bee.

Beitel, father of Charles, Roy, Frank and Albert Beitel.

Bennett, father of John, David, Jim, Joe, Jordan, Gramel and Margaret Bennett.

Bennett, W. A., father of Sam Bennett & Mrs. Yoakum.

Biesenbach, Peter, father of August and Ed. Biesenbach.

Bihl, father of Charles T., George D., and Walter Bihl.

Bitter, Henry, father of Albert and John A. Bitter, Tax Collector of Bexar County.

Bitter, Dan, father of W. H. and Charles Bitter.

Bonnett, father of Charles, Pete, Andrew, Dan and William Bonnett.

Booker, Dr.

Brackett, father of Mary, Ellen and Sarah Brackett.

Brackenridge, Colonel G. W.

Braden, Ed., father of Alderman Ed., Joe, Martin, Willie, Henry and Dr. Braden.

Bradley, John, father of Captain John Bradley, Mrs. Wilder, and other children.

Brahan, Major, father of Mrs. Ed Cunningham.

Briam, Louis, father of August, Louis and Hans Briam.

Brown, John and family.

Brodbent, C. L., father of Charles, Albert and Felix Brodbent.

Callaghan, Bryan, father of James and Mayor Bryan Callaghan.

Campbell, W. W., father of Charles and John Campbell.

Canterberry, Harvey, married Mrs. Wilson I. Riddle, children, J. W. and Mildred Canterberry.

Carolane, J. M., father of Mrs. Enoch Jones.

Cass, Josiah, and family.

Childers, George W., and family.

Childress, Jacques, father of Polk and Sam Childress.

Clements, Reuben, and family.

Colquhorn, Major.

Crawford, John C., father of Charles and John Crawford.

Cupples, Dr. George, uncle of C. E. Cupples.

Cunningham, Ed., father of Narcissa, Susie, Eva, Brahan and Ed. Cunningham.

Dangerfield, William H.

Dashiell, Maj. J. Y., father of G. R., T. P., D. H., and Y. F. Dashiell.

Dauchy, A. N., father of Malvina, Mary and Adelhirt Dauchy.

Dauchy, Carey.

Degen, Charles, father of Louis and Charles Degen.

DeMosie.

Denman, Coleman, and family.

Desmuke, Dr. and family.

Deussen

DeVillbis, Rev. J. W., and family.

Devine, Judge J. N., father of Netterville, Albert, and Joe Devine.

Devine, J. P., T. J., Gregory, and Daniel Devine.

Dial, Major ____, father of Mrs. Judge Shook.

Dietler, Frank, father of Henry Dietler.

Dietsch, Joe, father of Albert and Joe Dietsch.

Dignowity, Dr., father of Jim, Henry, Ed, Charles, and Frank Dignowity.

Dreiss, Albert, father of Edward and Adolph Dreiss, deceased.

Drier, and family.

Dryden, and family.

Duerler, father of Gus and Louis Duerler.

Dullnig, father of John, Christian, Jacob, Andres, and George J. Dullnig, president of the Dullnig Grocery Co.

Durand, J. A., and family. (He married Miss Rodriguez.)

Durand, W. C., and August Durand.

Dwyer, Joseph, father of Judge Ed., Joe, Sam, James and Pat Dwyer.

Eager, Robert, father of Mrs. Florence E. Roberts, Mrs. Blanch E. Badger, and Mrs. Fanny McCullough.

Eberhardt, B. C., father of Barney, Willie, Fritz, August, and Henry Eberhardt.

Edgar, Capt. Bill, father of several sons, and Mrs. Cotton.

Edgar, Jack, and James.

Edwards, Charles, and family.

Elder, father of Robert, Felix, and Albert, also of Mrs. Judge Devine and Mrs. Capt. G. Nelson.

Elmendorf, Charles, father of Henry, Emil, Edward, and Dr. Elmendorf.

Enderle, Fritz, father of George and Fritz Enderle.

Evans, family.

Ewell, General R. R.

Felder, William, father of Adolph, Charles, Joe, and Ed. Felder.

Fest, Henry, father of Ed, Henry, and Simon Fest, deceased.

Fischer, Charles.

Fisk, James, father of James, and Ben Fisk, Justice of

the Peace.

Ford, Capt. J. S. (Old Rip), father of Mrs. Maddox and other children.

Fournier, Anton, father of Anton Fournier.

Foutrel, father of Leon, Emil, and J. F. Foutrel, also of Mrs. E. T. Tschirhart.

Frazier, Dr., and family.

French, Marcellus.

French, J. H.

Fries, father of John, Louis, George, Fred, Walter, and Rudolph Fries.

Froboese, Ed., father of Ed., August, Julius, and Herman Froboese.

Gilbeau, Francisco, father of Frank and Edward Gilbeau, and Mrs. Bryan Callaghan.

Gimbel, Christian, father of Ernest and Gus Gimbel.

Giraud, F., and family.

Graf, Louis, father of Charles, Emil, and Ludwig Graf.

Grenet, Honore, and family.

Griesenbeck, Charles, father of Hugo and Eugene Griesenbeck.

Grimsinger, Frank, father of Joseph and Frank Grimsinger.

Graves, Dr. R. L., and family.

Groesbeeck, J. D., father of J. N. Groesbeeck, of San Antonio, and H. S. Groesbeeck, now deceased.

Gutzeit, Frank, father of Joseph, Charles, and Edmond Gutzeit.

Hall, Samuel.

Harney, Gen'l.

Harrison, T. S.

Hart.

Hatch, Dr.

Hays, Col. Jack, and family. (He married Miss Sue Calvert, of Gonzales.)

Hebgen, father of Otto Hebgen.

Heggers.

Herff, Dr. Ferdinand, father of Ferdinand, Charles, William.

August, and Dr. John Herff, deceased.

Herman, Dr. Thomas, and family.

Hertzberg, Theodore R., father of Dr. E. F., and lawyer Hertzberg.

Hettler, Joe, father of James, Michael, and Victor Hettler.

Higginbotham, R. T., and Aunt Martha Higginbotham.

Hoefling, Rudolph, father of Rudolph, Henry, and Willie Hoefling, deceased.

Homer, George.

Horn, Anton, father of Joe, Leo, and Henry Horn.

Horn, Charles, father of Julius and Charley Horn.

Horner, George, father of Kasper and Herman Horner, also of Mrs. F. A. Piper.

Houston, Dr. G. J., father of Augustus, Reagan, William Bryan, deceased, and J. W. Houston, also of Mrs. J. W. Frost and Mrs. R. B. Minor.

Howard, Russel, and family. (He married Miss Mary Elliot.)

Howard, Thomas H., and Volney.

Huntress, John, father of Frank Huntress.

Huppertz, Herman, and family.

Hutchinson, Judge.

Hutzler, father of Anton, Joe, and John Hutzler.

Jackson, W. C., father of Alvin and Zulo.

James, Judge John, father of Vinton, Sidney, Scott, and Judge J. H. James.

Jett, Capt. William E., father of Willie, Thomas, Stern, and Stephen Jett.

Johnston, Gen'l. Albert Sidney, and family.

Jonas, Peter, father of Albert and Peter Jonas.

Jones, Enoch, father of Griff Jones.

Jones, William E.

Judson, George H., father of Will, Mose, and Mrs. Si Pancoast.

Jordan, David, John, Jim, and Joe.

Kalteyer, F., father of George and Dr. Fred, also an uncle of W. C. Kalteyer, the druggist.

Kampmann, John H., father of Herman and Gus Kampmann.

Kerr, Uncle Billy, father of William, Thomas, Newton, Caroline, and Virginia Kerr.

King, family.

Kingsbury, Dr. , and family.

Knox, Gen'l. William B., father of Capt. W. R. and "Big Henry" Knox.

Koenigheim, E., and Sam.

Krempkau, Charles G., father of Gus, Henry, Adolph, Albert, John, and Willie Krempkau.

Kuhlmann, H., father of Henry and Adolph Kuhlmann.

Kunzman, Henry, father of Theodore Kunzman.

Laager, Henry, father of Henry Laager, Jr.

Lacoste, J. B., father of Lucian, and Mrs. Ferdinand Herff, Jr.

Ladner, Nick, father of Ladner Bros., of Eagle Pass.

Landa, Joe, father of Harry Landa, of New Braunfels.

Lee, Gen'l. Robert E.

Leslie, Jack.

Lewis, Nat., father of Nat., Jr., and Dan Lewis.

Lockwood, A. A.

Lytle, "Uncle Billy," father of Capt. Sam and Charles Lytle.

Luckee, W. F., father of William, Mary, Emily, Samuel, Julius, Eugene, Cornelius, George, and Ella.

Ludwig, father of Albert Ludwig.

Mackay, Dr.

Martin, George, father of George, Jr., Jack, and Miss Belle Martin.

Mauermann, father of Alderman Ben and Marshal Gus A. Mauermann.

Mays, N. D., father of Allie and Garland Mays, also of Mrs. Capt. Gosling and of Mrs. Judge Tom Mays.

Maverick, Samuel A., father of Sam, Lewis, George, Albert, and William Maverick, also of Mrs. Dr. Terrell.

McAllister, Sam, father of Willie, Joe, and Ed. McAllister.

McCullough, Sam, father of Robert and Clark McCullough.

McCullouch, Gen'l. Henry E.

McCullough, Gen'l. Ben.

McDonald, John S., father of John McDonald.

McLane, _____.

McLane, H. H.

McMullen, John, and family.

Menger, S., father of August, Dr. Rudolph, and Alderman Eric Menger.

Menger, William, father of Gustav and William Menger.

Menger, George.

Merick, M. L., father of Martin, Wolfe, and Julia Merick.

Meyer, father of Albert, Emil, and Edward Meyer.

Miles, Ed.

Minter, Major, and family.

Mitchell, Asa, father of Nathan ("Old Nat"), Caroline, William, Milam, Hiram, Martin, Laura, Madison, Jack, and Wallace Mitchell.

Moore, Sam, and family.

Muenzenberger, C., father of Ernest Muenzenberger, Gen'l. Agt., Nat'l. Lines of Mexico.

Nauwald, C. H., father of C. H. and E. A. Nauwald.

Neighbors, Major ___ and family.

Nelson, Capt. G., father of T. C. Nelson.

Nette, A., father of August Nette.

Neubauer, Fritz, father of Fred, Willie, Adolph, and Louis Neubauer.

Newton, Frank, father of Joe, Lee, Charley, and Frank Newton, Jr., County Clerk.

Newton, S. G., father of S. G., and Tom Newton, County Attorney.

Niggli, John, father of Emil, Fritz, and Ferdinand Niggli, deceased.

Noonan, George H., father of George B. and Ralph Noonan.

O'Day.

Ogden, Duncan B.

Ogden, D. C.

Oge, Louis, father of George Oge, and Mrs. C. H. Bertrand.

O'Ray, William.

Pancoast, Josiah, and family.

Pancoast, Aaron, and family.

Paschal, Frank, father of Dr. Frank, ex-Mayor George, and Ernest Paschal, deceased.

Paschal, Judge J. A., father of ex-Congressman Tom Paschal.

Piper, , father of Fred, Julius, and A. C. Piper.

Pirie, James, and family.

Poor, Ira S., father of Capt. D. M. and Fred Poor, also step-father of W. W. and Colon D. McRoe.

Post, and family.

Powers, John ("Kentuck").

Pfefferling, Ed., father of Ed., Rudolph, Henry, and Abraham Pfefferling.

Pyron, Col. Charles L., father of Clara, Ella, Charlie, and Mot Pyron.

Rice, father of Howell Rice.

Richardson, Dean W. R.

Riddle, W. I., father of Sarah E. Riddle Eager and James W. Riddle.

Rische, Ulrick, father of Ernest, Duck, and Edward Rische.

Ritterman, father of Louis and Henry Ritterman.

Rossy, Charles, father of Charles Rossy.

Rothenflue, George, father of Peter Rothenflue.

Rummel, Fritz, father of Charles, and Fritz Rummel, Jr.

Rummel, Louis, father of Gustave, Fritz, Louis, and Adolph Rummel.

Russ, father of Max Russ.

Russi, Michael, father of Mrs. George R. Stumberg.

Russi, David, father of Fritz Russi.

Ryan, father of Joseph Ryan, City Attorney of San Antonio.

Sartor, Alex, father of Alexander Sartor.

Sauer, Justus, father of Paul, Charles, and Ernest Sauer.

Schaffer, Adam, father of Henry and Philip Schaffer.

Schleman, Dr.

Schmeltzer, Gustave, father of Herman and Gus Schmeltzer.

Schreiner, Fritz, father of Charles Schreiner, and brother of the well-known Capt. Schreiner, of Kerrville.

Schumacher, Anton, father of Henry, William, and Charles Schumacher.

Schunke, father of Louis, Max, Willie, Charles, Otto, and Ed. Schunke.

Seffel, Stephen, father of Emanuel Seffel.

Seguin, J. N., a sister married Ira Hewett.

Shiner, Peter, father of Joe, Henry, Mike, Charles, and Bee Shiner.

Schleuning, Theodore, father of Fritz Schleuning.

Schleuning, Herman, father of Herman Schleuning.

Simpson, I. P., and family.

Small, William, and family.

Small, L., father of Henry, Fred, and Montgomery Small.

Smith, Capt. J. W., and family.

Smith, Samuel S., father of Thad. and Robert Smith.

Smith, Erastus (Deaf), and family.

Staacke, A., father of Herman, Gustave, and Rudolph Staacke, deceased.

Stevens, father of Constable Charley and Ed. Stevens.

Stevens, John, father of Postmaster John, Jr., Tom, and Andrew Stevens, private secretary of the City Brewery.

Steves, Ed., father of Ernest, Albert, and Ed. Steves, Jr.

Strohmeyer, Emil, father of Rudolph Strohmeyer.

Stumberg, Diedrich, father of George R. Stumberg, also of Louis and Henry Stumberg, deceased.

Stuemke, August, father of George Stuemke.

Sutherland, Dr., father of Leven, Jack, and Rev. Sutherland.

Sweet, Colonel James R., father of Alex.

Tobin, William, father of William G., C. M., and Sheriff John W. Tobin.

Teel, T. T., father of B. F., Van, F. F.,,J. F., W. E.

Teel, also Mrs. Judge Haltom.

Teel, R. E.

Tengg, father of Nic Tengg.

Thiele, father of August Thiele.

Thomas, Ben, and family.

Thomas, Wiley, and family.

Trainor, James, father of John, Capt. James, and other children.

Trueheart, Thomas L., father of James L., A. B., and H. M. Trueheart.

Twohig, John.

Ulrich, Joseph, father of Lewis Ulrich.

Umscheid, Frank, father of Joe Umscheid, J. P.

Upson, Columbus, father of James and George Upson.

Vance, William, father of William and John Vance.

Vanderlip.

Waelder, Major Jacob, father of Bradley and Carlo Waelder.

Wallace, William, Alexander, Anderson ("Big Foot").

Weber, Jacob, and family.

Wefing, father of Louis and Otto Wefing, who are half-brothers of Adolph and Capt. Eugene Hernandez.

Weidemann, Dr.

Welter, father of Carl Welter.

Wernette, John, father of Josie, Charles, and John Wernette.

Weyel, Jacob, father of Albert, and Ferdinand Weyel, deceased.

Weyel, William, father of Willie, Louis, Theodore, and Punk Weyel.

Wilkins, John, father of John Wilkins.

Willie.

Wheeler, Judge , and family.

Whitehead, Thomas, second husband of Mrs. Urutia.

Wolcken, father of John and Christian Wolcken.

Wurzbach, Charles, father of William, Charles, Dr.

George, and Harry, County Judge of Seguin.

Worth, Gen'l. William, U. S. A., and family.

Zander, August, father of August, Julius, and Adolph Zander.

Zork, Louis, father of Ralph, Jack, and Julius Zork.

Chapter Twenty-Nine:
The Mexican Frontier

A supplemental history of the settlement of west Texas would be incomplete without a description of the four frontier states of Mexico, and three others in the interior lying south of them. But before entering into details I will call attention to the conditions of the country, also to some of the prejudices of the people before the age of railroads, when I was familiar with the country, and compare them with those that exist at the present time. In this connection the fact should be noticed that I became familiar with the states of Tamaulipas, Nuevo Leon, San Luis Potosi, Coahuila, Chihuahua and Durango, before and after the great Civil War in the United States, but I did not visit Queretaro until 1889, when going to the City of Mexico by rail.

Then there were no railroads leading into the Republic of Mexico and all the highways in those sections were not only rough, but it was dangerous to travel over them because there was always a great risk of encountering robbers and wild Indians. The settlements were separated by long distances between, the people were almost destitute of the necessities of life; and places of entertainment, except in large towns, were of the rudest description. Traveling was nearly all done on horseback or in private conveyances, and merchandise or other commodities was transported on carts or wagons over routes leading from prominent seaports to cities in the interior. European nations monopolized nearly all the trade of the country, and they controlled its exports in exchange for the manufactured goods received from those countries.

Commercial intercourse between the United States and

Mexico was restricted by popular prejudices on both sides, that was expressed in the trade relations between the two Republics until the transactions were not worth considering because of their insignificance. The causes which were responsible for the boycott may be traced through the histories of the past, and especially to the war in which the nations engaged, that provoked a bitter hatred between the two races, but there is no necessity for noticing them in this connection. It is sufficient to know that in Mexico the feeling existed against the United States in its most intense form, and it is a known fact that the better class of citizens disliked to visit Texas, and disapproved the idea of educating their children anywhere in the United States. For that reason many of their young men were sent to school in Europe rather than have them learn the English language or adopt American customs.

No effort was made to counteract this bad feeling in the United States where it was generally encouraged; and it was reciprocated by respectable Americans who visited Mexico occasionally on business connected with mercantile affairs or mining property. But a few Americans owned business houses in that country and introduced small lots of goods manufactured in the United States, although there was little demand for them. Foreigners of English, German, and French origin who engaged in business in the interior were liberally patronized, and the goods they handled were all imported from Europe in wholesale quantities; but in 1868 a demand was created for merchandise of American manufacture which gradually increased until they became a necessity. In this connection I will notice the fact that nearly all the freight hauled overland to Mexico, until 1880, was imported from Europe and passed through Texas under bond. I will also state that during my intercourse with the people of Mexico I rarely heard a word of the English language, and it was never spoken in business houses, but the conditions have undergone a perceptible change on account of business relations that have been established with the United States in recent years with the aid of railroads.

The changes were brought about by means of commercial enterprises which have made it possible for business energy to work untrammeled, and forced the intelligence of the two countries to realize that a closer union between them is unavoidable. Mexico is preparing for it by educating hundreds of her young men in the colleges of San Antonio, and Americans are showing their confidence in the prospects of the future by investing millions of dollars in that country where they own and control large properties. These influences have promoted trade, and the vast railroad systems which the necessities of commerce have created have linked the two countries together with bonds of steel that will encourage friendship and assure perpetual peace.

These efforts of a later generation to forget the wrongs and differences of the past, that are charged against both republics, have been successful from a commercial point of view, and in the course of time a more liberal feeling will be entertained by the masses. These amicable relations should be cultivated in Mexico, and Texans should be reminded that Mexico was the mother that sheltered their state in its infancy, until the constitution of 1824 was trampled under foot by a military despotism, before it seceded from that republic, and they should grasp the friendly hand that has been extended to them by the present government over the chasm in which all their past differences ought to be buried.

My personal relations with Mexico have always been pleasant, and I entertain grateful feelings because of the liberal and courteous treatment that was received by me from the government and people on every occasion, when I visited that country on business or pleasure. I have many warm friends who live there, therefore I would not say anything to offend or misrepresent them, and I trust that no information of mine will be misconstrued, either in what I have written or in the descriptions of the states which follow.

CHIHUAHUA

This state is bounded on the north by the United States, on the east by Coahuila, on the south by Durango, and on the west by Sonora and Sinaloa. It is the largest and the farthest north of any in the Mexican Republic. Its greatest width is 360 American miles, and its extreme length is about 450 miles. The area of the state is estimated at 83,746 square miles, and the census of 1900 gave it 245,657 inhabitants.

The city of Chihuahua is the capital of the state, and it is beautifully situated, near its center, in a large plain, at the base of the Sierra Madre range. The Mexican Central Railroad, which extends from Ciudad Juarez, opposite El Paso, to the city of Mexico, passes through the city; and another road is being constructed from there to Presidio del Norte, on the Rio Grande, and also westward to the Gulf of California, both of which will soon be completed. Many towns and villages are scattered over the state and some of them are destined to become places of importance on account of their favorable locations.

The western portion of the state is broken by several chains of high mountains, with a number of deep cañons between, from which flow numerous beautiful streams of clear water that empty in the gulf of California; but there are also many wide valleys of fertile land that produce luxurious grasses and timber in great variety. The surface of the country towards the east is less rugged and the country is more accessible. In the northern part of the state in the neighborhood of Juarez is a desert sixty miles square, that is difficult and sometimes dangerous to cross on account of the sand which is constantly drifting and forming hills called *madonos*. The Rio Concho, which rises in the Sierra Madre Mountains and runs through the state 360 miles to Presidio del Norte, where it empties in the Rio Grande, which is the state's boundary line on the north, below El Paso, is the longest river in the Republic. The greater part of the valley is in cultivation and the land under irrigation is very productive, and Irish potatoes grow wild.

The live stock interests in the state are very great and there are many large ranches on which vast numbers of horses, mules, cattle, sheep and goats are profitably raised on the untillable lands which afford an excellent pasturage.

The mineral wealth of the state is justly considered to be greater than in any other part of Mexico. The Spaniards worked the mines in early times and several of them were made to yield sixteen ounces of silver per cargo, of 300 pounds, but they were unprotected from the Indians, and when sufficient labor or timber for securing the shafts could not be had they were abandoned. Since the conditions have changed, through the facilities offered by railroad transportation, the old mines have been opened by American capitalists and are worked by modern machinery under the direction of skillful engineers so as to yield enormous profits. Many new mines in other localities have also been opened and American enterprise, backed by unlimited capital, has introduced new methods, and the mineral resources of that region are being developed into enormous proportions.

The government maintains two custom houses on the Rio Grande within the borders of the state, one at Ciudad Juarez and the other at Presidio del Norte, where all the duties are paid on imports subject to tariff, and the northern border is strictly guarded to prevent smuggling. These institutions were established for the collection of taxes on foreign imports long before railroads were built through that country, and they have become important ports of entry since the Southern Pacific was completed through Texas.

The present conditions in the state can not be compared to those that existed when I freighted to Chihuahua, but the room for improvement is still very perceptible. These changes have been brought about by railroads, which have developed the country and encouraged friendly and commercial intercourse with the United States and other foreign countries whose citizens have invested enormous sums of money within its borders.

Among the first foreigners that settled in Chihuahua, between 1848 and 1855, were Henry Mueller, Emil Schadlig, F. Feltmann, Carl, Gustave and William Moye, Frank Mollmann, A. F. Wulff, Frank, George and Edwin McManus, and J. P. Hickman, father of James P. Hickman, Jr., proprietor of the Southern Hotel in San Antonio, and Henry Creel and family, father of Henry Clay Creel, present governor of the state of Chihuahua.

These and other foreign-born citizens were prominent business men in the city when I was engaged in freighting; but since then the population of other nationalities has greatly increased, and a large part of the business is under their control. The country is being developed very rapidly, especially its mineral wealth which offers flattering inducements for the investment of capital. Important railroad lines are being constructed which will largely augment the resources of the state, and when the route leading from Presidio del Norte to Topolobampo is completed, via the city of Chihuahua, it will be the most direct route from San Antonio to the Pacific coast.

COAHUILA

This state is bounded on the north by Texas, on the east by Nuevo Leon, on the south by Zacatecas, and on the west by Chihuahua and Durango. The state has an area of 50,890 square miles and the population in 1900 was 144,594.

When the Mexican Republic was first organized Coahuila and Texas were united as one state and they became known as the "Twin Sisters." The boundary line between them was not clearly defined, and later the Medina and Nueces Rivers were both claimed on Spanish evidence as the eastern limits of Coahuila. The seat of government of the two states was originally at Monclova, but it was subsequently removed to Saltillo, the present capital of Coahuila, contrary to a petition of the citizens of Texas, who opposed its removal on account of its greater distance and the dangers of the route which made it almost inaccessible to their delegates.

Saltillo is an Indian name which means "highlands with much water," and as the town is situated on the declivity of a high hill that is the source of many gushing fountains, the appropriateness of the name is obvious. The city is of considerable importance and it has about 25,000 inhabitants. The most prominent of its numerous churches is beautifully ornamented with sculpture, and it has besides a number of important buildings and other interesting features that include an amphitheater, a public garden, a central plaza, around which the governor's palace and other government buildings are situated, also an alameda planted with beautiful shade trees. In its vicinity are several large factories that are successfully operated by water power.

Several large towns and many villages are situated in the state, which are sustained by about fifty manufacturing enterprises, including factories, flour, corn and sawmills, and other local industries. The principal importing point within the borders of the state is Ciudad Porfirio Diaz, that was formerly known as Piedras Negras, which is opposite Eagle Pass, where a Federal customhouse has long been established. A bridge crosses the Rio Grande at that point which connects the Southern Pacific system with the Mexican National Railroad and other important highways leading into Mexico.

The mineral wealth of the state has long been known and esteemed for its riches, though its development was interrupted many years by the Indians. Some of the high grade ores taken from the mines have assayed a very rich yield in silver, and others of copper, lead, etc., are producing profitable returns. All of the old mines are now worked and many new claims have been opened in recent years which foreign capital is developing with improved machinery in accordance with modern methods.

A large area of the state is mountainous and not suitable for cultivation, but much of the tillable land is irrigated and the soil produces abundant crops of corn, wheat, cotton, sugar-cane and all the fruits of a temperate climate; grapes are grown in quantities, and wine made in that region received the gold medal at the Centennial Exposition, also Mescal of the best quality is produced from the Maguey plant. The nutritious grasses of the grazing lands sustain large herds of animals and all kinds of live stock do well.

Don Evaristo Madero, who was governor of the state about twenty-five years ago, was distinguished for his liberality and enterprising spirit which his enormous wealth enabled him to exercise in many ways for the good of the state. He accepted the executive office contrary to his inclinations, and afterwards distributed his salary among the poor. I knew him well through business transactions and Carlos Griesenbach was his intimate friend. The governor has been an exhibitor at the three last International Fairs in San Antonio, and secured premiums on a great variety of liquors of all kinds, including wines, brandy, etc., of his own manufacture. This fact shows that he has broad views that are not confined to his own country and that he realizes the importance of cultivating commercial relations with the United States. The Sisters of the Ursuline Academy, in San Antonio, have good reasons for holding him in grateful remembrance because of the aid he extended to them during and after the Civil War in the United States.

NUEVO LEON

This state has a very irregular outline. It is bounded on the north by Texas and Tamaulipas, on the east and south by Tamaulipas and San Luis Potosi, and on the north and west by San Luis Potosi and Coahuila. The state has an area of 23,635 square miles and the census of 1900 gave it 650,000 inhabitants.

When the country was first organized under Spanish rule Nuevo Reino de Leon was a kingdom, as the name indicates, which embraced Nuevo Leon and all the adjoining states, with its capital at Monclova. Afterwards it was reduced to three of said states, which became a province, and now it is the smallest of the Republican states that were carved from its territory. Its greatest length is about 300 miles, and it is only about 125 miles across its widest part.

The historic city of Monterey is the capital of the state and it has about 90,000 inhabitants at the present time. The altitude of the city is 1,630 feet above the sea level, and it is situated in a delightful and healthful climate about 630 miles from the City of Mexico. Mountain spurs from the Sierra Madre range nearly surround the city and form valleys that lead out from it. The most attractive of these elevations is the Sierra de la Silla, or Saddle Mountain, which rises six miles distant in a southerly direction. All the railroads that connect with those which pass through Texas and others of equal importance center in Monterey. These national highways afford rapid transportation to all parts of the Republic, and they facilitate the commercial energy of its citizens who are making the city an emporium of trade for the northern part of Mexico.

Before railroads were dreamed of, its factories and other industries attracted attention on account of its natural advantages, but its prominence has since been largely increased by the benefits they have conferred. Manufacturing establishments are converting the raw material of the country into merchantable commodities and large foundries are fusing its valuable iron ore into steel rails, etc., for commercial and industrial purposes. The vast opportunities that a progressive policy has conferred on the city have given it an importance in Mexico equal to that which Chicago holds in the United States as a commercial center.

Some valuable mines have been developed in the state since 1890 which are yielding profitable returns. Before that date primitive methods, which involved a small outlay of capital, were commonly employed and all the work was near the surface. Mines have been discovered in which silver, copper, iron, sulphur and valuable marble are found and they will add to the wealth of the state in the course of time. The principal mining towns are Jimenez, Linares, Montemorelos, Salinas, Cerralvo, Vilaldama and many other important and beautiful places.

A considerable area of land is in cultivation and that under irrigation yields abundant harvests of corn, oats, wheat, beans, pepper and sugar cane. Irish potatoes grow wild in the mountains and a variety of other vegetables constitute a part of the tillable crops. Fruits of all kinds thrive to perfection and the oranges grown in the vicinity of Monterey are classed as the best that Mexico produces. Land not suitable for tillage is devoted to ranch purposes and large numbers of horses, cattle, sheep and goats are raised on the excellent pasturage that sustains them in good condition.

TAMAULIPAS

This state is the extreme northeastern division of the Mexican Republic and its boundary line on the north is the Rio Grande, which separates it from Texas. It is bounded on the east by the Gulf of Mexico; on the south by the states of Vera Cruz and San Luis Potosi; and on the west by Nuevo Leon. The state has an area of 30,225 square miles and its population in 1900 was 141,000 souls. The Nueces River, in Texas, was claimed by Tamaulipas as its northern boundary until that part of its territory was relinquished in 1848, under the treaty of Guadalupe Hidalgo.

Ciudad Victoria is the capital of the state, and it is beautifully situated near the base of a high mountain where it is almost surrounded by attractive gardens, orchards, and fields of sugar-cane and corn, which are irrigated from large streams of clear water. The Mexican Central Railroad that connects Tampico with Monterey passes near the city and affords direct communication with the outside world. Before it was completed the town had only about 10,000 inhabitants, when I visited it in 1863. There were no local industries in the town then and its trade was insignificant; there were no attractions and its only place of interest was an old church which was built in the eighteenth century, but never finished. Its walls are scarred by marks of shot and shell similar to those on the high loopholed walls which surround the grave-yard that occupies a commanding position and was evidently built for and used as a fortification. They are reminders of the civil wars that were constantly waged for many years in the state by the frontier generals, Canalles and Cortinas.

The railroad has added greatly to the prominence of the capital and its importance as a commercial city will increase when the state develops its latent wealth under the present liberal policy of the government. A railroad from Matamoras southward through the tropical regions, near the Gulf of Mexico, will become a necessity in a few years. Rapid transportation for the products of that country to the markets of the United States will be secured, and the road would establish another bond that will unite the common interests of the two republics.

Matamoras is one of the principal ports of entry and it is the largest city in the state. It is favorably situated on the south side of the Rio Grande, opposite Brownsville, in Texas, and thirty-five miles above the mouth of the river, which gives it a safe harbor near the Gulf of Mexico and makes it the most northern seaport in the republic. Before the Civil War in the United States the place was scarcely known, but after all the ports in the Southern Confederacy were blockaded the Southern troops held possession of the Rio Grande. Matamoras was a friendly port that was open to the ships of all nations, and they flocked to its harbor with cargoes of freight to exchange for the cotton which was hauled on wagons from the interior of Texas. Thousands of bales were conveyed across the river and passed through the custom-house, in Matamoras, before it could be sold; consequently it became the most important cotton market in the world. The demand was greater than the supply and the fleecy staple sold at fifty cents, or perhaps more, per pound in gold; but nearly all of it was spent in the purchase of goods by individual purchasers for home use at exorbitant prices.

The population of the city increased during that period to about 35,000, of all classes, in which many nationalities were represented. The greater part were Mexicans, but a large number were refugees or deserters from the Southern states and others were from the Northern states and from Europe. The duties received by the Mexican custom-house on imports and exports yielded an enormous sum to the government before United States troops occupied the lower Rio Grande country and cut off the trade from Texas.

The prominence that Matamoras acquired under such conditions, and later during the war against Maximilian, secured for it an important trade with the northern states of Mexico that has constantly increased. The National Railroad which extends up the Rio Grande valley and southwestward to Monterey, has established direct communication with the interior of Mexico, and the St. Louis, Brownsville and Mexico Railway connects it with all the important railroad systems in the United States. Other railroads to that point are being discussed and undoubtedly one or more direct lines from San Antonio to Brownsville will be completed in the near future.

Nuevo Laredo, on the Rio Grande, is another important port of entry within the borders of the state. The Mexican National, the International and Great Northern, and the Texas-Mexican Railroads, which connect Monterey with San Antonio and Corpus Christi form a junction on the bridge that spans the river between the old and new town of Laredo. Both are improving rapidly under the magic touch of progress and the destiny of the two towns is not involved in doubt because that point is an important gateway between the two republics.

The Cordilleras range that traverses the state from northeast to southwest and separates it from Nuevo Leon, forms a barrier toward the west that is almost impassable; but the spurs extending from the mountains enclose many lovely valleys of considerable extent which sustain a large population. The climate west of the mountains is temperate and dry, but that towards the east is moist and much warmer, and at certain seasons portions of it are subject to heavy rain storms which do much harm.

The mountainous portion of the state is rich in minerals, and the deposits of gold, silver, etc., seem to be inexhaustible. Many mines have been worked profitably for years, and probably others that were once abandoned because of unfavorable surroundings, have been developed by foreign capital since new methods have been introduced.

The cultivable land is fertile and produces cotton, corn, rice, sugar-cane, beans, Irish and sweet potatoes with little labor. Tropical fruit in great variety, and many kinds that are common in northern climates, grow to perfection. The timbered portion of the state is mostly confined to the mountains, but there is an abundance in other parts that is suitable for building purposes.

The eastern portion of the state and that bordering on the Rio Grande, is admirably adapted for ranch purposes, and large numbers of horses, cattle, sheep and goats are raised at small cost. The finest mules in the Republic are bred in the state and they always find a ready market.

Before closing the subject I will give a brief description of the states immediately south of and joining those bordering on Texas. They were once politically associated with Texas, when Spain held dominion over the country; and now they are related through commercial interests. My acquaintance with all that region will warrant my calling attention to it and justify me in noticing a few of its attractions with which I am familiar.

SAN LUIS POTOSI

This state is bounded on the north and east by Nuevo Leon and Tamaulipas; on the south by Hidalgo, Queretaro, and Guanajuato; and on the west by Zacatecas. It has an area of 23,635 miles, and in 1900 it had 210,000 inhabitants.

The city of San Luis Potosi is the capital of the state. It was once the capital of one of the intendencies into which Mexico was divided when under Spanish rule and Texas was one of its provinces, forming part of the tenth brigade. I have described its appearance as I saw it in 1862 in Chapter III, but since that date the Mexican National and Mexican Central have been built through the city, which connect it with the railroad systems in Mexico, and its importance as a commercial center at the present time cannot be underrated. It has always been noted for its local industries, and it is destined to become a manufacturing city. There are several other cities situated in rich mining districts with large populations.

The mines of the state rank among the richest in the country, and many of the metallic veins in various localities are now worked by foreign capital that is doing so much to advance the prosperity of Mexico. All of the precious minerals are found in paying quantities, and many of the baser metals, particularly iron ore, in large deposits.

The surface of the state is broken by chains of mountains which run across it and form many large and beautiful valleys. They are spurs of the Cordilleras range which extends over the eastern portion of the Mexican Republic and form a natural boundary between the state and Tamaulipas. The most remarkable chains are the Sierra de San Luis and Sierra Gorda, which bound the state on the south and separate it from the states of Guanajuato, Queretaro and Mexico.

Many varieties of valuable timber are native to the southern portions of the state; lemons, oranges, peaches, pears, apricots, and other fruit peculiar to Mexico, are grown in its temperate climate; corn, oats and all kinds of vegetables are successfully cultivated; and cotton, coffee, sugar-cane and tobacco are produced with profit.

A large area of the state is devoted to the raising of live stock and large numbers of horses, cattle, sheep and goats add to the taxable wealth of the state. One of the largest and most valuable estates in Mexico lies partly within its boundaries. It is situated on the table lands and it contains nearly 900,000 acres in one body, which extends into three adjoining states. The name of this vast estate is *San Rafael del Salado y Agua Dulce*, but it is commonly known as El Salado. General Don Juan Bustamente, ex-Governor of San Luis Potosi, owns the property.

QUERETARO

This state is bounded on the north by San Luis Potosi; on the east by Hidalgo; on the south by the state of Mexico; and on the west by Guanajuato.

The state has an area of 3,027 square miles, and according to the census of 1890, it had 203,290 inhabitants.

A great variety of minerals are found in the state and a number of mines that had been worked before I visited the country were then idle because of the lack of enterprise and the want of capital, but it is more than probable that the rich resources of the state have been greatly developed under more favorable conditions.

The state is well watered, but none of the streams are navigable. Fruit and vegetables in great variety and every agricultural product that grows in the United States flourishes in that delightful climate. Many species of timber are found in the mountains, and the untillable land affords an excellent range for live stock of all kinds which are raised in considerable numbers.

The city of Queretaro is the capital of the state, and it is situated in a temperate climate about two hundred American miles in a northerly direction from the City of Mexico.

The National and Mexican Central Railroads pass through the city and connect with all parts of the Republic. These great transportation enterprises have brought about many changes, but its ancient features are still attractive, and among them are several fine churches, a large hospital, and the convents of San Francisco, Santa Cruz, San Antonio, San Domingo, and San Augustin.

The water that supplies the city is brought from the neighboring mountains through a large aqueduct that is made of solid masonry laid in a native cement which has stood the test of centuries in Mexico, where it is in general use. The channel, that conveys the water to the city in a constant stream, is about ten feet in width and fully seven feet deep.

The canal was built on a certain level, but owing to the irregular surface along its course, it was necessary to make cuts from ten to fifty feet deep, and in other places the duct was sustained by masonry with arches, some of which are eighty feet high. The work was completed over one hundred years ago, and it is said that it cost $124,000. The surplus water after supplying the city is conveyed in ditches to the gardens, etc., in the vicinity, and the irrigated land produces all kinds of native fruits and flowers which grow to perfection.

Near the city is the factory of Hercules, that, when I saw it, was represented to be the finest and largest establishment of its kind in the world. It is said that it cost over $4,000,000, and in 1867 it was owned by Francisco Rubio. Water, steam, and horse-power were used to run the machinery, and some of its departments were continually at work. The daily output was about 1,800 bolts of unbleached domestic, and at night a large number of stones, run by water-power, were employed in grinding quantities of wheat. The grounds around the factory are beautifully improved, and one of the attractions is a statue of Hercules that was brought from Italy, which cost $15,000.

It was in the city of Queretaro that Maximilian sustained a siege against the liberal forces of Mexico under General Escobedo, which resulted in his betrayal, through the treachery of his bosom friend, Colonel Miguel Lopez, of the Empress' regiment, whom he had just made a general, and he surrendered to Generals Palacio and Escobedo on the 19th of May, 1867. Maximilian was subsequently tried before a military tribunal, and shot, with his unfortunate companions, Generals Mejia and Miramon, at the foot of "Cerro de la Cruz" on the 19th of June, 1867.

ZACATECAS

This state lies northwest of the city of Mexico. It is bounded on the north by Coahuila; on the east by San Luis Potosi; on the south by the states of Aguas Calientes and Jalisco, and on the west by Durango. Its area contains 22,998 square miles, and in 1890 it had 470,000 inhabitants.

The city of Zacatecas is the capital of the state. It is situated in the southern part of the state in a cañon that runs through a mountainous district, and its altitude is 7,500 feet above the sea level. The principal edifices consist of the governor's palace, the mint, a city hall, a jail, markets, a hospital, a theater and an amphitheater, a cathedral and a dozen or more churches. The Mexican Central Railroad passes through the city from the north to the City of Mexico, and it is connected with Tampico by the same system over another route.

The greater part of the state is mountainous, but in the eastern portion there are many fertile valleys that are capable of sustaining a large population. The climate is cold in the more elevated portions, but it is temperate in the valleys.

Many species of timber are found and it is abundant. Pears, apples, and grapes are grown and produce fruit of excellent quality. Corn, wheat and other small grain, and vegetables in great variety are cultivated with satisfactory results.

The state has numerous haciendas of great extent and a large number of farms and ranches. The grazing lands are favorably adapted to live stock, and horses, mules, sheep and goats thrive on its mountainous pastures. The mineral wealth of the state is so great that it ranks among the first in the Republic, although all of the mines have been worked at a great disadvantage, and many, for various reasons, were abandoned. Some of them are very rich in precious metals and they also produced all of the baser kinds, but it does not appear that many of them were very profitable.

DURANGO

This state lies in a northwest direction from the City of Mexico, and it is bounded on the north by Chihuahua; on the east by Coahuila and Zacatecas; on the south by Jalisco; and on the west by Sinaloa, from which it is separated by the Sierra Madre range that sends out spurs of high mountains which also divide the state. It has an area of 42,510 square miles, and the census of 1900 gave it 200,000 population. The climate on an average is temperate, but it varies with the altitude.

The city of Durango is the capital of the state, and when I knew it in 1872 it had about 28,000 inhabitants. The government buildings are similar to those in other state capitals, and it also had a mint, three or four churches, a fine hospital, a theater, a place for bull-fighting, etc. The place was of considerable prominence as a commercial center, although it had only a few industries, and all the freight to and from the place was hauled on wagons, etc.

I suppose since the Mexican National Railroad was completed from C. P. Diaz to that point, and beyond to Tepehuanes, that the city has been greatly improved. It only needed transportation facilities to make it one of the most important cities in the Republic, and when the road is completed to its destination on the Gulf of California, its ocean outlet and connections with all the railroad systems in the country, the benefits the city will receive cannot be overestimated.

The state is known to be rich in minerals of all kinds, but the mines have only been developed successfully in recent years. Its gold and silver mines were worked profitably until they were abandoned on account of Indian incursions and civil wars. Valuable mines of copper, lead, and other metals have been discovered, and the inexhaustible iron mountain, known as *Cerro del Mercado*, is said to be one of the richest deposits of iron ore on the American continent. Movements have been recently made towards utilizing the ore by establishing one of the largest steel plants in the country.

The principal river is the Rio del Nazas, that runs through the state one hundred and fifty American miles, and on both sides of its wide valley are many beautiful haciendas and plantations that produce every variety of grain and other agricultural products adapted to that region. The Rio del Tunal and El Reno de las Palmas also have large valleys of tillable land through which they flow. These and other streams afford an abundance of water for irrigating purposes and the cultivable land in the state is capable of sustaining a large population. Live stock of all kinds do well, and there are many large ranches devoted to the raising of cattle, horses, sheep and goats.

APPENDIX

Names of the Mayors and Aldermen of
the City of San Antonio, Texas

From its incorporation, June, 1837, to the present time.

* precedes names of Aldermen who did not serve entire term.
† precedes names of Aldermen elected to fill vacancy.

September 19, 1837, to March 9, 1838.
Mayor. John W. Smith.
Aldermen. Manuel Martinez, Francisco Bustillo, Ramon Trevino, Pedro Flores Morales, Gabriel Arreola, Rafael Herrera, Francisco Grenado, Francisco A. Ruiz.

March 9, 1838, to July 20, 1838.
Mayor. William H. Dangerfield, and from July 20, 1838, to January 8, 1839, Antonio Menchaca, pro tem.
Aldermen. Antonio Menchaca, W. E. Houth, Jose Flores, Rafael Garza, Manuel Yturri, Leander Arreola, Ambrosio Rodriguez, Manuel Ximenes.

January 8, 1839, to January 8, 1840.
Mayor. S. A. Maverick.
Aldermen. Jose Cassiano, Vicente Garza, Francisco A. Ruiz, Domingo Bastillo, John W. Smith, Manuel Perez, George Dolson, Luciano Navarro.

January 8, 1840, to January 9, 1841.
Mayor. John W. Smith.
Aldermen. Cornelius Van Ness, George Blow, Francisco A. Ruiz, Jose A. Navarro, Miguel Arcienega, Manuel Perez, John McMullen, Ambrosio Rodriguez.

January 9, 1841, to April 18, 1842.
Mayor. Juan N. Seguin; and from August 17, 1841, to September 7, 1841, Francis Guilbeau, pro tem.
Aldermen. Man'l. Perez, Marcus A. Veramendi, Pedro Flores, Antonio Menchaca, Jose Cassiano, Juan A. Urutia, L. Smithers, Bryan Callaghan, Jose M. Flores, Francis Guilbeau, John R. Black, Diego A. Taylor, Francisco Bustillo, Antonio Lockmar, J. L. Trueheart, Augustin Barrera.

April 18, 1842, to March 30, 1844.
Mayor. John W. Smith.
Aldermen. J. McMullen, Rafael Garza, B. Callaghan, S. A. Maverick, E. Dwyer, J. A. Urutia, C. Rivas, B. Bradley.

March 30, 1844, to February 18, 1845.
Mayor. Edward Dwyer.
Aldermen. Rafael Garza, Ambrosio Rodriguez, Jose M. Flores, Robert Lindsay, Juan A. Urutia, Antonio Menchaca, James Goodman, Thomas Whitehead.

February 18, 1845, to January 1, 1846.
Mayor. Edward Dwyer.
Aldermen. Ygnacio Chavez, J. B. Lee, Augustin Barrera, Jose Cassiano, C. Rivas, Francisco Bustillo, Thomas Whitehead, Ambrosio Rodriguez.

January 1, 1846, to January 1, 1847.
Mayor. Bryan Callaghan. *C. F. King, pro tem.
Alderman. George Van Ness, J. A. Urutia, Charles
F. King, Pedros, A. J. McClelland, M. A. Veramendi,
William B. Jaques, Antonio Rodriguez.

January 1, 1847, to January 1, 1848.
Mayor. Charles F. King, *and from January 27,
1847, to January 1, 1848, S. S. Smith, pro tem.
Aldermen. W. G. Crump, S. S. Smith, M. Trumble,
J. A. Urutia, A. Rodriguez, O. B. Brackett, R. Herre-
ra, Ygnacio Chavez.

January 1, 1848, to January 1, 1849.
Mayor. Charles F. King, *and from April 3, 1848,
to January 1, 1849, S. S. Smith, pro tem.
Aldermen. S. S. Smith, A. Menchaca, J. N. Fisk, A.
H. Martin, Bryan Callaghan, A. Rodriguez, J. A.
Urutia, R. W. Peacock.

Janury 1, 1849, to January 1, 1850.
Mayor. J. M. Devine.
Aldermen. S. S. Smith, Bryan Callaghan, J. N. Men-
chaca, N. Lardner, Luciano Navarro, J. N. Fisk, Jose
A. Urutia, Win. Lytle, G. T. Howard, J. D. Groes-
beeck, J. H. Beck.

January 1, 1850, to January 1, 1851.
Mayor. J. M. Devine.
Aldermen. Chas. Hummel, S. A. Maverick, S. S.
Smith, Wm. Lytle, O. Evans, J. A. Urutia, G. L. Pas-
chal, A. A. Lockwood.

January 1, 1851, to January 1, 1852.
Mayor. J. S. McDonald.
Aldermen. S. A. Maverick, J. H. Lyons, J. A. Urutia, John Vance, G. L. Paschal, George Cupples, F. Giraud, J. D. McLeod.

January 1, 1852, to January 1, 1853.
Mayor. C. F. King.
Aldermen. A. A. Lockwood, Peter Odet, M. G. Cotton, Rafael Herrera, H. D. Stumburg, James R. Sweet, H. Huffmeyer, J. A. Urutia, J. S. McClellan.

January 1, 1853, to January 1, 1854.
Mayor. J. M. Devine.
Aldermen. A. A. Lockwood, C. N. Riotte, M. Lopez, H. Huffmeyer, F. Herff, B. Callaghan, J. B. Lacoste, A. Navarro, J. R. Sweet, Charles Hummel, G. M. Martin.

January 1, 1854, to January 1, 1855.
Mayor. John M. Carolan.
Aldermen. C. F. King, F. Guilbeau, J. A. Urutia, J. A. Navarro, J. M. West, H. F. Oswarl, J. Hackett, J. Ulrich, August Sellingsloh, B. Brady.

January 1, 1855, to January 1, 1856.
Mayor. James R. Sweet.
Aldermen. C. F. King, A. W. Desmuke, Asa Mitchell, J. S. McDonald, J. G. Viall, B. E. Edwards, A. Deffenbaugh, B. R. Sappington, J. D. Groesbeeck.

January 1, 1856, to first Monday of January, 1857.
Mayor. J. M. Devine.
Aldermen. G. T. Howard, A. Nette, G. Soto, I. A. Paschal, S. S. Smith, G. P. Post, F. Giraud, D. C. Alexander, John Fries, E. G. Houston, N. A. Mitchell, L. Zork.

January 1, 1857, to June 30, 1857.
Mayor. J. M. Devine. June 5, 1857, to June 30, 1857.
Mayor. J. H. Beck, pro tem.

July 1, 1857, to January 1, 1858.
Mayor. A. A. Lockwood.
Aldermen. D. C. Alexander, W. B. Knox, Jose Rodriguez, J. G. Gardner, W. Aj Menger, Owen Clark, David Russi, W. W. Campbell, J. A. Urutia, J. H. Beck, N. Lardner, S. W. McAllister, George Horner.

January 1, 1858, to January 1, 1859.
Mayor. A. A. Lockwood.
Aldermen. J. E. Gardner, J. M. Chaves, John Sturm, W. A. Menger, D. Russi, J. Earl, J. M. Penaloza, M. G. Cotton, H. Canterbury, G. Thiesen, C. Byrn.

January 1, 1859, to January 1, 1860.
Mayor. James R. Sweet.
Aldermen. G. Persh, W. W. Campbell, H. D. Stumburg, W. C. Tynan, C. Byrn, L. M. Penaloza, D. Russi, M. G. Cotton.

January 1, 1860, to January 1, 1861.
Mayor. James R. Sweet.
Aldermen. M. H. Campbell, D. Russi, Wm. Vance, Thos. H. Stribling, G. Persh, H. D. Stumburg, W. C. Tynan, W. W. Campbell.

January 1, 1861, to January 1, 1862.
Mayor. James R. Sweet.
Aldermen. E. Braden, F. Galan, C. F. Fisher, J. Hoyer, D. Russi, J. M. Fenaloza, Wm. Vance, Thos. H. Strebling, P. L. Buquor, G. C. Patching, E. A. Florian.

January 1, 1862, to January 1, 1863.
Mayor. James R. Sweet, *from January 1, 1862, to May 26, 1862.
Mayor. S. A. Maverick, from May 26, to January 1, 1863.
Aldermen. E. P. Alsbury, D. Russi, F. Schreiner, G. A. Patching, E. A. Florian, E. Hickman, A. Sartor, E. Braden, C. F. Fisher, Chas. Hummel, G. Persch.

January 1, 1863, to January 1, 1864.
Mayor. P. L. Buquor.
Aldermen. F. Cassiano, Jose Martinez, C. E. Fisher, E. A. Florian, C. Hummel, E. Hickman, G. C. Patching, A. Sartor, E. Dewey, S. Sampson, E. Miles.

January 1, 1864, to January 1, 1865.
Mayor. P. L. Buquor.
Aldermen. E. Braden, E. Hickman, A. Moye, E. Schenck, W. B. Jaques, S. S. Robinson, C. F. Fisher, F. Cassiano, Jose Martinez.

January 1, 1865, to October 1, 1865.
Mayor. J. H. Lyons to August 15, 1865.
Mayor. C. F. Fisher, pro tem, from August 15 to October 9, 1865.
Aldermen. F. Cassiano, D. Russi, C. F. Fisher, S. W. McAllister, W. B. Jaques, A. Moye, E. Braden, F. Schenck.

October 9, 1865, to August 23, 1866.
Mayor. D. Cleveland.
Aldermen. H. D. Stumberg, M. H. Campbell, F. W. Poppey, C. F. Kaiserling, P. Shiner, G. Persch, C. Seabaugh, F. Schreiner.

August 24, 1866, to December 31, 1866.
Mayor. J. H. Lyons.

Aldermen. J. F. Cassiano, W. B. Jaques, Ed. Braden, S. W. McAllister, A. Moye, D. Russi, C. F. Fisher, C. E. Jefferson.

January 1, 1867, to November 8, 1867.
Mayor. J. H. Lyons.
Aldermen. M. Yturri, A. M. Ruiz, D. Russi, S. S. Smith, F. Wonderschack, C. F. Fisher, A. Sartor, S. W. McAllister.

November 8, 1867, to March 8, 1870.
Mayor. W. C. A. Thielepape.
Aldermen. A. Sartor, C. F. Disher, E. Pentenreider, J. M. Chanez, Frank Rose, J. P. Newcomb, P. H. Braunback, Thos. Hertzberg, V. Lieffering, C. G. Artzt, A. Dillon, F. Groos, A. Bucchette, James Callaghan, R. C. Norton.

March 28, 1870, to November 12, 1872.
Mayor. W. C. A. Thielepape from March 28, 1870, to March 12, 1872.
Mayor. S. G. Newton from March 13, 1872, to November 12, 1872.
Aldermen. E. Pentenreider, James Callaghan, F. Groos, W. W. Gamble, D. Bell, C. Elmendarf, J. P. Newcomb, R. C. Norton, F. Guilbeau, F. Schreiner, J. W. Mozee, J. A. Duerler, Jose Flores, Ed. Steves, J. H. Kampmann, C. L. Probandt, N. Lewis, E. Cole, William Reed.

November 13, 1872, to January 13, 1873.
Mayor. F. Giraud.
Aldermen. J. Sweeney, H. Collman, F. Kalteyer, S. S. Smith, C. F. Fisher, H. W. Tong, A. Michel, C. J. Hupperts.

January 14, 1873, to January 19, 1875.
Mayor. F. Giraud.
Aldermen. J. Sweeney, T. T. Teel, S. S. Smith, Frank Rose, C. F. Fisher, Louis Briam, F. Groos, F. Schreiner, J. H. Kampmann, Phil Shardein.

January 19, 1875, to January 19, 1877.
Mayor. James H. French.
Aldermen. J. Sweeney, G. R. Dashiell, T. T. Teel, P. Scheiner, S. S. Smith, F. Schreiner, E. J. Chavez, F. D. Faville, E. Degener, W. Frescott, F. Hahn, S. W. McAllister, T. Kiolbassta, M. Muench, A. F. Wulff.

January 19, 1877, to January 25, 1879.
Mayor. James H. French.
Aldermen. T. T. Teel, P. Scheiner, F. G. Smith, John Monier, F. D. Faville, F. Schreiner, F. Hahn, E. Degener, W. Prescott, M. Muench, A. F. Wulff, G. Hoerner.

January 25, 1879, to January 25, 1881.
Mayor. James H. French.
Aldermen. L. Bergstrom, *A. Bruni, B. Callaghan, E. Froboese, J. P. Newcomb, F. Schreiner, R. Wulfing, *W. Prescott, P. Jonas, A. I. Lockwood, W. H. Maverick, George Homer, *W. Heuermann, M. Muench, Edward Steves.

January 25, 1881, to January 25, 1883.
Mayor. James H. French.
Aldermen. *L. Berg, A. Bruni, Geo. Caldwell, B. Callaghan, H. L. Degener, Win. Heuermann, P. Jonas, A. I. Lockwood, E. Niggli, F. Schreiner, E. Steves, R. Wulfing, †M. C. Shiner.

January 25, 1883, to February 1, 1885.
Mayor. James H. French.
Aldermen. Eli Arnaud, *J. N. Gallagher, *Jos. E.
Dwyer, August Belknap, F. Schreiner, W. R. Story,
J. H. Bolton, J. T. Hambleton, A. I. Lockwood, H.
Pauly, C. A. Richter, J. H. Smye, †Juan T. Cardenas,
†J. N. Gallagher.

February 1, 1885, to February 1, 1887.
Mayor. Bryan Callaghan.
Aldermen. T. E. Conner, J. N. Gallagher, *Juan
Cardenas, J. H. French, F. Schreiner, A. Belknap,
A. I. Lockwood, J. T. Hambleton, *J. H. Bolton,
*Henry Pauly, *Martin Muench, J. H. Smye, †M. F.
Corbett, †N. Mackey, †Hans L. Degener, †L Berg-
strom, †S. W. McAllister.

February 28, 1887, to February 28, 1889.
Mayor. Bryan Callaghan.
Aldermen. *A. Belknap, Fritz Schreiner, Dan Lew-
is, J. N. Gallagher, †J. H. Schaefer, †J. H. Presnall,
C. Guerguin, T. E. Conner, E. L. Richey, Geo. H.
Kalteyer, H. L. Degener, Gus Mauermann, G. A.
Reiman, *J. H. Smye.

February 28, 1889, to February 28, 1891.
Mayor. Bryan Callaghan.
Aldermen. A. I. Lockwood, Henry Fest, A. F. Wulff,
John H. Bolton, Charles Guerguin, T. E. Conner, Ja-
cob Weber, Geo. H. Kalteyer, Joseph Boelhauwe, F.
F. Rogers, Gus A. Reimann, Alex Sartor.

February, 1891, to February, 1893.
Mayor. Bryan Callaghan.
Aldermen. A. I. Lockwood, F. Schreiner, *M. F.
Corbett, †W. S. Anderson, L. M. Gregory, C. Guer-
guin, T. E. Conner, Jacob Weber, *Aug. Santleben,

Jos. Boelhauwe, *H. W. Bitter, Albert Persch, Albert Backmann, †Thos. E. Dougherty, †W. Muth.

February, 1893, to February, 1895.
Mayor. George Paschal.
Aldermen. Chas. Schreiner, W. S. Smith, *C. B. Hill, G. W. Russ, *S. G. Newton, Jas. H. French, Wm. Hoefling, H. Limburger, J. A. Daugherty, Albert Beckmann, H. Eltnendorf, N. Mackey, Joe Beckmann, Erich Menger, *John W. Tobin.

February, 1895, to February, 1897.
Mayor. Hy. Elmendorf.
Aldermen. F. Guerguin, Aug. Robin, Erich Menger, Jos. P. Devine, Wm. Hoefling, C. Fahey, Ad. Dreiss, A. F. Beckmann, W. C. Robards, N. Mackey, Louis Oge, W. Holt.

February, 1897, to February, 1899.
Mayor. Bryan Callaghan.
Aldermen. G. A. Duerler, B. J. Mauermann, J. N. Rome, W. B. Hamilton, Lee Kilgore, W. L. Richter, Geo. Surkey, Marshall Hicks, L. Mahncke, John Miller, C. A. Denny, W. W. Johnson.

February, 1899, to February, 1901.
Mayor. Marshall Hicks.
Aldermen. L. Mahncke, F. A. Piper, Geo. Surkey, T. E. Mumme, J. K. Lamm, W. L. Richter, J. A. O'Connor, R. F. Alexander, Aug. Thiele, Wm. Davis, W. L. Barker, A. P. Rheiner.

February, 1901, to February, 1903.
Mayor. Marshall Hicks (Elected to State Senate October, 1902).
Mayor. Dr. Frederick Terrell (Elected to fill vacancy).

Aldermen. W. L. Barker, Aug. Lewy, J. F. Hickman, Walton Peteet, J. K. Lamm, W. L. Richter, J. A. O'Connor, R. F. Alexander, Fred Terrell, A. Seidel, Frank Weber, A. P. Rheiner.

February, 1903, to May, 1905.
Mayor. J. P. Campbell.
Aldermen. W. L. Barker, V. P. Brown, W. L. Richter, N. T. Wilson, J. R. Lambert, J. D. Seamands, Rud. Krisch, J. H. Kirkpatrick, J. F. Fentiman, H. B. Salliway, F. M. Gloeckner, Ed. Steves.

May, 1905, to May, 1907.
Mayor. Bryan Callaghan.
Aldermen. W. L. Richter, B. J. Mauermann, John Bauer, J. T. Hambleton, J. R. Lambert, Eli Arnaud, E. Menger, M. A. Davis A. I. Lockwood, C. S. Robinson, Ed. Braden, E. A. Kuehn.

May, 190T, to May, 1909.
Mayor. Bryan Callaghan.
Aldermen. B. J. Mauermann, W. J. Richter, *John Bauer, †Ernst Dietzmann, J. T. Hambleton, J. R. Lambert, E. Arnaud, E. Menger, *L. C. Thompson, †C. C. Smith, A. I. Lockwood, K. J. Carey, Ed Braden, E. A. Kuehn.